JOSÉ ORTEGA Y GASSET'S
METAPHYSICAL INNOVATION

SUNY Series in Latin American and Iberian Thought and Culture
Jorge J. E. Gracia, Editor

JOSÉ ORTEGA Y GASSET'S METAPHYSICAL INNOVATION

A Critique and Overcoming of Idealism

ANTONIO RODRÍGUEZ HUÉSCAR

*Translated and Edited
by*

Jorge García-Gómez

State University
of New York
Press

Published by
State University of New York Press, Albany

Production by Susan Geraghty
Marketing by Dana Yanulavich

Printed in the United States of America

For information, address State University of New York Press, State University
Plaza, Albany, N.Y., 12246

Library of Congress Cataloging-in-Publication Data

Rodríguez Huéscar, Antonio, 1912–
    [Innovación metafísica de Ortega. English]
    José Ortega y Gasset's metaphysical innovation : a critique and
overcoming of idealism / Antonio Rodríguez Huéscar ; translated and
edited by Jorge García-Gómez.
        p.   cm. — (SUNY series in Latin American and Iberian thought
and culture)
    Includes bibliographical references and index.
    ISBN 0-7914-2235-6 (alk. paper). — ISBN 0-7914-2236-4 (pbk. :
alk. paper)
    1. Ortega y Gasset, José, 1883–1955. I. García-Gómez, Jorge.
II. Title. III. Series.
B4568.O74R62413 1994
196'.1—dc20   93-50570
                                                             CIP

10 9 8 7 6 5 4 3 2 1

CONTENTS

TRANSLATOR'S PREFACE

Why write a book on José Ortega y Gasset so late in the century? Because he is, simply and bluntly put, one of the major philosophers of our time. This may come as a surprise to some who know him as a great essayist or as a noted historical and cultural critic. It is not my intent, however, to impugn such an impression as being wrong or superficial. One only has to point to *El tema de nuestro tiempo* (1923),[1] *La deshumanización del arte e ideas sobre la novela* (1925),[2] *La rebelión de las masas* (1930),[3] *Una interpretación de la historia universal* (1948–49),[4] and "De Europa meditatio quaedam" (1949),[5] among other prescient works of his, to dispel any such possible misunderstanding. Yet that approach to Ortega proves insufficient even to do justice to his actual cultural and historical analyses. This is not the place, of course, to inquire into the reasons therefor, which are by no means incidental. Some nevertheless suggest themselves at once: as to content, one can mention the burning interest of some of the topics examined by him, and, as to form and context, one may refer to his beautiful style and to the venue of many of his pieces, originally composed, as they were, as essays or articles for the regular press. Be that as it may, what is now perfectly clear is that Ortega's grasp of the absolute roots of experience (insofar as it underlay such analyses) did not lack the required rigor, and that his capacity to name those foundations was not bereft of inventiveness. Accordingly, other factors must have been the source of the distractedness of some of his readers, as well as of the consequent limited influence exerted, where it mattered most, by his philosophical work proper. This did not mean, of course, that Ortega was not acutely aware of the problem, for in fact he went as far as to identify nearly the opposite reasons to explain why Wilhelm Dilthey, his most relevant predecessor in matters of ultimate and common concern, came to be in a similar predicament.[6]

By contrast, my contention is that the origin of those and other writings of Ortega is not so much his concern with the cultural and historical phenomena he discussed in them, no matter how important and even urgent they were, as it is his preoccupation with the ultimate foundations of reality. Indeed, it was his practice of metaphysics or first philosophy, which began quite early in his career and certainly had achieved a first level of maturity by the time his first book, *Meditaciones del Quijote* (1914)[7] saw the light, that increasingly served to shape the body of his work, whether published in print or in the lecture hall.

In that book Ortega advanced a thesis that was to play the role of radical basis and motivation for his subsequent, life-long inquiry. I mean the formula, "I am I and my circum-stance,"[8] by means of which he gave expression at once to his assessment of modernity and the insight in terms of which to overcome it. That assessment was twofold: on the one hand, that the philosophical doctrine characteristic of the Modern Era was idealism and, on the other, that idealism had by then run its course or exhausted its historical virtualities.[9] One must bear in mind that just one year earlier Edmund Husserl had developed, in the first volume of his *Ideas*,[10] an idealistic interpretation of the phenomenology he himself had practiced in his *Logical Investigations* (1900–1901).[11] As Ortega saw it, even Husserl's most exacting version of idealism had to be transcended, inasmuch as it did not do justice to the absolute dimension of experience that the founder of phenomenology had been seeking to identify and essentially describe. Considered as the science of such an absolute, Husserl's phenomenology, or the "doctrine of transcendental subjectivity engaged in the constitution of the world and everything contained therein," as Jan Patočka for one came to give it expression years later (1973), "*is not sufficiently radical,* in the sense that it presents us not with the *appearing* of a being, but with a given being, with something already disclosed, however fluid and refined it may be."[12] "Appearing," or the ultimate datum concerning the universe (as Ortega will characterize it in 1929),[13] could not then be identified either with the *world* (as had been already demonstrated in idealism, both classical and phenomenological) or with *subjectivity* of any kind (as idealists of all stripes had claimed in one way or another), for those two realms presuppose something more fundamental, namely, what Ortega called the "fundamental reality,"[14] i.e., the event in which something appears to someone. This event, amounting as it does to the experience in which something befalls me absolutely,[15] is irreducible both to the apparent (or world) and to the someone before whom the world appears (i.e., subjectivity), for it is precisely the awakening of subjectivity in my life in its quest for meaning in the world and with the things of the world. I find, at every turn, that I cannot do away completely with the originary sense of living, which is the "finding . . . [of myself] shipwrecked in the world, the nature of which I do not know. . . ."[16] Accordingly, I am alive in the ultimate human sense of being intrinsically in need of guidelines to survive in the world, i.e., to live and go on living meaningfully.

But how was it possible in principle to overcome the insufficiency of idealism? Ortega realized soon enough that the critique of that doctrine (and therefore the endeavor to go beyond modernity) could not successfully be brought to term unless, at the same time and by the same token, he found a reality that showed itself to be both fundamental and systematic in character, and which was accessible as such to essential description. In his opinion, such a reality is no other than every individual life. No wonder, then, the development of the critique of idealism and the elaboration of the categorial analysis of human life went for him hand in hand. In that attempt at clarification, my life appears, always and everywhere, as an "entitative reflexivity."[17] My life is not an individual affair in some accidental or contingent sense, but rather "something" unique, and it is so by virtue of "having absolutely to refer itself and everything to itself."[18] In other words, my life is the "operative uniqueness" (*werktätige Einzigkeit*)[19] in which the "surrounding world and I constitute an indissoluble and absolutely existent organism."[20] Neither myself nor my world is my life, at least not originarily; rather, these two spheres are the coexistent and mutually referring constituents thereof.[21]

To arrive at a nontrivial understanding of Ortega's axiom to the effect that "I am I and my circum-stance," one must be able to establish that the successful completion of his critique of idealism is already the beginning of the articulation of the Idea of Life *qua* radical reality. A superficial inspection of Ortega's thesis will show that it contains at least two expressions for selfhood,[22] one which is originary, another derivative. The latter, as conveyed by the second "I" of the formula, points to me insofar as I am directed upon the things of the world and objectivate them. The former, as conveyed by the first "I" of the formula, is coextensive with my life as a "sphere of reflection in itself, wherein everything, absolutely speaking, is engaged in 'being-for-itself,'"[23] whether what is involved is the realm of the "secondary" self or the things of the world. Accordingly, in the usual or derivative sense of the word "I," it cannot be said of me that I "am the *locus* of reflection; rather, I find myself, as a matter of course, immersed as it were in a medium of light."[24] Therefore, human life, in the radical or first sense of selfhood, is precisely the ongoing, nonobjective, or entitative self-presence of being, which is thus nonmediately given as universal, necessary, and unique. But this is consistent with what philosophy as the search for the absolute dimension of experience requires, namely, the *dis-closure as achievement*—Ortega called it "performative being or presence"—[25] of that which Patočka expressed either negatively (by saying that it "cannot be any being at all")[26] or positively (by asserting that the structure of "*appearing must rest upon itself*").[27] In other words, ". . . *subjectivity itself must show itself as something which appears as part of a deeper structure* . . . ,"[28] and such a structure is to be given as the bearer of the appearing, which may only be rationally distinguished from it (and then with the greatest and most perilous of theoretical efforts).[29] Originarily, then, my life is not an object appearing before me, but "something" which is for itself. Accordingly, the radical reality is my own life, and yet it is "no such thing insofar as it is an object of mine [for] . . . it is an object to the extent that [thought] entertains it as that which is no-object for me, but rather that which is for itself. . . . The one living cannot but exist, since it may not be nonexisting for itself."[30]

Metaphysics or first philosophy is thus henceforth to be understood as the categorial analysis of human life. In fact, the first essential-descriptive theorem resulting from such a radical treatment is the one given expression by Ortega by means of the axiom that has just been considered. The book by Antonio Rodríguez Huéscar, which is here being presented in English translation, is precisely the exposition of the fundamentals of Ortega's metaphysics taken as the analytic of human life. And yet this is a task that he has not merely discharged in a straightforward way but likewise, and most perceptively, as a function of Ortega's critique of idealism. Indeed, in this lucid and penetrating study, the author has succeeded in showing *in actu exercito* the necessary interrelation and mutual relevance of both pursuits.

All that notwithstanding, a word should be added, if one wishes to avoid any confusion about first philosophy, as understood and practiced by Ortega. To express it positively and in principle, one would again have to stress, first and foremost, that it is the essential-descriptive doctrine of human life as appearing and, secondly, that it is the categorial examination thereof. And yet that may not prove sufficient to grasp Ortega's far-reaching philosophical position readily but exactly, to which end it might not be without some utility to attempt to place Ortega in his immediate historical context within twentieth-century philosophy. Were one to do so, even if only cursorily, one would arrive at certain negative results, such as the following, which would be helpful in avoiding error:

Ortega's notion of metaphysics cannot be considered synonymous with Heidegger's "thinking of Being," even though the latter is a persistent endeavor to arrive at an ultimate clarification of appearing, and it cannot be so regarded because Ortega's aim has been the rational or categorial analysis of life as the first datum concerning the universe.[31] Nor can it be construed as if it were an ontological inquiry, whether in the form of Heidegger's fundamental project in *Sein und Zeit*,[32] or in that of Nicolai Hartmann's regional investigations,[33] or in that of J.-P. Sartre's existential examination of human experience.[34] Nor, finally, is it to be regarded as somehow equivalent to the systematic consideration of the rootedness of human experience in the embodied ego's life in the world, as was the case for example with M. Merleau-Ponty,[35] a point that must be insisted upon even if it is true that Ortega, following M. Scheler's example, quite early recognized the importance of such an implantation. But then such negative conclusions find their validation, in the final analysis, in the fact that those manners of thinking, however proximate and akin to Ortega's own they may be, nonetheless presuppose, without exception, a more basic stratum, namely, the event of appearing, which indeed cries out for a suitable clarification. And that is precisely what Ortega intended to accomplish by means of metaphysical reflection, if understood as the categorial analytic of human life qua radical reality.[36]

The characterization of the problem set examined in a book can never be reasonably satisfactory, unless one turns to its author and at least makes a gesture to present him to his would-be readers. Antonio Rodríguez Huéscar is no exception to this rule. In fact, he is a paradigmatic exemplification of it, for the understanding of his *José Ortega y Gasset's Metaphysical Innovation,* being as it is a study of Ortega's ideas deliberately conducted in an Orteguian manner, intrinsically requires its being placed in the context of the author's life. Naturally, this is not equivalent to the inconsequential exercise consisting in merely establishing a relevant schedule of events, dates, and places; rather, it involves at least a minimal effort to think narratively but essentially about a man's life and work, one which would indeed follow the threads of motivation and intent. My purpose at this time is not, however, to engage in a full-fledged biographical inquiry concerning don Antonio, as his recent death would seem to demand. I take the liberty of leaving a task of that magnitude for a more fitting opportunity, when my mind will have regained its composure. In this connection, I trust that Julián Marías's "Prologue"[37] to the book may provide the reader with a sufficient portrait of the man and an able reconstruction of the general sense of the author's philosophical objectives.

But neither am I going to conduct here a close analysis of the author's book, much less an examination of his work as a whole. Again, this is not the appropriate setting to brave such a difficult enterprise. I will have to confine myself to what I have already done, namely, to providing the general framework which, in my estimation, is essential to grasp the fundamental aims and procedures that are consistent with Ortega's metaphysical stance. If this has been accomplished with a modicum of success, then such an introduction to Ortega's first philosophy cannot but cast some light on a study of it, such as this one, which has been carried out in the Orteguian style. Fortunately, however, the reader may not be ultimately disappointed, for this book is its own best commentary and a genuine expression of Rodríguez Huéscar's position and spirit. In my judgment, it will allow anyone reading it—insofar as it clearly captures *in actu exercito* the essence of the author's mind—to form a most definite idea of the scope and depth of don Antonio's philosophical origins, interests, and accomplishments.

In what follows, then, I intend only to take a global look at his long life,[38] as well as at his work, from what I believe is a suitable standpoint. I shall be brief discharging this task, as I think he would have appreciated.

Let me say, first of all, that his was one of the finest and most complex creative minds devoted to philosophical thought that I have had the pleasure of encountering. It is no wonder, then, that Jaime de Salas, a professor of philosophy at the Universidad Complutense de Madrid and don Antonio's friend and former student, remarked on the occasion of his death that his work "places him among philosophers of the first rank in twentieth-century Spain."[39] It was a rare privilege for me to have known him for the last twenty-five years, a period coinciding with his maturity and the consummation of my youth. It was through the written word first (by means of his books, articles, and letters) and then face to face, by way of his actual example, that I came to appreciate certain important questions about living and reflection.

In a philosopher, it seems that these two dimensions are not essentially separable from each other, however distinguishable from one another they may be in various contexts. In this connection, the reader should keep alive to a notion of the greatest consequence (both theoretically and in terms of its effects in every life), namely, that living itself, even at the level of its unforged spontaneity, is already a "rational" affair, that is to say, an adventure in making sense of self and world, in which one's own life is at stake. This statement is meant without pathos, but it is certainly proposed to underscore the dramatic element at work in every life (philosophy being included as one of its highest forms). In other words, it is advanced as signifying that life—any and every human life—is a self-plotting and self-deciding actional undertaking, wherein one's character and happiness always remain in the balance as functions of truth and justification. These concerns of reflection (which include many a terror and uncertainty) may culminate—and should do so in a philosopher's life—in a systematic analysis of living, or at least ought to point in the direction of such an examination under the guidance of life's spontaneous reflexivity and rationality, which it would seek not to distort.

Now, these are no idle remarks for a solemn occasion. On the contrary, thinkers inspired by Ortega's philosophy can only regard their encounters, in whatever medium or shape, as truly biographical events. But to understand this contention aright, one must realize that "biographical" is not a word employed in this context to refer—whether in regard to encounters in general or philosophical ones in particular—to some anecdotal or trivial occurrence, merely consignable to a given date and location. By contrast, living encounters—to such men—*may* become invitations, indeed challenges to ponder, certainly not over the accidentals of meeting or event, but over the meaning *in fieri* that such contingencies may have and, above all, over the foundations and structures, intrinsic to living, that would render them possible. Don Antonio's work is precisely the embodiment and fruit of such reflections.

Secondly, I wish to place emphasis on his temper, as well as on the character he fashioned on its basis by delivering himself to a practice of philosophical thinking that would expressly accept no unexamined premises. Here I am not making a moral evaluation (at least not in the usual sense of the expression), much less a psychological assessment. Again, his living and his reasoning must be seen, if we wish truly to appreciate them, as striving to go hand in hand for the purposes of attaining truth and knowledge. As I see it, this man arose from his "incorruptible depths" (to use Ortega's phrase)[40] in order to think and rethink life and to attempt to justify his thoughts, but in a manner that would sacrifice no essential principle or relevant concretion pertinent to reality proper, taken individually or as a whole. In other words, I am asserting that don Antonio was a man with a vocation for integrity, provided one understands this locution in its most radical or far-reaching sense, namely, when it signifies the willed convergence of personal destiny and justifiable truth.

At this point, consider, if you will, a particular section of Plato's *Republic*.[41] I have in mind the passages in which he briefly sought to identify, among other things, the essence of courage. After he appeared to have reached a conclusion, he nevertheless continued to pursue his goal most paradoxically, for his relentless search after the *eîdos* seems to have kept its driving force even past that moment. This perplexing impression is dispelled, however, as soon as one realizes that Plato was ultimately seeking to contemplate "intellectual courage," or those abiding wellsprings of deliberate spiritedness which exceed valor. If there was a man intrinsically marked in his life and work by this dianoetic virtue, that certainly was Antonio Rodríguez Huéscar, who recognized no social or political master or any authority in matters philosophical, even at the price of great renunciation or at the cost of personal obscurity. This attitude applied, no doubt, even in the case of his profound relation of discipleship to Ortega, whose doctrine he never ceased to clarify, articulate, deepen, and, in many significant respects, surpass. This notwithstanding, I must say that his nobility as a thinker and a man did not rest on that alone, but, more precisely, on what he achieved with it, for he turned his vocation for integrity into the deepest layer of his thought and transformed it into the furthest horizon to which his reflections were conformed. In fact, he carried out this work with "exemplary courage," as he himself has said of Ortega.[42] Accordingly, I would contend that the foundational problem defining his life and inquiry is no other than the question of the existence and nature of the nexus of *lógos* and *éthos,* when it is carried to its final consequences. Salas, for one, has clearly seen this point, but he has also, most subtly, grasped the results necessarily deriving from it, for he has remarked that don Antonio's intellectual calling to seek after ultimate principles "led him, in a spirit of total impartiality and generosity, to devote his time and attention to, and exercise his judgment about, anyone promoting the cause of philosophy. In this manner of conduct, he reminded one, on occasion, of the naïveté, as well as of the lucidity, exhibited by Spinoza in some of his letters."[43] No wonder his example as a thinker and a man—in this case, indissolubly interlocked—has been so inspiring, and his loss so grievously felt.

To conclude, let me refer to the fact that the translation of this book,[44] which I had initiated with don Antonio's approval and support, was almost halfway when his unexpected death occurred. Although we had discussed my work in progress both in person and in long telephone conversations, he only had the opportunity to examine the resulting text in part. I have taken into account the marginal notes he scribbled for himself on his copy of the incomplete draft of my translation of the first part of his work, and I have followed his suggestions to the extent I have been able to. Unfortunately for me, the working sessions planned never materialized, for, had they taken place, he would have given me invaluable advice, I would have been able to pose a number of questions to him, and, in consequence, I could have effected improvements in the translation, especially so far as the second part of the book is concerned. I have nevertheless striven to be faithful to English expression, Spanish idiom, and philosophical nuance, but I may not have completely succeeded. I have also tried to assist the reader by providing sources, citations, cross references, and even at times

some explanatory remarks in the footnotes, or by supplying clari-
fying expressions in brackets, although I have reduced these addi-
tions to a minimum. I would like to point out as well that I am
responsible for the translation of all passages by Ortega and other
authors whom Rodríguez Huéscar quotes, except where it is otherwise indicated. I wish to add, finally, that the entire English version
of the book has been read and revised at least twice by my wife,
Sara, whose suggestions have always been taken into account and
often incorporated into the final text. It goes without saying that I
am most grateful for her help and encouragement. If I originally
conceived this project as a way of doing don Antonio homage in
the measure open to me, now that he has died I would like to pay
him tribute by means of the completed translation of his book,
however imperfect the product of my labors may have turned out
to be.

PROLOGUE

Julián Marías

Antonio Rodríguez Huéscar's is one of the very few books about Ortega y Gasset which is written on the basis of a "full knowledge of the facts." In other words, it is one of those rare books built on the grounds of total responsibility. The reason for this is not hard to find.

Antonio Rodríguez Huéscar was born in La Mancha, Castille, in 1912. When he arrived in Madrid to pursue his studies, he was a young man characterized by modesty and a firm attachment to his place of birth. His was a genuine acquaintance with the life in a small Spanish town, with its vineyards, cereal fields, and melon patches. His was a refined aesthetical, visual, and literary sense: he was a painter and writer of true vocation. His nature was not bookish at all; he was shy and lived on deep resources of silent joy. His inclination to appear less substantial than he in fact was has only become stronger with the passage of time. He is now seventy years of age.

He began his studies at the School of Philosophy and Letters of the University of Madrid about the time of the establishment of the Republic. His arrival coincided with the moment of greatest glory in our university life, especially at that school and particularly in its extraordinary Division of Philosophy. We were together in attendance for five years and were awarded the degree of master of arts at the same time, a month shy of the civil war.

Rodríguez Huéscar felt attracted by the literary, artistic, and intellectual climate characteristic of Madrid at the time, a period of exceptional brilliance, and yet he never forgot his place of birth, as if he could always manage to keep both his feet firmly on the ground of his native La Mancha. This is the reason why, despite his youth, he possessed a clear sense of quality and relevance and of

the relative value of things. At the School of Philosophy and Letters, he enthusiastically and attentively assimilated the teaching of
his masters. They were Manuel García Morente, on occasion Julián Besteiro and Juan Zaragüeta, and José Gaos thereafter, but his
most important teacher was Ortega.

He devoted his efforts to the study of the various philosophical
disciplines, the history of philosophy, and the works of the great
philosophers. And he conducted such studies according to the
standards set by Ortega in his lecture course and seminars, that is
to say, on a level with the creative power proper to contemporary
philosophy, as formulated in Spanish and in view of the circum-
stances then prevailing in Spain. As it happened with the rest of us,
he was progressively won over by a body of thought that vindicated
its claims and displayed the evidence to support them before us
with irresistible force. And I use the word "irresistible" advisedly,
for our critical sense made us resist the would-be lure of anyone's
sheer brilliance of thought.

Antonio Rodríguez Huéscar never experienced that strange,
peculiar manner of resentment that some harbor in their hearts
when they cannot but bow to the self-evidence of truth. It is interesting to note that there are even some who manage to keep this
feeling alive after half a century has elapsed. In fact, any upset in
their lives serves them as an occasion to make it manifest, perhaps
because the truth they had once to confront conflicts with some
recent but unjustifiable love. By contrast, Rodríguez Huéscar felt
overjoyed by the fact that things—at least some of them—could be
exhibited with clarity, with a rational clarity that could be shared
and justified. In other words, he felt enriched by such truths as
Ortega had discovered or was engaged in discovering with us, in a
dialogue he kept going with us. And yet such truths were fully and
legitimately Ortega's own. After a few years, the young man who
had arrived from La Mancha was in possession of an intellectual
wealth greater than that of those who had not endeavored to make
their own such riches as were offered them.

This left Rodríguez Huéscar marked for the rest of his life. He
was so affected not only intellectually, but in the totality of his
person as well. A word of caution is here in order, however, for
when I say "intellectually" I take the word in a sense consistent
with Ortega's concept of "living reason," which is identical with
life itself, insofar as life consists in giving an account of reality.

Ortega's thought essentially included the evidence pertinent to establishing the thesis that human life is intrinsically ethical, i.e., moral or immoral. But this position implied the view that any comportment of self-deception, any endeavor to substitute others' convictions, valuations, aims, or desires for one's own is tantamount to a self-falsification, to being other than what one truly is. Those who really underwent the experience of meeting Ortega in the context established by the demanding closeness characteristic of his classes in the Department of Metaphysics were no longer capable of self-deception, for, if they ever attempted to deceive themselves again, they would have done so knowingly and, as a result, would have carried for the rest of their lives the burden of vexation and remorse.

At this point, it would not be useless to bring up the fact that only those who had the experience of partaking in Ortega's classes in metaphysics, especially when the experience was prolonged, are cognizant of a special dimension of his personality and therefore of his thought and manner of thinking, a dimension that is perhaps the most important about him. Not many have been acquainted with him in this fashion, since the courses taught by Ortega enrolled only a small number. The youngest of those who are presently alive and had this experience are about seventy years of age. In other words, those who still remain are few, and among them the emulators of Esau are not unknown.

Hardly had we graduated, when everything we had gained, i.e., our capacity for understanding and our moral strength, was put to the test by the civil war. Antonio Rodríguez Huéscar fought as a soldier in the armies of the Republic, in a simultaneous exercise of loyalty and disillusionment. He was shot in the leg, spilled his blood, and lost a great measure of his hopes, arriving at the conclusion that he would be defeated regardless of the outcome of the war, for no one could any longer expect freedom, generosity, or respect for the truth to prevail.

Since that time, he has been a man gifted with a lesser endowment of joy; he has become a person characterized by a decreasing measure of ambition. During the postwar period, he was content with leading his own life and making it possible for his wife and three daughters to lead theirs, for he had married quite early. He made sure he would never have to be ashamed of anything. He entrusted his life to obscurity. He limited himself to teaching a few unpretentious courses on a private basis, which meant for him little financial reward and even a smaller degree of success. His publications were few and far between, since they rendered "profit" to no one and were not forceful enough to tear through the puzzling cover of silence that hung in Spain over almost everything that was truthful.

For fifteen years, Rodríguez Huéscar taught philosophy at the University of Puerto Rico, then under the inspired presidency of Jaime Benítez, a remarkable man who transformed that institution into a Caribbean center of higher learning conceived after Ortega's ideas, and made it into one of the leading universities of the Spanish-speaking world located in the midst of an island the size of the province of Madrid. There Rodríguez Huéscar had the opportunity of personally seeing to the formation of students and of increasing the range of his intellectual influence by means of courses, essays, and books. Among the latter, his *Perspectiva y verdad* deserves special mention.[1] He would afterwards return to Spain, a land to which he was bound by an unbreakable allegiance. Once arrived in this country, he was entrusted with the responsibility of teaching at the preuniversity level, as many a distinguished man before him had done. (Among them I may refer to Antonio Machado, Vicente García de Diego, Samuel Gili Gaya, Gerardo Diego, and Manuel Seco). He was then able to impart lessons in philosophy to young minds just awakened to reason.

Antonio Rodríguez Huéscar set himself, above and beyond this, the intellectual task of coming to terms with Ortega's thought, of satisfactorily understanding his philosophical position. He proposed to do so by determining the ways in which its various components were linked, by rendering explicit the countless allusions found in his work, and by drawing consequences from that which only lay implicit therein. By means of courses characterized by careful and detailed analyses and by way of writings that are the result of perhaps excessive elaboration and reflection, he has been able, throughout fifty years of effort, to make progress into Ortega's philosophical system. Time and again, he has refused to remain on the surface of Ortega's thought and has rejected any enterprise seeking to adorn it in ways designed to elicit unthinking praise. He has focused his critical acumen on the analysis of certain parts of Ortega's work which in his estimation are of decisive importance and has then attempted, by means of a truly philosophical endeavor, to search after their contents and implications.

For the longest time, Rodríguez Huéscar's reflection has been directed to coming to terms with the concepts of "perspective" and "truth," which are so closely connected. His effort to unravel the web of implications bearing on apparently simple notions is worthy of our admiration, since he has been able to show that, given the systematic nature of philosophy, they "complicate," that is to say, coimplicate all there is. Now, by means of his new book, he comes to consider the problem of overcoming idealism, in an endeavor that mirrors his mature work, in so many respects already anticipated by him in various university courses. I am not, however, going to discuss that question, since it is the purpose of his book to do so. I only wish to emphasize the fact that it is an accomplishment traceable to the very philosophical beginnings of the author.

When Rodríguez Huéscar and I made our first acquaintance with Ortega, he used to begin his courses precisely by posing the problem of overcoming idealism. In my as yet unfinished book, *Ortega: las trayectorias,*[2] I direct the reader's attention to the moment when Ortega, in his attempt to define his philosophical position and to distinguish it from others that in his judgment were erroneous and insufficient, underscored the gulf separating it from vitalism, rationalism, and, finally, idealism. According to Ortega, idealism became the philosophical stance characteristic of the Modern Era, except in the significant cases of Spinoza (who was not a European) and positivism (which was not a philosophy). Even the philosophical position attendant to Husserl's phenomenology, which is the greatest philosophical innovation of our times, still constituted a manner of idealism, though it was a veiled expression of it and, to be sure, the most refined form thereof. The Modern Era began with Descartes, who was already moving in the direction of idealism, and idealism culminates in Husserl. But by 1900 the Modern Era had virtually come to an end. In fact, Husserl's work marks the beginning of our times, and yet error is reborn in the midst of the new dawn in the form of phenomenological idealism, which essentially is the same as the error that gnawed at the heart of modern thought throughout its entire history, and which prevented it from being freed—once and for all—from the shortcomings of realism.

This was Ortega's own perspective during that period, precisely the time when Rodríguez Huéscar took his first steps into Ortega's thought. For half a century, Rodríguez Huéscar has not been faithful so much to Ortega's philosophy as he has been to the perspective out of which it flows. He has devoted the better part of his talent and work to the task of mastering the philosophical system he encountered in his first youth. After fifty years, he has written a whole book that is a clear demonstration that he has fully understood the sense of those first lessons he took in philosophy and which have marked his destiny. This is why we will have to single out his writings as an essential component of the basic set of indispensable works contained in the vast bibliography devoted to Ortega.[3]

INTRODUCTION

I

The presentation of Ortega y Gasset's critique and overcoming of idealism may prove to be a good way of access to his metaphysical thought. In fact, it may even be useful as an introduction to his whole philosophy, provided the undertaking be carried out on the basis of a sufficiently broad outlook.

Ortega's metaphysical system is indeed built on the insight or, if you will, the strong sense—already developed very early in his career—that the philosophical positions characteristic of the Modern Era were hardly adequate [to the tasks for which they had been proposed]. After being in force for nearly three hundred years, such theses entered a period of decline that began in the late nineteenth century, a phase leading to the extinction of their historical virtualities. During their extended tenure, those views underwent a series of vicissitudes or were faced with various alternatives. The most profound among them was attributable to Kant, a fact that explains why Ortega found in him, as placed within the unfolding philosophical tradition, the most proximate origin of the dialectical conflict motivating his own thought. Since his first youth, then, Ortega harbored the conviction that he was witnessing the advent of a new epoch, a new sensibility, a new way of facing life and world, indeed a new style [of thinking and feeling] that would be "very much of the twentieth century but not modern in the least," if one chooses to phrase it after the title of his 1916 article in *El Espectador*.[1]

Accordingly, what is involved in this change is not just philosophy, but a whole historical situation as well, one which Ortega would soon characterize as critical, indeed as the times of a great crisis. It is to the examination and evaluation thereof that he devoted, throughout his life, an extensive and essential portion of his thought. In point of fact, the totality of Ortega's thought was motivated by his deeply rooted awareness of crisis and his need to adopt a position with regard to it. Now, in order to succeed in this enterprise, he had no choice but to scrutinize the given situation with serenity, since his aim was to understand its complex and disconcerting structure. Ortega had been alive to this requirement since his early youth, and in this respect he was far ahead of European thought. In fact, he took such a task not only as a historical necessity but as his unavoidable personal mission as well, indeed as a necessity and a mission to which his philosophical thought responded and to which it is conformed from its very roots.

In his early writings, in fact already with the publication of his first article in 1902,[2] it is possible to detect a fundamental insight of that sort guiding and moving his whole meditative effort. This becomes most apparent if we look at Ortega's early work retrospectively, i.e., from the vantage point of his mature thought. He was to render specific his guiding intuition soon enough by coming to a new metaphysical idea, namely, the notion of human life understood as the radical reality. This idea is as rich in developmental possibilities as it is complex and difficult to formulate and grasp by means of inflexible concepts. I hope to show how it signals an epoch-making philosophical turn, certainly a transformation that allows for the possibility of establishing a new period in the history of metaphysical thought, one which can only be compared, on the one hand, to ancient-medieval thinking as a whole and, on the other, to modern thought. Obviously, an idea of this magnitude—as is the case with any other of similar intellectual breadth and depth—could not have arisen only in Ortega's mind, as a solitary phenomenon so to speak. On the contrary, its birth was attended to and supported by a vast and manifold intellectual movement.

One can say, first of all, that this current of thought ultimately sought just one thing, namely, to return to the sphere of metaphysics, a discipline greatly spurned and disregarded during the second half of the nineteenth century by virtue of the then prevailing positivism. A quest of that kind was pursued by adopting various attitudes and approaches and even at times in terms of involuntary misconstructions. Secondly, one can find, as the most genuine source of the intent and general orientation of such a return, a profound need to relate thought and life—and assuredly not in any haphazard way, but by definitely establishing the primacy of life over thought and by abandoning thereby the "intellectualistic" principles (and even the presuppositions at their basis) on the grounds of which philosophy had proceeded since its origination in Greece, but especially since such principles and their presuppositions had been subjected to reinterpretation in "modern" philosophical reflection. Accordingly, bringing thought, indeed philosophy itself, to be at once a function of life and a process of reflection focusing on life itself became the new mission, in fact the novel desideratum felt and, above all, "seen" by Ortega before anybody else, no doubt more clearly than anyone who was an active participant in the intellectual life of the first half of the twentieth century.

Philosophers have always known and acted upon the conviction that their discipline is not just a theoretical endeavor, but a way of life as well, in the sense that such a determination would belong to the very essence of philosophy. I have in mind the *bíos theoretikós* or theoretical way of life which Aristotle, optimistically reaping the fruits of a first harvest, made into the substance and fullness of happiness. And yet the clear and express consciousness of the fact that, in the context of the philosophical way of life, theoretical reflection had to focus on "life itself" was to be a prerogative of our times, although this realization had already been anticipated—however obscurely—at certain "significant" moments of the history of philosophy, among which I wish to underscore those corresponding to the figures of Socrates, St. Augustine, Descartes considered as a moral thinker, Kant insofar as he was concerned with anthropology and the primacy of practical reason, Fichte, Nietzsche, and, to be sure, Dilthey, a well-nigh contemporary of ours.

This could not have been, however, otherwise, for the "dialectical" process involved in coming to this realization first demanded the occurrence of many an intellectual experience, the nature of which is, strictly speaking, metaphysical. Later in this study I shall subject to a detailed analysis the well-known fact that Ortega attempted to convey the substance of this process by articulating it into two extended periods of thought. The first phase began with Parmenides in the fifth century B.C., that is to say, with the very inception of philosophy. This phase lasted up to the time of Descartes in the seventeenth century. The second one started then and came to an end at the beginning of the twentieth century. Moreover, Ortega did characterize these two periods as realism and idealism respectively. And finally, he developed his now renowned conception of the two "major metaphors," about which I will speak in due course, in order genuinely to come to terms with the two historical periods in question.

According to this interpretation, we have been for some time running the last mile of the developmental race of idealism. Actually, Husserl and his phenomenological philosophy were but the swan song of idealism. The European mind was caught up in this predicament already in 1914, a year in which Ortega's major metaphysical idea had already reached its first mature formulation. We nevertheless find ourselves in a position to overcome idealism. In fact, our state of readiness to do so presents us with a task that Ortega did not hesitate to propose as the *theme of our times*, inasmuch as it expresses an urgent historical need.

In not so distant a future, we will have seriously to take up the challenge of carefully defining that most complex process involved in overcoming idealism, that is to say, in determining the many historical and intellectual errors that are encompassed by its sweep. I have in mind errors that are relevant to problems of the greatest consequence and not to matters of academic import, since our most uncertain future depends on their resolution. The fact that such errors endure precisely today, despite the fact that they should have been eradicated or "overcome" in Ortega's company, or according to the clear indications he began to provide us more than fifty years ago, could explain many of the implausible, stupefying, and absurd phenomena that form part of our present condition, one that indeed displays itself as chaotic and bereft of guiding lights. I cannot presume to undertake this task in these pages, not only by reason of the thematic limitations inherent in this book (insofar as it is focused on the critique and not on the overcoming of idealism), but also because it would then become a very ambitious project, which could be carried out successfully neither by one person alone nor by means of one single study.

To say it again: during the first thirty years of our century, the need to overcome idealism was generally felt in disparate philosophical quarters. One finds it present as much in the self-styled "philosophies of life" (e.g., those of Bergson, Dilthey, and Simmel) as one does in the so-called "existential" philosophies (e.g., those of Jaspers, Heidegger, Marcel, and Sartre). But one also encounters it in the "spiritualistic" philosophies (such as those of Le Senne and Lavelle), even in certain positions deriving from phenomenology (say, those of Scheler, Hartmann, and others), and in the last or penultimate developments of Husserl's thought (I have in mind the stage corresponding to his notion of the *Lebenswelt*), just to mention the most important figures. In fact, one could say that a new metaphysical climate of thought seems to have prevailed throughout this widespread movement, even though some of its representatives did adopt self-proclaimed extra- or even antimetaphysical positions, which they however embraced in the name of certain "ontological" assumptions, despite the great differences in direction observable among them. This climate of thought was indeed quite depressing, broody, or "anxiety"-ridden (if we are to use an expression that was fashionable then). This was particularly obvious in the quarters of existential philosophy. As a matter of fact, Ortega did exercise his ironical wit at the expense of the "lovers of anxiety" of those days. As opposed to their characteristic somber disposition of mind, he adopted an attitude [of serenity, that mental bent corresponding to] *ataraxia* or *halcyionism*,[3] of which Julián Marías has written so well and provocatively. What is at stake here, however, exceeds the sphere of mere inclination, as can be appreciated in the fact that some of the most significant and representative philosophers of the period made certain profound contributions that will have to be reckoned with and kept in view, if we are to understand that moment in history.

Today it is fashionable to hold up to scorn and even mock those philosophical positions in the name of others that are presumably new and "scientific." I could mention, for example, such trends as linguistic analysis, logical empiricism, dialectical philosophies of one stripe or another, structuralism, and other movements of lesser magnitude or importance. And yet all these schools of thought are rooted in certain metaphysical presuppositions, since no philosophy can evade having such foundations, although some of these schools may not be able to deal with and cast some light on them, as they are in principle required to do. In fact, their presuppositions are so anachronistic as to belong squarely in the nineteenth century. During the period lasting approximately from 1900 to 1960, the questions confronted by the philosophical schools proceeding on the basis of a new metaphysical foundation were rooted, to be exact, in the problem of the essence of man, of his historical sense, of the meaningfulness or meaninglessness of his life, which was then becoming unintelligible in the midst of the raging storm of the prevailing crisis. In those years, philosophical and literary movements of the "absurd" multiplied, and irrationalistic positions of all kinds prospered and blossomed as well. But of the men who embodied that philosophical turn of mind, however, no one can say—except through sheer falsification or in absolute ignorance of what they stood for—that they did not respond, on the basis of their inherent attitude, to the profound demands placed on them by their times. Indeed they personified their own philosophical turn of mind, which was a special *Stimmung*,[4] understood in Heidegger's sense of the term or not. This has to be acknowledged, whether or not the *Stimmung* at work involves an exaggeration or a deviation, and regardless of the fact that one may or may not use it as a basis for developing a philosophical doctrine.

Confronted with this situation, Ortega reacted in a more complex manner, indeed in a way that was at once more serene and (thereby) more effective. He knew how to evade the pitfalls of irrationalism and how to avoid any retrogression into the impracticable "ontologism" seemingly characteristic of such philosophical positions. He managed to find the intellectual key required to safeguard the rights of life and history, without thereby renouncing reason. This is why one can find only in Ortega the genuine formulation of the terms necessary to succeed in overcoming the crisis, a need sensed or felt by all, but actually fulfilled to a sufficient degree only in him. In so doing, Ortega reached a new metaphysical level, that is to say, a new practicable way to philosophize, if by "philosophy" one still understands the radical attempt to determine the sense of world and life that essentially consists in *giving an account* of them.

In my opinion, one must say that an achievement of this kind is precisely Ortega's own. Perhaps this is so not only because of his personal genius (though, of course, without genius no such result would have been forthcoming), but also by reason of the most special "circum-stances" in which he had to carry on with his effort. (And though this may sound like a paradox, it is really one of the major and most striking confirmations of his famous principle, "I am I and my circum-stance.")[5] In fact, it may very well be that Ortega would have never been able to go as far as he did in doing justice to his own metaphysical intuition, had he been fated to be born and lead his life in Germany or France. It may very well have been possible only for a Spaniard to have come fully to uncover the fact that human life is the radical reality, and completely to realize the sense of the new philosophical principle, by means of which the process of overcoming idealism could achieve—to say it again—its manifest and totally clear consolidation. But when in this context I speak of a Spaniard, I mean of course a European, but one who lived in the circumstances typical of the Spain of the time, an environment certainly devoid of a strong philosophical tradition. Such a placement gave him a freedom of thought and response that was not at the disposal of other European philosophers, immersed as they were in their own circumstances and traditions and especially conditioned by them. One must also keep in mind, no doubt, the role played by Ortega's very special talents and personal and biographical determinants, among which I would like to emphasize those that led him to take on the intellectual endeavor of "saving" the circumstances then prevailing in Spain, a requirement constitutive of his own circum-stantial world as the "destiny" or "mission" of his own life. I mean precisely the effort to bring philosophy in Spain to the level commensurate with the times and in the only way possible then: *habent sua fata philosophiae!*[6]

In fact, Ortega's bold metaphysical achievement consists in having realized—an event that took place quite early in his career—that reality *itself,* or reality given "in person," as Husserl used to say—in other words, the truth and (thereby) the reality the philosopher is seeking—cannot be found either *outside* or *inside* himself. And yet, since the times of the Greeks, philosophy has come precisely to one or the other result, indeed it has placed reality first outside, then inside the self. No other answer seems to have been possible, except to declare the philosophical quest itself impossible. Now then, both answers can only be forthcoming as the product of a far-reaching process of abstraction. Here I take "abstraction" in the twofold sense given to the term by the Scholastics. First and above all, it is the effort to set reality forth by casting something aside, by dispensing with one of the two great "components" of reality to the benefit of the other. Secondly, it is a manner of thinking that consists in generalizing, a procedure the final issue of which is the most universal of concepts, namely, the notion of being. As Ortega realized, this abstractive use of thought lies at the beginning of philosophy as one of its original errors, even if it proves to be a necessary one. But that is another question.

Like all originary errors, it is most difficult to eliminate or correct. Actually, it constitutes the burdensome and persistent Greek heritage—ultimately, the Eleatic inheritance—that philosophy to date has not succeeded in relinquishing. Ortega did thus become aware of the need to establish a new style of thinking or, as he also put it, to carry out a reformation of the mind or proceed to a new way of employing reason. Consistent with its new use, reason would have to operate at once on two fronts, for it would have to function both as an instrument of analysis (since the analytical service it renders cannot be waived) and as an organ of concretization, i.e., of directly and constantly keeping in touch with reality *itself*. Now, it is just in this second operation of reason that its "living" condition is essentially rooted, a character Ortega attributed to it as opposed to those exhibited by "pure" or "abstract" reason. But in order to have been able to postulate this new form of reason, Ortega would have had first to discover the truly originary or, as he said, "radical" reality metaphysics has always sought. This is no other than the reality of my own *living,* i.e., *my life* proper, a reality that we have never succeeded in seeing because of its immediacy and transparency. In fact, the moment we set out after it, we have already left it behind. Such a reality—a reality that is permanent *presence* and maximal transparency—implicates me and my circum-stance or world in an indivisible and dynamic unity of reciprocity. Both I and my circum-stance equally belong in my life, no side showing any sign by which to ascribe it priority or preeminence over the other. In my life, *I* am no "thinking thing" or "mind" or "consciousness," but simply someone who finds himself in a certain world and is already dealing with certain things at every turn, in the manner of having to *do* something precisely with the things available in the world and just in the here and now. In my life, neither my circum-stance nor the so-called "things" are anything at all *in themselves*. Rather, they are what they are *for me;* they are specific urgings or functions rendering my life possible—they are the "possibilities" facilitating my doing or becoming obstacles to it in my life. To use Ortega's own term, they are *prágmata,* i.e., "facilities" or "difficulties," serviceable means or their opposite.

Accordingly, the "radical" reality is, originarily speaking, both a duality and a mutuality; it is an originary and active interdependence that cannot therefore be located either outside or inside the self. Terms such as "immanence" and "transcendence" have now totally changed their meaning. In point of fact, similar transformations have been undergone by most of the terms of traditional ontology, even though we may keep using them out of inertia. The world and I transcend one another, and yet both the world and I are immanent in my life. My life is then a peculiar reality, for it is neither being (or substance) nor even existence; rather it is the "absolute event," to use Ortega's very own term, an event by which I already find myself living, that is to say, having at every turn to do something—like it or not—with and in my concrete circum-stance, so as to be able to go on living the next instant. Furthermore, it so happens that my inevitable doings are not "given" or established beforehand. On the contrary, I have to decide what to do at every juncture and, in order to accomplish this, I am in need of knowledge about my own self, as well as of knowledge concerning the possibilities my circum-stances open up or foreclose for me. This "knowledge about that which I can abide by" (as Ortega characterized it) concerns what I *can* do with things (i.e., it is the "blueprint of the universe") and what I *want* to make of myself[7] (i.e., it is the life project which I have to "invent" to some extent or other—in other words, more or less originally, but always without recourse).

This most brief and elementary description of the reality I call "my life" will, I hope, prove sufficient at this point to show how much Ortega's model differs from all metaphysical or ontological proposals that have been advanced so far. To begin with, it allows us to see that what Ortega characterized as a "radical datum" and as "the fact of all facts" happens to be a *given* which is not a "gift" (except as a problem to solve) and a *fact* which is not yet done (it is no *factum*) but something "to be done," indeed something we "have to do" (it is a *faciendum*).[8] On this basis, it is not difficult to see that, if we wish to think this sui generis reality, we are in need of fashioning new categories, for those belonging to traditional metaphysics or its derivatives have become invalidated by this new approach. At least, we must assign new significations to the terms traditionally employed in categorial analysis, so as to render them apt to grasp and express the fundamental structures of this new reality which is at once, to say it with Ortega, the oldest one. But it goes without saying that, upon drastically altering the idea we have of reality, we would be confronted not only with a transformation of the content of the categories, but with a change in the very notion of category as well. In other words, we are to experience not only a conceptual variation, but also a modification of the role concepts themselves are to play.

II

For the time being, this presentation will have to do [as an introduction to Ortega's position]. I will of course have to return to many of the questions I have touched upon here. To them I shall devote detailed analyses throughout my exposition of Ortega's doctrine, and I will even have to insist on some of them, especially in the concluding sections of this book. First of all, I will endeavor to show that Ortega came to formulate the views I have just sketched, and I will do so specifically on the basis of his critique of idealism or by means of it. Secondly, I will indicate how a critique of idealism implies a critique of realism, as well as of a set of attitudes and views that are essentially connected with both positions, almost all of which can be expressed by means of antitheses. Every such attitude and position can be overcome in the light of Ortega's stance, an accomplishment bearing, more or less proximately, on the fundamental antithesis of realism vs. idealism. Furthermore, one can say that Ortega focused his attention and critical effort on idealism as defined within the area of this antithesis; he was able to do so to the extent that the critique of realism had been brought to term, historically speaking, by idealism itself, insofar as the latter is a philosophical doctrine that arose on the grounds of a critical analysis of realism. This notwithstanding, Ortega did also subject realism to a critique, particularly in respect of those objectionable aspects of it that idealism had not been in a position to criticize, inasmuch as they were errors shared in common by both ways of thinking.

It was in idealism, therefore, that Ortega found the major danger threatening us today. (On occasion he even referred to it—as we shall have the opportunity to see—as the major "infirmity" or "vice of our times.") Its perilousness to us lies in the fact that it has outlived itself. At a time when it has already fulfilled its historical mission, it can only enduringly shape the European mind as a source of serious errors and deviations or, simply, as an obstacle or hindrance standing in the way of our adoption of new standpoints, namely, those required of us to come face to face with a new set of living and (thereby) social and historical problems.

To be sure, Ortega did not stand alone in opposing idealism. Since the end of the nineteenth century, philosophers belonging to various and sundry schools of thought have done likewise. And yet those philosophers, especially the most renowned and remarkable, Moore and Russell among them, carried on with their opposition in the name of a new realism. Actually, this is a factor common to the varied cohorts of "critical realists" and "neo-realists" which did form in continental Europe, Britain, or the Americas from the end of the nineteenth century to the middle of the twentieth. But Ortega held the view that if there is anything foreclosed in our rejection of idealism, it is any manner of relapse into realism, no matter how critical or new the garb it would don could be. In fact, the only form of realism that may be concurrently held with Ortega's position (and then never at the level of ultimate foundations) is the so-called "realism of the will," the most distinguished precedent for which is found in Maine de Biran's doctrine, a stance with which the names of Dilthey and Scheler are usually associated in our century. As a matter of fact, Ortega has devoted analyses and critical evaluations to Dilthey's and Scheler's views, thus clearly bringing to the fore the virtues and positive aspects of their positions, as well as their shortcomings and the dimensions along which they involved theses irreducible to Ortega's own. Finally, there are those who also criticize idealism without however postulating a new form of realism as an alternative, and yet such philosophers are nevertheless incapable of giving shape to a firm metaphysical position, on the basis of which they could clearly surmount both traditional doctrines. Now, this is possibly due to various reasons, for the philosophers in question may deny the legitimacy or possibility of metaphysics itself, espouse some form of irrationalism, or fall back on an ontologistic doctrine which is incompatible, according to Ortega, with the thorough reformation of philosophy that our situation demands. I hope to show how each and every one of these points arises and is dealt with in Ortega's critical analyses.

Let us now take a look at the most important antitheses to which I have alluded. I mean those which, more or less proximately, are rooted in the fundamental antithesis of realism vs. idealism, and which are only to some extent analogous to it. One can in fact take Ortega's thought as having overcome them.

[In a nutshell,] these are the antitheses in question:

A. *In the metaphysical order:*

1. Realism vs. idealism;
2. substantialism vs. psychologistic phenomenalism, biologistic vitalism, and so on; and
3. ontologism (including its existential variety) vs. antimetaphysical stances (above all, those developed on a positivistic basis).

The overcoming of these antitheses leads to Ortega's novel metaphysical doctrine concerning human life, which is biographically and historically understood as the radical reality.

B. *In the epistemological or metaphysico-epistemological order:*

4. Objectivism vs. subjectivism;
5. rationalism vs. irrationalism (in its vitalistic, existential, or other forms);
6. rationalism vs. relativism (particularly in its historicistic variety);
7. intellectualism vs. voluntarism; and
8. intellectualism vs. pragmatism.

The overcoming of these antinomies leads to Ortega's perspectivism, which is another, more encompassing version of his doctrine of living or historical reason and circum-stantial thought.

(At this juncture, one could well expand the list above by pointing to other ways in which Ortega has characterized the kind or kinds of thought that his own doctrine is designed to overcome. Among them, one can mention naturalistic thinking, progressivism, absolutistic thinking or thought sub specie aeternitatis, utopianism and uchronianism, thinking *ad calendas graecas,* and so on.)

Before turning our attention to our specific topic of concern, it is still necessary to make some general remarks concerning the antitheses just identified. First of all, it is to be noted that the epistemological antinomies or antitheses are almost always based on those belonging to the metaphysical order. In fact, they may be set forth concurrently with them. The same may be said of the attempts to overcome them. Accordingly, there is between them, as I pointed out before, a connection that is usually, if not always, essential. As is to be expected, this is of consequence for any critical analysis applicable to the antinomies belonging in those two orders. (The nexus between rationalism and modern idealism is a case in point.) Furthermore, the members of each pair of opposites do not correspond to the members of other pairs on a one-to-one basis. For instance, substantialism, as understood in the second metaphysical antithesis, is not a position exclusively associated with either member of the first antinomy, i.e., the antithesis of realism vs. idealism; in fact, it is a stance which can be connected with either side of the antinomy. From the outset, one must give up any attempt to establish a perfect symmetry between the respective members of this set of pairs of opposites, for, as I indicated above, they are only *to some extent analogous* to each other. (In philosophy, schematic formulations have not always been grounded in reality; in fact, not infrequently have they been propounded out of sheer eagerness to achieve conceptual symmetry. Kant and Hegel are well known in this regard: let us bring to mind the renowned Hegelian triads, a precedent for which is found in the no less renowned Kantian triads and tetrads.) Moreover, one could say that some of the theses in question (to keep to traditional terminology) may figure in more than one antithesis (as can be seen, for example, in the cases of rationalism and intellectualism). The reason for this is found in the fact that the respective concepts (or, possibly more exactly, the terms signifying them) are subject to a certain semantic oscillation, depending on the context in which they are employed in any given case. But this is quite a normal occurrence, which could be formulated by saying—according to present fashion—that the way terms are used is a condition determining their meaning. Briefly: pragmatics conditions semantics. (In point of fact, Ortega himself placed great emphasis on this sort of dependence, which is at the root of his theory concerning the universalization of "occasional expressions."[9] I mean of course the view according to which it is necessary to understand each and every concept referring to human life "as a function of the given occasion.") Finally, and to return to my first point, in Ortega's position one must underscore most forcefully the priority of the metaphysical over the epistemological order. Or to put it in his own words: any intellectual perspective must be inserted in a context constituted with reference to a more fundamental standpoint, namely, the "living vantage point," or that of life itself. Strictly speaking, one has to assert that Ortega's thought is metaphysical through and through, a contention that is tantamount to saying that it is the exact correlate of a concern, an ultimate intention, and, in the final analysis, a doctrine which are all metaphysical in nature.

III

Having completed this basic introduction, it is now time to turn to our own immediate topic of interest, namely, Ortega's critique of idealism. In what follows, I shall always have in mind a metaphysical position or thesis whenever I employ such terms as "idealism" (and "realism" too, of course, if and when the need to refer to the doctrine it signifies should arise). Unless otherwise indicated, I am leaving out of account any other connotations those locutions may have, be they philosophical or not, ranging from the acceptations they possess in everyday and literary language to those they acquire in epistemological, ethical, and other philosophical areas. I am also setting aside any of the senses they may be associated with within special sectors of discourse that are defined in terms of specific technical questions, such as that of realism as it is employed in the context of the problem of universals. (I do not mean to assert, of course, that the various meanings assignable to those terms cannot often be used concurrently, or even to deny the possibility that the pertinent concepts may be connected by means of relations of strict logical consequence.)

Accordingly, one may say that Ortega regarded realism and idealism—in the various forms they have taken up throughout history—as the two major solutions proposed so far to the problem that has seemingly been the basic preoccupation, indeed the prime "mover," of philosophy. In point of fact, this question has formally defined, since the times of the Greeks, the scope of the fundamental philosophical discipline, which Aristotle called *protê philosophía* or "first philosophy," and which later came to be known under the name of metaphysics. As is well known, Ortega modified the posing of the basic question by reason of his distinctive manner of understanding or conceiving reality and our cognition of it. In so doing, he thought he had taken up in his own statement of the problem the valid aspects of the intent inherent in traditional formulae, beginning with the *ti tó on*[10] of Greek philosophy, while at the same time believing that he had discarded any unjustified assumption at work in them. We are then dealing with a restatement of the matter, in which words such as "being" or "entity" are for the most part deliberately eliminated, or used only after having been subjected to a suitable critical elaboration, or employed in contexts where it is unmistakably apparent that they are rid of their traditional significations and endowed with a new sense. I have in mind such new expressions as "What in fact is-there?" or the more succinct, "What is-there?"[11] or again, arguably, his most original formula, "Which *reality* is the *radical* one?"

At this juncture, let us disregard the differences in outlook that are embodied in the various answers history has recorded as proposed to the question regarded almost to this day, let me say it again, as the fundamental problem of philosophy. If we do this, we may discover, believed Ortega, that all such answers reduce to only two, namely, the two major positions or classical theses that respectively go by the names of realism and idealism. The resulting dual scheme would fulfill, according to him, the conditions that an extreme procedure of this sort should abide by. Such conditions are the following:

1. The scheme advanced must be comprehensive enough to encompass the entire history of metaphysics until the given moment.

2. The two components of the proposed scheme should refer to solutions found or, as I indicated before, at least advanced as keys, to one and the same problem. To be more exact, one should say that they are to be solutions proposed for a metaphysical question formulated in the same fundamental way throughout history, although one should allow for the unavoidable differences as to particulars. This way of posing the problem would determine, in various respects, the *kind* of solution adopted, whether it takes the form of realism or idealism. These various respects shall be specified in due course.

On the basis of this understanding, it is possible to draw the following consequences:

3. On the one hand, the scheme would in fact have to exhibit the nature of an "antithesis," since its two components would have to be related by way of a "dialectical" opposition.

4. On the other hand, the opposition in question would operate and become established within a frame defined in terms of common metaphysical constants, although without reaching the same level of radicalism in each case. Those metaphysical constants could be specified with reference to the three standpoints signified by the terms that are most closely associated with the scheme of realism vs. idealism in the table of antitheses presented above. They are substantialism, ontologism, and rationalism (or their opposites).

Let me now take another step. I still have to mention the fact that Ortega approached this problem or theme—as he did any other found in the classical or traditional stock or list of philosophical questions—by means of the adoption of successive views that are, to some degree or other, motivated by "occasion" or "circumstance." In other words, he dealt with such problems or themes by placing them in different contexts, or by variously connecting them with other questions. Now, this is an *essential* feature of Ortega's thought, indeed one observable throughout his entire philosophical career. Despite appearances to the contrary, this way of proceeding is intrinsic to his manner of thinking, and even a methodological requirement of his thought. Therefore, there is nothing fortuitous, arbitrary, or capricious about this comportment, as some however have tried to show. In the present discussion, I cannot examine this special dimension of Ortega's method, which I have analyzed elsewhere with some care.[12] Suffice it to say that the essential and *deliberate* "circum-stantial" nature of Ortega's thought is responsible for the fact that his philosophical doctrine did develop according to an iterative-evolutionary and (so to speak) dynamically expansive style. In other words, his doctrine did achieve an increasing depth of insight into its themes and a growing conceptual mastery of them. This was accomplished on the basis of a set of fundamental intuitions available to Ortega since the very beginning of his intellectual career. (As I did point out at the outset, this was, in a certain sense, already the case with his first article entitled "Glosas.") Accordingly, if one wishes to carry out the exposition—and therefore proceed to study—any of the themes found in Ortega's thought, one is then required to follow a procedure that includes the analysis of the chronological-biographical development of the problem under scrutiny, while keeping in view the totality of Ortega's work. In other words, one has to follow through with a re-constitution of the topic on two fronts, namely, by regarding it both in itself and systematically. This is done by abstracting it from the varying "circum-stantial" contexts in which it appears, but without ever losing sight of them, since it is precisely the context that will allow us fully to come to terms with the specific features displayed by the particular doctrine of Ortega then under consideration, thus in the final analysis enabling us to *justify* them. Or equivalently stated: the history of the unfolding of the basic philosophical themes within the compass of Ortega's thought, or our seeing them according to the living perspective of their author, is decisive for the understanding of the *systematic* character specific to his doctrine. This doctrine finds its *ultima ratio* [or final ground] in the fact that the systematic character exhibited by Ortega's philosophical doctrine is nothing but the intellectual transcription of the systematic character of life itself, to which the former is intimately bound by a process of inherent justification, which is the fundamental nexus of *living reason*. By the same token, the methodological comportment that proceeds by means of the adoption of successive "views" concerning a reality one seeks to know is perfectly adequate to Ortega's manner of "circum-stantial" thinking and to his oft-iterated approach to the same themes, even when there may have been great intervals between his repeated attempts to consider them. This understanding applies whether one is dealing with a particular reality or with reality as such. I have in mind Ortega's way of besieging reality by closing in on it by means of a "progressive encirclement" or "spiral" approach, a way of proceeding Ortega called "Jericho's method" and also referred to by various other names, such as the "method of dialectical sequences," the "threading method," the "method of life urgencies," and so on, depending on the aspect of it he wished to underscore.

To be sure, it is not going to be possible for me faithfully to abide by all these methodological requirements, given the limitations of space under which I am working. I will focus only on certain essential texts of Ortega, but my presentation does nevertheless presuppose my acquaintance with the entire corpus of his work and my familiarity of long standing with his thought. It goes without saying that I will have to do without all—or nearly all— the "interpretive" fringe considerations motivated by the "circumstantial" and biographical examination of the origins of such texts. I am of course keenly aware of the truncations and shortcomings an omission of this kind would entail, particularly in a thinker like Ortega, who has elevated the "circum-stantial" nature of thought to the status of a principle properly so called, and whose doctrine cannot be adequately understood without having become sufficiently acquainted with *who he was* and the specific set of circumstances of his life, to which, in every case, the advancement of his views was a determinate response. Taking up ideas he had propounded long before, Ortega devoted himself in 1942 to giving thematic formulation to our need to carry out a general reformation of the history of philosophy.[13] A demand of this sort must be regarded as a particular application of his method of living or historical reason, which places us under the obligation to understand human facts—and ideas are certainly human facts—by situating them within their specific living contexts. By 1921 Ortega had already said as much:

> To date, philosophy has always shown a utopian face. This is why every system involved a claim to validity for all times and all men. *Abstracting from any living, historical, and perspectival dimension,* philosophy renewed, time and again and in vain, its effort to become definitive. In opposition to this tendency, I have proposed a theoretical account in which the role of standpoints [is acknowledged. Accordingly, I contend that] a system should incorporate into itself, in an articulate fashion, the living perspective from which it originated. . . .[14]

And in the piece referred to just before this one, he made this further point:

> A doctrine is a series of propositions, and propositions are utterances. . . . Now then, it is a mistake to assume that an utterance "has a sense all its own", which would remain after one abstracts from the time when it was said or written and from the man responsible for it. There is nothing which is "intelligible by itself". But the histories of philosophy that are usually available

to us are based on the opposite assumption: doctrines are presented there as if they had been formulated by "an unknown
philosopher", by someone bereft of birthdate or dwelling
place. . . .[15]

These citations, to which I could add countless others, will suffice
to make it apparent that there could be nothing more alien to
Ortega's spirit than to attempt to expound his thought as if it were
the work of an "unknown philosopher." And yet, even though it is
true that Ortega continues to be unknown to most people, including those devoted to intellectual subjects and, among the latter,
even those who speak or write about him, it is nonetheless the case
as well that he is no longer unknown to many others. Furthermore,
anyone may become acquainted with Ortega who shows an interest in his person and work, provided it is a concern sufficiently
strong to make him turn to the pertinent sources of information at
our disposal today, however few and unsatisfactory they may prove
to be. In fact, an abundant bibliography devoted to Ortega is
presently available to us in which we can select firsthand and
trustworthy reports about him, many of them originating with his
disciples. These sources are good enough to sketch out an outline
of Ortega's figure that would enable us to answer the following
two questions with some significant measure of accuracy: *Who
was Ortega? What was his circum-stance?*[16] We can even find,
especially for the young Ortega, a report of exceptional value, both
as to its intrinsic content and the nature and quality of the witness,
indeed a work that has become the norm to follow in studies of this
kind, and which we are obliged to read as the greatest accomplishment so far among them. I have in mind, of course, Julián Marías's
Ortega, I: Circunstancia y vocación,[17] a book of almost six hundred pages composed to initiate the efforts to answer such questions. I only hope he will crown his achievement with a second
volume of similar proportions and makeup.[18] On these grounds
alone, I may then dispense with the task—at least for the purposes
of this investigation—of having to conduct the relevant work of
exegesis and commentary that would be required in a more ambitious endeavor.

PART I

A Textual Exposition of Ortega's Critique of Idealism

Exclusively for the purposes of this investigation, I propose to differentiate three stages in the development of Ortega's critique of idealism. Let me proceed to specify them as follows:

First, one finds a phase which, in my opinion, serves to prepare the way. I would like to deal with it as "A Conceptual Introduction to Ortega's Critique of Idealism." It lasts approximately fourteen years, a period the boundaries of which are marked by the publication of "Renan"[1] in 1909 and "Las dos grandes metáforas"[2] in 1924. Together with these two, I would single out, as the most significant texts, his "Ensayo de estética a manera de prólogo"[3] and *Meditaciones del Quijote*,[4] both of 1914, and "Conciencia, objeto y las tres distancias de éste,"[5] published in 1916.

Second, one would come then to the straightforward critique of idealism properly so called. Reverberations of it are detectable already and above all in *Meditaciones del Quijote*, where it functions as a living and effective presupposition of the doctrine expounded by Ortega throughout the book. It comes expressly to be elaborated particularly in the following texts: "Kant. Reflexiones de centenario"[6] of 1924, which signals the beginning of the development of his critique of idealism; *¿Qué es filosofía?*[7] of 1929, which carries it out formally and thoroughly, in a manner especially relevant to the first or Cartesian version of idealism; "En el centenario de una universidad"[8] of 1932, where Ortega underscores the critical examination of the Cartesian form of idealism, but also brings up other matters connected with idealism; *Unas lecciones de metafísica* (1932–33),[9] in which he continues to elaborate his critique of Cartesianism from various standpoints, and *Sobre la razón histórica*[10] of 1940, where he returns to his critique of Cartesianism, although he complements it at that juncture by means of new approaches.

As one can gather from these texts, the point of view I have adopted in identifying this phase cannot be strictly characterized as chronological, for I have attempted to bring it to unity by assembling in it everything that is of significance to understand Ortega's critique of the first historical and, so to speak, originative form of idealism, namely, the Cartesian version of it. Had I envisioned a more comprehensive study, I would have had to take into account Ortega's critical analysis of substantialism, ontologism, and rationalism by devoting to them sufficient time and space, since they have to do with his critique of idealism. Among others, the texts useful to that end are the following: "Sensación, construcción e intuición"[11] of 1913, where Ortega presents his critique of ontologism; El tema de nuestro tiempo (1921–23)[12] and "Ni vitalismo ni racionalismo"[13] of 1924, writings relevant to the critique of rationalism; again "En el centenario de una universidad" (1932), which is pertinent to the critique of rationalism and voluntarism; "Historia como sistema"[14] of 1935, in which Ortega considers rationalism once more and elaborates a critique of intellectualism and ontologism; "Meditación de la criolla"[15] of 1939, in which idealism is examined as the "infirmity" and "vice" of our times; and El hombre y la gente (1949–50),[16] where the critique of substantialism is taken up. (One would also have to take into account portions of texts already mentioned, where these matters are regarded as well.) In this connection, one could also add his "Prólogo para alemanes"[17] of 1934, in which he elaborates his critique of German and Neo-Kantian idealism, although I shall especially avail myself of this remarkable piece both in the "Conceptual Introduction" and in my examination of the third stage of the development of Ortega's critique of idealism.

Third, one would finally have to regard as a distinct phase of Ortega's critique that in which he addresses the last historical form of idealism, namely, phenomenological idealism. For this purpose, his "Prólogo para alemanes" (1934) is crucial, but one would also have to consider other texts, the most significant of which are the following: one would again have to refer to Sobre la razón histórica (1940), but in conjunction with "Apuntes sobre el pensamiento, su teurgia y su demiurgia. Anejo"[18] of 1941 and La idea de principio en Leibniz[19] of 1947. At this stage, the space devoted to the critique of idealism is much smaller than in the second one; however, the sharpness and depth it achieves, the closeness of phenomenology to Ortega's position, and the special significance of the stance here subjected to criticism for the purpose of casting light on essential aspects of Ortega's new metaphysical idea are such that they amply justify dedicating to it a section of its own. (As belonging in this phase, one should take "Sobre el concepto de sensación"[20] of 1913 into consideration, for it is there that Ortega made a first presentation of the idea of phenomenology. Indeed, one finds sections of this series of articles in which the principles of the critique of idealism he will later expressly elaborate are already suggested.)

Let us then take up, one by one, the three stages of Ortega's elaboration of his critique of idealism.

CHAPTER 1

A Conceptual Introduction to Ortega's Critique of Idealism

An exponent of Ortega's doctrine[1] has characterized the initial or youthful stage in the development of his thought as an "objectivistic" phase. That interpreter had in mind the period running from 1902 to 1913, one that would culminate in Ortega's 1909 essay, "Renan." Now, the notion of such a would-be objectivistic phrase is highly questionable, as I have attempted to show elsewhere.[2] Rather, what one finds is a sort of Platonizing realism, the shape of which is not well defined, but which nevertheless contains certain "rudimentary" intimations of what would soon become the fundamental idea of his philosophical system. This phase of his thought displays, to be sure, some objectivistic features, but their uncertain character proves insufficient to define this stage in terms of a specific doctrine with which Ortega could be identified—not even remotely—at this point.

Accordingly, one could say that this is a transitional period in which Ortega is moving in the direction of certain fundamental and definitive conceptual determinations of his thought. For example, take the role played by the notion of *thing* in establishing the meaning of *res* in the context of the realistic position of which I spoke above. A thing, no doubt, becomes individualized in the process, and yet, by the same token, it paradoxically acquires universal signification and value. This is related, in principle, to the idea of "universal connection" that will later unfold in "Adán en el paraíso" (1910)[3] and in *Meditaciones del Quijote* (1914). During this period, Ortega unquestionably attacked subjectivism; in fact, he did so in the strongest of terms. This is particularly true of his "Renan," an essay in which his reaction against personalism was almost one of annoyance, but Ortega himself came later to acknowledge that his extreme formulations at the time were in fact

5

quite ambiguous. In any case, the whole attitude then adopted by Ortega pointed, no doubt, in the direction of a critical analysis of idealism, although, to be sure, it could not be construed as already being a definite elaboration of it. It only amounted to implicitly taking up a mind-set according to which the ego would subject itself, so to speak, to the lawfulness of things, indeed a position by means of which the propensity to arbitrariness or capriciousness to which the ego is liable when it abides solely by itself would be opposed. It was a question, then, of prescribing a regimen tantamount to the "imitation of things," as a way of replacing the "imitation of subjectivity" or, more exactly, of complementing both manners of imitation.

Without ignoring relevant differences, one can nevertheless say that Ortega's prescription here is in keeping with his later view that "we should think by means of things," a stance arrived at in his maturity, when idealism had already been rejected by him after a thoroughgoing critique. There is no denying that, in this formula, the term *thing* has undergone a transformation in meaning. In Ortega's "Renan," the word did not yet signify *prágmata* or "concerns," i.e., "facilities and difficulties"; it just had the sense of "cohering units of significance." And yet at this point Ortega already regarded the ego or subjectivity as inherently open to things or as given to objectivity. In fact, he managed then, somewhat obscurely to be sure, to make out the reality of human life by employing the concept of "verisimilar world." Accordingly, the significant (and not merely material) reality of things is responsible for the fact that the intimate nexus, bond, or solidarity obtaining between things constitutes a historical world properly so called, or a world established historically. Now, acknowledging that the significance of things is the "true" reality of life, or the "world" in which we truly live, seems to anticipate, albeit only in a rudimentary fashion, an initial understanding of the thesis that ego and "things" are doomed to coexist in essential reciprocity. Moreover, the task of subjecting idealism to a critical analysis, and certainly the goal of finally overcoming it, are proposed, whether by implication, postulation, or express contention, whenever the new idea of human life comes to light (and to the degree that it does). In Ortega, one thing is unquestionably a function of the other.

Only approximately one year elapsed between the publication of Ortega's "Renan" (1909) and that of his "Adán en el paraíso"

(1910), and yet, in the latter, one can already find Ortega's idea of life in full-blown operation, although its formulation in that essay is still rudimentary. Furthermore, the correlative concept of thing also underwent a profound transformation in that piece, for Ortega did not use the term there to signify substantial being, but to refer to relations and, in the last analysis, to functions dependent upon human life. At this point, a thing is regarded as a "universal nexus" or as the hub of a network of relationships with the rest of reality. Moreover, it is in this context that one can unmistakably identify, for the first time, the idea of perspective or the notion of standpoint, which is, among other things, a new major metaphor designed to signify and grasp the reality of life. If one were to abide literally by some turns of phrase employed in this essay, one could take Ortega's move as a relapse into idealism resulting from having withdrawn from his [previous] objectivistic position, but the sense of the piece as a whole—and even the letter of the text, if one excludes the ambiguous turns of phrase just alluded to—would render that interpretation impossible. On the contrary, his discovery of life qua radical fact inspires the entire essay; one even finds in it Ortega's first effort to try his hand at the description of life.[4]

The presence of Neo-Kantianism, under the influence of which Ortega found himself during the periods in which he stayed in Germany [at the beginning of the century], is ascertainable in this writing only as a meager vestigial trace without consequence. We are fortunate to have at our disposal a most valuable resource concerning Ortega's abandonment of Neo-Kantian idealism, indeed an account attentive to circumstances of time and place. I have in mind Ortega's "Prólogo para alemanes," which he composed around 1934. It is an exceptional autobiographical piece, which he himself characterized as unique in his entire literary output. There he described in detail the kind of education he received in Marburg and the positions he adopted in response to it. More than once, he refers to 1911 as the year in which he finally renounced Neo-Kantianism; he did so at the same time as Nicolai Hartmann and Heinz Heimsoeth, his contemporaries and fellow students. They all were then about twenty-six or twenty-seven years old, a fact that, according to Ortega, has the greatest importance for a person's intellectual development, since it is at that age that a human being "for the first time leads his life according to a mold that has not been merely received . . . [for] his spontaneity begins [then] to take hold."[5] It is at that point in his life that he came to understand the nature of the grounds on which his mind had already settled unknowingly. By way of an unconfessed will or "decision," he had by then adopted grounds that proved to be definitive, inasmuch as they "measured" the level of the mind-set proper to his generation. For him and his fellow students, that level was marked precisely by the "abandonment" of Neo-Kantianism. In 1911, says Ortega, they "were no longer Neo-Kantians." And yet one may wonder whether in fact they had ever adopted that conviction. In Ortega's case at least, it is perfectly clear that his "reception" of that philosophy, directly from Hermann Cohen and less so from Paul Natorp, was a merely external and "scholarly" event in his life, since he never came to identify himself with it. In his judgment, this was so much so that the only thing that prevented the whole learning experience he had been involved in from becoming a complete waste of time was that it afforded him the opportunity of seriously studying Kant's philosophy. Or to put it in his own words: "We had not completely wasted our time, however. We had seriously studied Kant's philosophy, and that's no trifle."[6] (Another matter entirely is, of course, what the encounter with such masters and fellow students and, in general, what the two periods in which he stayed in Germany, while he was a young man, signified in his life as a valuable human experience.)

In most instructive pages, Ortega passed judgment on post-Kantian or Romantic idealism, in which he saw an odd marriage between great philosophical genius and a peculiar and unusual lack of truthfulness. Even as he acknowledged the correctness of the purpose animating Neo-Kantianism, he underscored its insufficiency and ultimately emphasized the fact that it had been "infected" by the authoritarianism characteristic of Romantic idealism, precisely the doctrine it had striven to reform. Ortega also stressed its "excessive eagerness to be right." Moreover, he avowed having always had the feeling that Neo-Kantianism was strongly dogmatic in nature and that it functioned as a kind of prosthetic appliance.

Using Ortega's own words, one could briefly characterize both his response to idealism and that of his fellow students by saying that it amounted, first of all, to "opting for truthfulness"; secondly, to displaying a "will to systematic thought," and, finally, to holding "the conviction that one had no choice but to weigh anchor and leave behind not only the land of Romantic idealism, but the entire continent of idealism as well."[7] And to these points he added the following remark: "Abandoning idealism is, without question, the most serious and radical option open to Europeans today. The rest is just a side show. But exercising this option means not only giving up an area but an epoch as well, namely, the 'Modern Era.'"[8]

Now then, the problem vexing anyone embarking on a voyage without conceivable return can be formulated by the question, "Where can one put ashore?" since one would be making sail precisely "toward the unknown." Ortega himself acknowledged the fact that no one among them was then in possession of "*specific positive reasons* that would have allowed them to *know* that idealism was no longer true. . . . To be sure, we had at our disposal many *negative* reasons, many objections to level against idealism. But this is hardly sufficient. Living truth is not governed by the rules of scholastic disputation. Indeed, one has not come fully to establish the erroneousness of an idea until one is already in possession of a clear and positive idea by means of which to replace it. But this we certainly did not have. And this is what was odd about our situation, for we were aware of the perfectly recognizable and unmistakable outline or contour of the new idea, in the way the missing piece of a mosaic becomes conspicuous by its absence."[9] But Fortune chose to smile on the voyagers, who were embarked on a venture hazardous in nature and riddled with difficulty. She provided them with "phenomenology, a wondrous instrument." Ortega thus acknowledged his debt, but at the same time he formulated his caveat: those young men who, "strictly speaking, had never been followers of Neo-Kantianism . . . did never yield completely to phenomenology either," precisely on the grounds of their commonly shared will to systematic thought, which is incompatible with phenomenology. "This is the reason why, so far as we were concerned, phenomenology was not a philosophical doctrine; it was [just] . . . good luck."[10] From that moment onward, the members of the group followed their own separate ways, each seeking after "his own singular destiny which, at bottom, cannot be shared."[11]

After a couple of years had elapsed, Ortega's vessel had however managed to make port. He tells us that "in 1913 I wrote my first book which I entitled, *Meditaciones del Quijote.* There my natural reaction with respect to all I had received from my German education, which could be essentially reduced to Neo-Kantian idealism, was to become apparent . . . .[And] my reaction against . . . [it] was radical and unmistakable . . . .[I proposed the thesis that] an individual life. . . , each and everyone's life . . . , life *qua* immediacy . . . [is] the radical reality. And yet one's life *qua* radical reality is not consciousness or *Bewusstsein,* but . . . the dynamic dialogical intercourse between 'me and my circum-stances'. . . ."[12] Now, every ". . . cultural endeavor consists in *interpreting* life, i.e., it is the effort to clarify, explicate, or develop an exegesis of it. Life is an abiding text . . . [and] culture its [running] commentary. . . ."[13] And further on he adds: "As one can gather, twenty-one years ago I found myself for sure in possession of something analogous to what has only been recently discovered in Germany and is there called 'existential philosophy', a name that in my opinion is an arbitrary misnomer."[14] But "the boat in which I was sailing did not bring me to the uncertain shores of 'existential thought', but to those of the land I myself would soon refer to as the 'philosophical doctrine of living reason', where reason is meant to be, on the one hand, intrinsically and radically *vital* and, on the other, equally rational."[15]

Immediately thereafter, Ortega proceeds to relate how he came to the discovery of living reason, his narrative account of the achievement amounting precisely to conducting a critical examination of phenomenological idealism,[16] a position he overcame almost as soon as he assimilated it. (In 1912, he informs us, he devoted himself to a thorough analysis of it.) Later I shall return to the critical examination contained in this passage, which is of fundamental importance to understand Ortega's intellectual biography. Provided one does not overlook the differences due to time and place, one could even say that these lines bear some resemblance to portions of Descartes' *Discourse on Method,* especially if viewed in terms of the similar role such texts do in fact respectively perform as direct reports of an important intellectual discovery. Indeed, this section of Ortega's piece allows us, with sufficient accuracy, to locate a period of decisive importance for the constitution of his metaphysical system, since by means of it one can see that idealism had been completely overcome by him in 1913, the year when his *Meditaciones* were composed. The passage in question makes it apparent that Ortega was then in full possession of the metaphysical idea that would embody his overcoming of idealism, although one does not find him there explicitly carrying out a critical analysis of this doctrine.

Two other [significant] writings also belong to Ortega's 1913 production. Although they are not critical but strictly expository in nature, one should nevertheless avoid neglecting them, for, in accordance with the manner of expression so characteristic of Ortega's creative mind, one may always find instructive passages therein where a personal contribution is made. This is true regardless of the subject matter under consideration, even when the manner of presentation is apparently most objective, as it happens when the piece in question is devoted to the exposition of the doctrine of others. In this instance, however, it is no less than phenomenology, and not just any doctrine whatever, that falls under the author's focus of attention. Now, [the choice of topic is of signal importance,] since Husserl's publication of [the first volume of his] *Ideen* took place too in 1913.[17]

The first writing is "Sensación, construcción e intuición,"[18] the text of a speech delivered by Ortega at a congress convened by the "Spanish Association for the Advancement of Science." He devoted his presentation to an exposition of the empiricistic conception of sensation (according to Mach and Ziehen), the Neo-Kantian "constructivistic" form of idealism, and, finally, the phenomenological notion of "intuition." The consideration of the latter is most brief and is conducted almost entirely by way of allusion, even though the whole speech is conceived from the point of view of the phenomenological understanding of intuition and moves in the direction of it. The second writing, entitled "Sobre el concepto de sensación," presented Heinrich Hoffmann's *Investigations Concerning the Concept of Sensation.*[19] In this series of articles, Ortega gives us one of the first clear and accurate formulations of the fundamental idea characteristic of phenomenology, then a most novel philosophy and soon to become a decisively influential philosophical doctrine. It is worth noting how Julián Marías passed judgment on Ortega's accomplishment in "What is Phenomenology?," one of the articles mentioned. This is what he had to say: "I seriously doubt that anyone has attempted to answer so exactly the question [formulated in the title], and done so on the basis of such intimate knowledge. Certainly this did not take place outside Germany at that time."[20]

We have to bring these two texts to bear on our discussion, even though, to say it again, they are not expressly critical, except here and there. The justification for this decision lies in the fact that, by means of these pieces, one can clearly see how far Ortega had proceeded in distancing himself from the doctrines he was there endeavoring to expound. This is hard to believe, especially concerning the issue of phenomenology. Particularly in the second writing, to which I shall return in the "third wave" of my presentation, one can find such concepts as the notion of "performative value" [*ejecutividad*], a fact also underscored by Marías, and even the first version of what Ortega will later call "Jericho's method" or the "method of dialectical sequences." This is undoubtedly sufficient to point to the metaphysical ground to which Ortega had already advanced, and on the basis of which he approached the doctrines he was expounding, doctrines that, in the final analysis, reduce to one or another form of idealism. This ground is no other than that of his definitive philosophical position, which he so forcefully and brilliantly gave expression to in his *Meditaciones,* a book roughly contemporary with these pieces.

Actually, in his "Ensayo de estética a manera de prólogo" (1914), composed to introduce José Moreno Villa's *El pasajero,* Ortega used the notion of performative value once again, but there he already endowed it with the distinctive and innovative metaphysical connotation that henceforth is to be the proper meaning of the term. Accordingly, when in that context he spoke of "the 'ego' *qua* performance,"[21] he was implicitly referring to his eventual and decisive critique of realism and idealism, although without having arrived as yet at the full realization of its significance. His express intent was then to free reality itself (that is to say, the necessary and irreducible polar duality constituted by ego and things) from the shackles of intellectualism, to rid it of any intellectualistic distortion, especially in its idealistic or extreme form. By means of the concept of "performative value," Ortega therefore "sensed" the pulsation of life itself (which is prior to any intellectual interpretation of it, or to anything given or presented to it), namely, that which is other than I. The concept of performative value or "performative being" came thus to have pride of place in Ortega's thought, precisely as the key idea of his metaphysical view of reality. Strictly speaking, it is another title for the very notion of radical reality or human life, a concept or idea the paradoxical nature of which lies precisely in the fact that it points to a reality free from—or itself not subject to—any form of conceptualization or "ideation." Carried to its ultimate consequences, Ortega's critique of idealism is equivalent to the rejection of any interpretation or idea of reality that takes reality not only as if it were an idea, but even as something that would be tinged by the slightest idealistic coloring. Seeing reality as performative being is tantamount to placing oneself before reality from a vantage point prior to the event of making the distinction between the two sides of reality, namely, between ego and things. In other words, it corresponds to a perspective applicable to the two dimensions of reality, since performative being encompasses them both. This manner of procedure is equivalent to adopting in every case a point of view irreducible to that of any concept or image, for it consists in placing oneself in the position of the very thing that is being conceived or imagined as it is itself [*en su mismidad*]. According to Ortega, an image (or a concept) cannot possibly be identified with what is imagined (or with what is conceived). In terms of this formulation, one is then able clearly to appreciate Ortega's effort in his attempt to overcome both the realist's and the idealist's standpoints—or, to use his terminology at the time, to go beyond the objectivistic and subjectivistic points of view. One may thus say that he sought to supersede subjectivism by treating the particularity of each thing with the utmost deference, that is to say, by taking things as they are themselves and according to their independent status. Or to put it in his own words: "every thing is *ego* when it is regarded from within."[22] But he also sought to surmount objectivism by means of a conceit in terms of which a thing is taken as "*ego*," a procedure presupposing that one has grasped the most intimate and originary reality of the "*ego*." Now then, this comportment implies two things: on the one hand, it means that one has become aware of the impossibility of thinking of an ego as if it were "totally disengaged" and "in isolation"; on the other hand, it signifies that what one postulates when one regards a thing as it is itself necessarily refers to its being present to an ego, however paradoxical this may seem.

Here one can also find the essentials of an argument that will prove decisive for Ortega's elaboration of his critique of idealism. It is a form of reasoning which is, no doubt, especially applicable to phenomenological idealism, even if in the present context he speaks only in general terms. In fact, he uses expressions like "subjectivism," the "original sin of modernity," and the "mental ailment of the Modern Era," although one should not forget that he characterized subjectivism too as a "source of no insignificant number of virtues and accomplishments." Ortega contended that the adoption of a subjectivistic standpoint

> consists in assuming that I am that which lies in closest proximity to myself—in other words, that, cognitively speaking, my own reality is, or I am, insofar as I am real, closest to myself.[23]

On that basis, it is possible to formulate Ortega's argument in a nutshell as follows: "When I feel pain, when I am engaged in loving or hating, I do not *see* my pain, nor do I see myself engaged in loving or hating,"[24] for, in order to carry out that observation,

> . . . I must no longer be in pain and have to become an "ego" that is engaged in seeing. The "ego" now engaged in seeing the former "ego," i.e., the ego then in pain, is at this point the only genuine or performative "ego" actually present. Strictly speaking, the "ego" in pain is no more; it has now been reduced to an image, thing, or object confronting me.[25]

But "an image is irreducible . . . to that which is imagined [thereby] . . . pain, while it is felt, is the opposite of an image of pain."[26] (And this point can be equally made with regard to things or the "ego.") According to Ortega, the subjectivistic trend of thought reached its climax with Fichte, after whom a period of decline set in, "perhaps now heralding our arrival at new shores then only vaguely anticipated, or at a novel manner of thinking freed from that concern."[27]

In terms of these first fruits of Ortega's original thinking, one can see that he was not ready to grant the ego any metaphysical privilege, since it is the case that I am acquainted with other human beings and with things no less directly than with myself. In fact, he went as far as to make the following statements, where the new manner of reality he was after and his new metaphysical perspective become fully manifest:

> Only with . . . our lives are we in intimate terms . . . but this intimate relationship of ours is no more whenever it becomes an image. . . . *Genuine intimacy, consisting as it does in self-performance,* is no image at all, neither of something external nor of something internal [to our lives], but rather it is something equally distant from both extremes.[28]

We already have before us the *new approach* that is characteristic of Ortega's thought as a whole, and which is as different from realism as it is from idealism. To be sure, Ortega did not then have the required conceptual instrumentality at his disposal that would have allowed him adequately to work out the new intuition he already possessed, and yet he clearly grasped the difficulty corresponding to it, or the basic problem motivated thereby. Let me put it in his own words: "Whether and how it is rationally possible . . . to turn into an object of our thought that which appears destined never to become an object at all."[29]

Unable at the time to deal with this problem on its own terms, Ortega turned to art to consider the role it could play in allowing us to come into contact with genuine reality.[30] First of all, he proceeded to reject Theodor Lipps's doctrine of *Einfühlung* [empathy], characterizing it as "an error born of the subjectivistic offense of which I spoke before." Instead, he postulated the existence of a *presentative function* that would be exercised by things whenever they are "engaged in self-performance."[31] A function of this sort, however, would not be introduced to replace *cognition,* since, after all, Ortega's position was not irrationalistic; it would rather complement it, or render it possible. Now, the basic instrument for the discharge of that function would be the "aesthetical nucleus" or *metaphor.* In this context, we thus come across another concept among Ortega's fundamental notions, the first formal mention of which can be found, as far back as 1909, in his essay "Renan." The development of this idea, taken as an essential component of a significant theoretical formulation, can be retraced along a well-defined path. In his "Conciencia, objeto y las tres distancias de éste" (1916), Ortega confronted the strange character of consciousness, noting with special emphasis the particular *dual* nature it exhibited. As he then said, "I am face to face, as it were, with something different from or other than me."[32] But he also insisted upon the indivisible *unity* characteristic of this dual totality. This brief and penetrating analysis of consciousness and its [correlative] object, which was carried out already by means of the employment of tools provided by phenomenology, involved an inchoate formulation of Ortega's new metaphysical doctrine, although it was advanced only at the most abstract level of discourse, namely, that concerning the indissolubility of the nexus of reciprocity formed by ego and things, a nexus which constitutes a higher-order reality that equally encompasses both elements. But inasmuch as the facts in question were difficult to handle conceptually "in a straightforward fashion," Ortega proceeded to develop his notion of metaphor precisely in connection with the idea of consciousness. This is particularly evident in his 1924 essay, "Las dos grandes metáforas,"[33] where the problem is formulated in a specific and strict fashion and at a higher level of maturity and precision. As contrasted with his initial attempts, as found in his 1909 essay, "Renan," here Ortega makes progress, for he is now able to find a rightful place for metaphorical speech in the context of the most rigorous employment of scientific and philosophical discourse. In fact, it is in this writing that he expressly tells us that metaphors are "essential mental instruments" and constitute "a manner of scientific thought."[34] There he also defined for us the "two ways of employment, of unequal standing, . . . [that they] find in scientific discourse," namely, as a "means of expression" and as an "instrument essential to intellection."[35] Accordingly, one must say that metaphorical discourse would allow us to have precise knowledge of realities.[36]

In the context of our discussion, it is not possible to make available, even in outline form, Ortega's doctrine of metaphorical discourse.[37] I bring it up, however, for it is in terms of the notion of metaphor that Ortega arrived at the correct formulation of the conceptual introduction that is a prerequisite for his critique of idealism (and for that of realism too, of course). He came to it by way of his attempt to present to us again the idea of consciousness. A metaphor is, he tells us, "an instrument necessary to engage in the process of abstraction." But "abstraction" is the name for a comportment consisting in thinking of something as if it existed separately, a procedure that would isolate the thing in question from everything else with which it appears joined, and that would result in forming a clear and distinct concept of it.[38] Now, a practice of this sort is all the more difficult to follow the more abiding the presence of the object under consideration, or "the greater the number of combinations in which it plays a role."[39] There is, however, nothing more abidingly present than consciousness, for it is a "phenomenon that is the unavoidable concomitant of every other phenomenon, one which is uniformly and unfailingly associated with it and appears always in attendance with it."[40] To this Ortega added the following reasoning:

> On account of consciousness . . . everything else appears to us, we become aware of everything else. . . . Consciousness is the very fact of appearing, the event itself of our becoming aware. . . . Accordingly, there is nothing more difficult to understand, perceive, describe, and define than this universal, ubiqui-

tous, omnipotent phenomenon. . . . The employment of metaphors is unavoidable in the case of consciousness, if anywhere.[41]

This is the reason why people have resorted to metaphors whenever they have attempted to think of something, or to translate it
into concepts. Now, Ortega contended that all the metaphors thus
far employed in the history of philosophy reduce fundamentally to
two, to which he referred as the "two major metaphors." On the
one hand, we have that which prevailed since the time of the
Greeks and up to the Renaissance, that is to say, throughout Antiquity and the Middle Ages; on the other hand, we find that which
predominated throughout the Modern Era up to the present times.

Let me now attempt to formulate the problem being dealt with
here. Object and subject, that is to say, that which is perceived and
the mind perceiving it, display "opposite features," by virtue of
which they exclude each other. And yet in the phenomenon of
perception they *coincide,* a contradictory state of affairs if there is
one, a fact which thus becomes a problem (analogous to the one
that exists in the case of the stick [partially] submerged in water).
Actually, the problem in question is twofold.

On the one hand, we discover that perception discloses that
what is perceived is somehow present in us. "But how could it be
possible to find anything like a mountain two thousand meters
high enclosed within an unextended mind? The first stage of our
examination of this question would then have to be the attempt
simply to describe how it is that things are present in consciousness."[42]

On the other hand, we are to say that the "second stage of the
process would amount to providing an account of how . . . this
manner of presence . . . comes about. Now, one should endeavor
to keep the two dimensions in question separate from each other,
but one cannot identify an effort of this sort either in Antiquity or
in the Modern Era, for in both historical periods the description of
the phenomenon itself appears mingled with the attempt to render
an account of it."[43] One can appreciate this point in terms of the
two major metaphors by means of which men have successively
tried to *understand* this phenomenon.

First of all, we encounter the metaphor of the seal and the
wax tablet. According to "this interpretation, subject and object
are related to each other in the way any two bodily things can."
The two dimensions would exist independently of one another,

both before and after they came to be related, but, whenever in fact they are so related, the object would leave its imprint in the subject: "consciousness is [thus] impression."[44] This is the thesis of realism, to the critical analysis of which Ortega proceeded at once by noting its incongruity, for how would it be possible to compare a thing with the imprint it leaves in the mind? What we see is always the mental impression of the thing, which we are thus unable to circumvent in order to gain direct access to the thing itself. The view that objects may exist outside consciousness and apart from it cannot ever be anything but an opinion fraught with danger. It is certainly not a thesis marked by indubitability. In light of it, one could never distinguish between perception and hallucination. This realization is precisely the port of entry for Descartes, who "resolved to introduce a major innovation": in his hands, things turned into thoughts (*cogitationes*). The relationship between things and consciousness is now "interpreted in a manner opposite to that of Antiquity [and the Middle Ages]." The metaphor of the container and its contents is at this point substituted for that of the seal and the wax tablet: "thoughts are seen as being just states of the subject, of the [thinking] ego itself, of *moi même, qui ne suis qu'une chose qui pense* [of myself, who am but a thinking thing]. . . . Things do not come from outside consciousness, but are contents of consciousness; they are ideas. Hence the new doctrine is called idealism."[45] Imagination is given pride of place in this conception, which is proper to the Modern Era, just as perception was in the interpretation characteristic of Antiquity [and the Middle Ages]. But "as in the tales of the East," the ego, whose former station was that of a beggar, "awakens as a prince."[46]

This is the special path Ortega followed in posing the problem in 1924. In this manner of formulation, one may already identify the prerequisites according to which one may carry out a critical analysis of idealism, although they are advanced there only in their incipient form. Such prerequisites are:

1. One should clearly distinguish between the pure description of a phenomenon and the account one renders of it.

2. One ought to emphasize the radical difference, even the antagonism there is between the mode of being of things and that of subjectivity or consciousness.

3. One must deny the existence of the right to grant primacy or privileged status to any one of the two members in the pair "ego and things." In this manner, one does postulate an attitude of strict impartiality.

4. One should never lose sight of the metaphorical nature of any interpretation. In this fashion, one would be able to strive not to take interpretations *in modo recto* [literally].

On the basis of this conceptual introduction, let us then proceed now to examine the critical analysis to which Ortega subjected idealism.

CHAPTER 2

Ortega's Straightforward Critique of Idealism Properly So Called

By means of his 1929 essay, "Kant. Reflexiones de centenario,"[1] Ortega embarked on his critical analysis of idealism. He chose to develop, as his point of departure, an understanding of the German soul. He found it to be characterized by a peculiar proclivity towards self-absorption, reflection, or subjectivism, in contrast with that proper to the Mediterranean or meridional soul, namely, a marked sense of being pulled by things and other men. These two originary experiences or primordial impressions are radically opposed to each other: on the one hand, Ortega pointed to the state of aloneness, self-enclosure, or metaphysical isolation characteristic of the German soul; on the other hand, he spoke of the projection of the self upon the things of this world, the extrovertedness or call to the marketplace typical of the meridional soul. Ortega also underscored the peculiarity of the first manner of sensibility, to the point of regarding its sense of inwardness as well-nigh pathological, since the natural bent of attention is to focus, to begin with, on extramental objects, while the event of ". . . taking cognizance of consciousness, or of turning it into an object, is a secondary phenomenon that presupposes . . . [our taking cognizance of extramental objects]."[2]

According to Ortega, a philosophical doctrine in the "meridional style" sets out to construct the ego as if it were analogous to the body, but any subjectivistic philosophical system proceeds to construct the world intellectually as if it were analogous to the ego. Moreover, Ortega correlated these two points of view with the notions of "trusting soul" and of "distrustful or wary soul," respectively, although he also connected them with other concepts, such as those of the types of humanity known as the warrior and the bourgeois and the kinds of mentality proper to man in Antiquity and the Modern Era, respectively. A study devoted to the examination of these correlations would be of the greatest interest, but here I must concern myself only with the well-defined metaphysical subject of this investigation, and I shall do so in a somewhat inflexible manner by purposely subjecting Ortega's many-sided thought to a process of "desiccation" and a nearly relentless simplification.

Ortega contended that modern philosophy is coextensive with idealism, except for a few understandable cases. But Western man has already run through the entire gamut thereof and has touched the deepest reaches of the intellectual experience of modernity. In fact, he has traveled through all the possible avenues it opened to, until he finally came to discover that ". . . it was an error"—a magnificent experience and a fruitful error, without which "a new philosophical stance would . . . [have been] impossible," but an error nevertheless. And conversely: the *novel philosophical stance* and the *novel manner of living* may be guided only by one watchword, namely, the "overcoming of idealism."[3] Accordingly, one is entitled to regard Ortega's essay as the beginning of a new phase in his critical examination of idealism, one which will be developed by means of three basic texts: *¿Qué es filosofía?* (1929), *Unas leccciones de metafísica* (1932–33), and *Sobre la razón histórica* (1940). They correspond to three lecture courses in which Ortega approached the subject of this inquiry more broadly and closely than in any of his prior attempts thus far discussed.

In his *¿Qué es filosofía?* Ortega initiated his critical examination by pointing out that the novel style of philosophical thinking, as opposed to prior attempts to philosophize, is marked by the awareness at full that there is a radical qualitative difference between the seeing, imagining, or thinking subject and what is seen, imagined, or thought by it, whether the object in question is physical or "ideal" in nature. As I already had the occasion to note, this distinction is already found in Ortega's "Las dos grandes metáforas" and shall be reiterated elsewhere. This indeed comes as no surprise, since one may assert that Ortega's admonition to keep to this distinction—one which was indeed examined in depth by him in all its ramifications—is the very basis of his critical analysis of idealism.

The text under consideration places the problem of realism vs. idealism at the most fundamental metaphysical level, namely, at that of our search after (and would-be identification of) what Ortega calls *radical data.* Every intellectual performance, and particularly every theoretical formulation, must make its departure on the basis of certain *data,* since the motivation for thinking is always the awareness that something is *problematical,* and every problem implies the existence of data. Regarded in themselves, data are not problematical; their problematical condition arises, however, in view of the insufficiency, incompleteness, or contradictoriness they may exhibit. (Ortega often referred to the classical example of the stick partially submerged in water.) This is the usual state of affairs encountered when one is engaged in attempting to arrive at any theoretical formulation, but, when one is endeavoring to advance a philosophical or metaphysical theory, i.e., one which has the universe or the *totality of all there-is or is-available* as its theme or problem, the search after data becomes especially serious and difficult. While in any investigation conducted within the confines of a particular area (for example, that of a given science) "data are not problematical, the problem of [the identification of] the would-be data for the constitution of the universe does however loom large and unforgiving already at the threshold of philosophical inquiry. Philosophy must be concerned precisely with the question of determining what exists for certain or indubitably within the totality of all there-is or is-available."[4] In other words, the "radical data" philosophy is after are characterized, as opposed to any other sort of data, by the following features:

First of all, radical data, precisely insofar as they are radical data, are problematical in nature. In other words, data of this sort are not just given; one must seek to identify them.

Secondly, they must be radically indubitable. But this is equivalent to saying that, just as in traditional metaphysics one encountered the "modalities of being," in the novel style of doing metaphysics one is to find the modalities of what there-is or is-available. Accordingly, the reality given to us in a radical datum exhibits, within the totality of all there-is or is-available, a modality characterized by the following properties:

1. It renders the reality in question irreducible to any other.
2. It establishes it as a case of last resort, or as the most universal exemplar to which to refer any other reality within the totality of all there-is or is-available.

3. It is responsible for the fact that the reality sought is given to us without mediation.

4. Accordingly, it also accounts for the fact that it is self-evidently given to us, i.e., at a level of evidence marked by its radicalness or indubitability.

These last two features spell out what one could characterize as the "requisite of presence." In this context, Ortega employs terms like "unmediated presence," "intuition," "insight," or "evidence" as nearly synonymous. To the subject of evidence, he in fact has devoted the sixth lecture of this course, where one can see how he takes up Husserl's doctrine on the matter and carries it further. Ortega's treatment of evidence is guided by the goal of establishing the grounds of a novel form of metaphysics that would supersede the level of thought where Husserl was still situated, namely, that of idealism.

It is not possible to examine here this important passage, which I have analyzed elsewhere,[5] but I must at least underscore the fact that it is crucial for the question of determining the principles of Ortega's metaphysical system. Later I will have the opportunity of showing how, according to Ortega, "presence" is to be regarded as the "first category" to be identified in the attempt to specify the structure of human life, and how the strict observance of a regimen in which one would understand life in terms of this category is the primordial, indeed the literally fundamental, requirement to be complied with by "philosophical theory."[6]

These thematic indications are useful towards the end of making a descriptive presentation of some of the most important implications of the problem of "seeking after radical data," but they hardly exhaust the subject. At a juncture like this, Ortega proceeded to list those entities that have in fact been or may be proposed as radical data, only immediately to eliminate those that do not fulfill the above-mentioned requirements, which, in the final analysis, can be reduced to the requisite of "unmediated presence" or "intuitive evidence." Let me summarize as follows the various sorts of data that have been rejected by him as dubitable to some degree or other:

First of all, we have the objects of fantasy, the dubitability of which is so apparent that it deserves no special examination.

Secondly, we find the objects of physics (e.g., forces, atoms, electrons, and the like), the existence of which is only manifest in terms of a theoretical account, or as a result of it. Accordingly, their factual existence is a function of the truth-value of the theoretical account in question, the status of which is, at best, that of a problematic truth (at least insofar as it must be proven).[7]

Thirdly, we come across the sense-perceptible data, which gave Ortega the opportunity of formulating, in a most penetrating fashion, the well-known argument concerning the phenomena of dreams and hallucinations, in keeping with the most genuine Cartesian tradition.[8]

After the elimination of such dubitable data, one is left just with the experience of doubt. Accordingly, one thus finds oneself in the domain of thought proper. But this makes one come face to face with the idealist's stance, to which Ortega devotes an extended exposition, carried out by him with the utmost precision. But in order to be able to arrive at this result, he adopted the idealist's standpoint itself, since his goal was to achieve an intellectual understanding of idealism that could be characterized as most accurate and clear, for he wished, to put it in his own words, "to exalt clarity to the level of frenzy." The justification of this procedure lies in Ortega's view that anyone may find himself in the position of overcoming idealism only if he absorbs and assimilates it completely. Let us not forget that overcoming idealism was for Ortega no less than a personal, intellectual, and historical necessity. Now then, the attempt to overcome idealism will prove all the more difficult—and as well all the more genuine—the better one understands the firmness and solidity of the idealist's thesis, by which "consciousness" is proposed as the radical or primordial datum for the construction of the universe.

It is not possible to doubt the existence of thinking, inasmuch as doubting is a form of thinking and, therefore, of existing. Or as Ortega expressed it: ". . . of the entire universe, only thinking is given to thinking. Its manner of self-givenness is that of indubitability, since thinking consists only in *being given;* it is sheer presence, sheer appearance, sheer self-disclosure. To this amounts Descartes's great and decisive discovery, which becomes, as a sort of imposing Wall of China, the dividing line marking off two periods within the history of philosophy. . . ."[9] Before it, one finds Antiquity and the Middle Ages; after it, one faces the Modern Era.

In light of this, one is entitled to say that it is not true that something exists because I imagine or think of it, but that it is "enough that I think this or that for thinking to exist."[10] Therefore, thinking is ipso facto the positing of the being of thinking. In other words, thinking is a datum to itself. Over against what may be the case with the rest of the universe, one may assert that thinking is sui generis, because only "thinking and existing are one and the same."[11]

Now, our certainty about the existence of thinking (*cogitatio*) "cannot be compared to that of any other affirmation of existence."[12] Accordingly, the absolutely first truth is this: *cogitatio est* [thinking exists]. "But [the implication of this position is clear:] the mind becomes the center and support of reality." Modern philosophy since Descartes is then coextensive with idealism, given its point of departure, namely, the interpretation of everything that appears not to be a thought or an idea as if it were precisely that—a thought or an idea. In Ortega's opinion, idealism is, as a philosophical doctrine, superior to realism, precisely on the basis of its having made the discovery of a modality of being that consists in being-for-itself. This is the act of self-awareness or self-reflection, or the event of withdrawing into oneself or of being internal to oneself. Thinking is thus sheer inwardness or reflexivity. Its manner of being is radically different from that of anything other than thinking, and it is particularly different from bodily existence. A body will henceforth be regarded as a mere idea entertained by the mind, in direct opposition to the former view according to which the mind (or the spirit or the soul) is something located in the body. We are witnessing here a reversal of perspectives.

Ortega again underscored the fact that these two modalities of being are radically different from one another, indeed that they are opposite to each other. And yet he placed no lesser emphasis on the "strange character" of this discovery, since it implies an attitude that runs counter to that by which we naturally live. According to him, it is an "unnatural turn" of mind. Moreover, Ortega brought to the fore the fact that advancing the thesis of consciousness presupposes that the mind is divorced from the world—that it is self-enclosed, self-imprisoned, essentially and radically *alone*. He wondered how it was possible in the first place for human beings to have arrived at such a strange discovery.[13] To make this determination, Ortega strove to identify the historical forces responsible for the occurrence of such an event, among which forces he pointed especially to skepticism and Christianity.[14] Presently, however, we find ourselves living in a historical situation opposite in kind, one in which we are required to overcome idealism, a task the importance of which can be appreciated in the fact that Ortega considered it no less than the "theme of our times," as I have already pointed out. Or to put it in his own words:

> Accordingly, saying that in our times we live by the need or desire to overcome modernity and idealism is equivalent to giving vent, by means of humble words and penitent's gestures, to what could be otherwise expressed more nobly and solemnly if one were to assert that overcoming idealism is the major intellectual task, the lofty historical mission of our century, the "theme of our times."[15]

But accepting this task is tantamount to "accepting our destiny."

It would be enlightening to engage in a comparative analysis of the various formulations Ortega gave to the *theme of our times* since the 1923 publication of his book bearing that title. Such a study would allow us to come to an understanding of aspects of the philosophical innovation brought about by Ortega which are of major importance, as well as to uncover the specific forms of relationship existing between his innovative contribution and the various historical interpretations and prognostications he advanced, the sociopolitical standpoints he adopted, and so on. But unfortunately it is not possible for me to dwell on such formulations. Suffice it to say that Ortega always approached the theme of our times as an intellectual task which, if performed, would produce a profound renovation or transformation of the entire philosophical tradition or, even more comprehensively, of our whole intellectual or spiritual heritage. The great significance of this venture is rooted in the fact that it would be the unavoidable response to the most serious historical challenge confronting us. What is involved therein is not then a question of mere academic interest, but a matter of fundamental and vital importance for us, since it amounts to having to replace the rule of pure reason by that of *living* or *historical* reason, or to "the ordering of the world from the standpoint of life"[16] and, therefore, to the process of overcoming idealism.

Now, idealism is essentially conjoined with rationalism and other trends of thought, the overcoming of which is as problematical as it is urgent. This is particularly true today when, having fulfilled their historical mission, they "corrosively penetrate" our lives down to the smallest detail, thereby "dispossessing life of its vitality." In the text under consideration, one encounters formulations also found elsewhere. Let me mention some of them. Ortega asserted that the

> . . . major philosophical task of the present generation must be the unification of the eternal and temporal dimensions of things. . . . Truth is a historical affair. . . . The major question . . . the theme of our times . . . lies in determining how, that recognition notwithstanding, it is possible and necessary for truth . . . to be supra-historical.[17]

In this connection he referred to his own doctrine, which "has been called 'perspectivism' . . . in Germany."[18] The overcoming of idealism is precisely tantamount to, or implicates, all this.

In the strictly metaphysical or, more exactly, ontological order, what would be involved in this process is the reformation of the idea of *being* and therefore the "radical reformation of philosophy."[19] Again, I have to refrain from crossing the threshold leading to this *magna quaestio*. Suffice it to say that Ortega enters upon its examination by means of a brief exploratory sally into the novel concept of "being" he is proposing. Let me now present this notion in summary fashion.

To begin with, it seems that the concept in question should be applicable to thinking. Moreover, it would present being as marked by essential features that are opposite to those comprised in the connotation of the traditional notion bearing the same name. The latter seizes being as static (in contrast with the presumptively unabiding and accidental character of what is subject to becoming and change) and as sub-stantial (in contrast with the presumptive irreality of appearances or phenomena). Ortega contended instead that one should understand thinking as a manner of being devoid of a sub-stantial basis. He pointed however to the perils with which any position is fraught which seeks to approach thinking itself in terms of the category of sub-stance, but he indicated as well that they can be avoided, provided that one abides by thinking insofar as it is *pure act,* or as long as one regards it as actuation or performance (again we come across the concept of performative being). Now, this is easier said than done.[20] Let me then turn to the "evidence" adduced by the idealists in support of the position that the first truth concerning what there-is or is-available would assert that "thinking exists," or that *cogitatio est*.[21]

It is here that Ortega's decisive critical examination of idealism, understood in the Cartesian sense of the term, finds its point of departure. In other words, his critique is directed to the *cogito* itself along two correlative dimensions, namely, that concerning the subject of thinking (i.e., the *cogitans*)[22] and that pertinent to the object thereof (i.e., the *cogitatum*).[23]

First of all, in order to understand the sense of the *cogito*, Ortega found it useful to replace Descartes's formula by another, to wit: "*thinking exists, therefore I exist.*"[24] Let me now endeavor to present the first part of Ortega's critique on the basis of it. Accordingly, turning one's attention to the "ego" or subject of thinking, it is possible briefly to summarize Ortega's critical analysis as follows:

1. It appears that a thinking subject and an object of thought are given in conjunction with thinking. In other words, every thought would imply three terms, namely, the thinking *act* itself (which is the only genuinely unmediated datum), the *subject* of the act, and the *object* thereof.

2. And yet the idealists proceed to commit, first of all, an error of interpretation concerning the sense of the notion of the thinking subject, since they still labor under the weight of "cosmic categories." In other words, they have not succeeded in freeing themselves from the metaphysical standpoint proper to realism and "above all . . . from the classical or naïve concept of being."[25]

3. It was on such grounds that Descartes engaged in an illegitimate process of inference, which *a radice* invalidated any of his subsequent metaphysical conclusions. I have in mind the procedure by means of which he came to posit a subject for the pure act of thinking merely because of the existence of such an act, inasmuch as he interpreted the ego or subject of the act as its substrate, i.e., as a sub-stance or thing (*res*), of which thinking would be just an attribute or phenomenon, or at best an operation. At the basis of this argument, one may identify

inveterate Scholastic schemata, according to which *operari se-quitur esse* [an operation or performance flows from being] or *actiones sunt suppositorum* [acts or actions are the underlying subject's].

4. Ortega contended that the notion of sub-stantial being necessarily finds its origin in the standpoint adopted by the realists. The realistic conception of being is, in principle, an understanding of being as sub-stance. But it could not have been otherwise, for realism and substantialism are two positions that are essentially connected, as one can gather from the three notes that are part of the definition of the concept of substance, to wit: a. it is the bearer or substrate of accidents; b. it is that which abides through change, and c. it is self-sufficient. Now then, the application of the categorial schemata that are consistent with the standpoint adopted by the realists, but in a context conformed to the point of view characteristic of the idealists, cannot yield anything but a series of countersensical conclusions, as in fact it happened with Descartes.[26]

5. As the net result of the first part of his critique, Ortega came to the view that, by virtue of turning the subject of thinking into a sub-stance, Descartes cast it out of the sphere of thought, thus transforming it into a cosmic, external being, the essential status of which is neither that of an object of thought nor that of the activity in which one thinks of oneself. In other words, the subject of thinking would have lost its inwardness, which it had so bravely earned for itself, no longer being capable of the feat of endowing itself with being, just as the stone is unable to appear as a stone before itself. And yet, as Ortega forcefully summarized the point, as opposed to the stone, "I am nothing but what I think I am. This is the essence of the matter, to put it drastically and bluntly. The rest is so much illusion."[27]

The second part of Ortega's critical analysis has to do with the question of interpreting the sense of the object of thinking, i.e., the *cogitatum*. Let me again endeavor to summarize Ortega's reasoning:

1. The idealists take the objects of thinking, or the "things" given therein, as being simply "contents of consciousness."[28] This position is both right and wrong, since, as Ortega argued, "it is

beyond question that the presumptive reality of the external world has only a presumptive status,"[29] for indeed I cannot perceive it by stepping out of myself, and yet it is unwarranted to conclude that the reality of the external world is part of my mind or thought, merely on the basis that it essentially depends on my becoming aware or "conscious" of it.

2. This erroneous conclusion is rooted in the fact that the idealists pose the problem of knowledge in terms of an exclusive disjunction, namely, that consisting in contending that the object of thinking must be either inside or outside my mind or thought. But these are terms denoting categories applicable to the spatial, external, corporeal world. To say, then, that something external (for instance, this room) is a "content of consciousness or of the mind" is, "strictly speaking, countersensical," just as it would be to speak of a "round square."[30]

3. As a matter of fact, no external thing (say again, this room) is either outside or inside my thinking, but is given in conjunction with it, "inseparably connected to my act of thinking it," as any two correlative terms would be (for instance, as the obverse and reverse sides of a coin, or as the right-hand and left-hand sides of a picture in fact are). If this is so, then the object of thinking cannot be understood either in terms of the concept of sub-stance: "the world is no self-subsistent reality existing independently of me . . . but that which is *for* me or before me; in other words, it is, to begin with, nothing else. Up to this point, I concur with idealism."[31] Or equivalently stated: one has in this fashion legitimated the thesis that the being of the world is nonindependent and apparent. One can "concur with idealism" concerning this point, but only in part, for, having rejected the applicability of the exclusive disjunction by which one would place the object either inside or outside one's thinking, one has already advanced beyond idealism.

4. Consequently, we have in this manner arrived at a new metaphysical formulation that gives expression to the fact of having overcome idealism. I mean the twofold realization that the idealists are right in affirming that no world is conceivable independently of an ego, but that they are wrong in believing they are entitled to conceive of the ego independently of the

world, or to reduce the latter to the former. I am the one who is now engaged in seeing or conceiving the world; in fact, I *am the act of seeing it*. Accordingly, without the world there-is no ego—or expressed in the usual terminology: without objects there-is no subject. In other words, the relationship of dependence between ego and world is one of reciprocity. "To be sure, I always keep company with myself," but the world is my permanent companion as well. This means, therefore, that my own manner of being is that of *being-with-the-world*, rather than that of *being-in-the-world*, to use Heidegger's expression.[32] Or to put it in Ortega's own words:

> I am for the world, and the world is for me. If there-were nothing to see, think or imagine, I would not be seeing, thinking or imagining, which is tantamount to saying that I would be nothing.[33]

Accordingly, one must assert that the radical datum on the basis of which one is to construct the universe, the only thing there-is or is-available indubitably, is a "primordial and fundamental fact that is self-positing and self-warranting . . . , namely, the joint existence of an ego or subjectivity and its correlative world. It is not possible to have one without the other. I do not come to self-consciousness except as a consciousness of objects, of a surrounding world."[34] (Here one ought to keep in mind Ortega's formula, "I am I and my circum-stance.")[35] "Understood as a subjectivity and as the performance of thinking, I find myself as a component of a dual totality, the other side of which is precisely the world. Therefore, the radical datum that cannot be argued away is not the fact of my existence, or that I exist, but that of my co-existence with the world."[36] "Consciousness is not self-imprisonment; it is just the opposite. . . . Consciousness is the fact that I, this particular someone, am myself precisely when I become aware of things, of a world. . . . There is nothing more alien to the ego than the concept of self-enclosure, for the ego is rather *openness* par excellence."[37] Now, "the radical fact is this: . . . [I am] engaged in seeing, loving, hating, and desiring a world, in which . . . [I am] moving, by virtue of which . . . [I am] suffering, and in terms of which . . . [I am] striving. But this is what has always been called 'my life', to employ the most unassuming and common of expressions. . . . The simple fact of the matter is that it is 'my life', never my own self alone, or my consciousness conceived as a non-communicant sphere, that constitutes the primordial reality, the fact of all facts, the radical datum on which one is to construct the universe, or what is genuinely given to me. Such things as 'my own self alone' or 'my non-communicant consciousness' are nothing but idealistic interpretations of this radical fact."[38]

Consequently, the "first task imposed on philosophy is thus the endeavor to define a datum of that nature . . . , namely, the radical modality of being [that life is]. Anything else, any other modality of being is precisely encountered in or within my own life, as a part of it and as essentially referring to it. . . ."[39] "The expression 'my life' denotes a fact of major importance which is prior to the establishment of biology, of any science, of culture itself—I mean the imposing, radical, indeed the awe-inspiring fact that every other fact presupposes and implicates. . . . Now, this primordial reality . . . is no abstract concept, but my most individual being itself. For the first time, philosophy makes its departure on the basis of something non-abstract."[40] Philosophy "can now be regarded as the mode of life it intrinsically is. . . . In short, it reverts to life and submerges itself in it—to begin with, philosophy is the meditative contemplation of our own lives. The oldest of landscapes thus constitutes itself as the most novel of vistas. In fact, this is so much so that it amounts to being the most significant discovery of our times." Indeed, its novelty is so great that one is in need of forging new categories that would be suitable to the modality of being proper to human life: to this end, ". . . none of the concepts belonging in the philosophical tradition is of any use: new categories are required to articulate living as a modality of being. The categories which have been employed from time immemorial to deal with cosmic being are inapplicable; in fact, the novel task consists precisely in sidestepping them in order to find the categorial structure of living, i.e., the essence of 'our lives.' "[41]

In effect, Ortega devotes the last two lectures of this course to the goal of identifying such concepts, to describing this new manner of reality. At this point, however, it is not possible for me to follow him along this path, since, if I did, I would be entering into the development of his metaphysical system, while my present objective is only to determine the proper point of departure for it. Actually, we have just come across some of the most significant expressions used by Ortega himself to convey his novel understanding of the matter, an understanding that results from overcoming both traditional approaches. If I now attempted to come to terms with this novel understanding, down to its ultimate implications and consequences, I would be required to expound not only the contents of these two lectures, constituting as they do a source of the greatest significance for that purpose, but I would have as well to develop Ortega's metaphysical system in full. To discharge a task of such magnitude is, of course, impossible in this context, and yet, as I advance with my presentation of Ortega's critique of idealism, I will be able to achieve greater clarity and precision in the understanding of the first and fundamental thesis of Ortega's metaphysics, for nothing else is involved here. By the same token, we will proportionately learn to appreciate the difficulties involved in doing justice to the theory of which it is the principle, as well as the high degree of complexity that such a theoretical formulation would exhibit.

As I have already indicated, one can find, in a series of lectures delivered in Madrid from 1932 to 1933, another source of significance for the elaboration of this phase of Ortega's critique of idealism. I am referring to a course, the preparatory notes for which were later published under the title of *Unas lecciones de metafísica*.[42] For the sole purpose of considering Ortega's critical analysis, only the last four lectures are of interest to us. Again, the text in question is of fundamental importance; in fact, it contains the most extensive version of Ortega's critique of realism, although my presentation of it will be as short as possible.

From the point of view of the topic of this investigation, one may say that Ortega follows in these lectures an order of exposition that is the opposite of that we saw him abide by in *¿Qué es filosofía?* In this work, the critical examination of idealism led us to the "discovery" of human life as radical reality, and thence to the endeavor to describe it. In *Unas lecciones de metafísica*, by contrast, the inquiry concerning the nature of metaphysics makes us, to be sure, "stumble" upon the reality of human life, which Ortega then proceeds to describe, but it is only at the end of the exposition that one does see how the discovery of the fact of life presupposes the invalidation of realism and idealism, that is to say, the critical examination and overcoming of their respective theses.

Again, I shall avail myself of a method of exposition consisting in summarizing select passages of the work under scrutiny, although I am fully cognizant of the fact that a procedure of this sort simplifies the wealth of argumentation found in those texts, especially insofar as they complement ¿Qué es filosofía?

In his *Unas lecciones de metafísica,* Ortega showed us that it is (vitally) necessary for human beings to adopt a radical standpoint, an event which would presuppose that a state of perplexity is constitutive of living. Now, adopting such a standpoint cannot amount to anything except coming to live by a "system of certainties," truths, or theses, a fact demanding the existence—in the theoretical order, naturally—of a first thesis meeting requirements already familiar to us, namely, those of universality (or *pantonomy*) and radicalness (or *autonomy*).[43] As a first position proposed to satisfy these conditions, one encounters realism, to the exposition and critical evaluation of which Ortega then proceeded.[44] According to that doctrine, things or the world would constitute being, reality, or what there-is or is-available genuinely. This manner of being would display the features characteristic of sub-stance. In other words, the thesis of realism is equivalent to assigning to the modality of being exhibited by things[45] the role of prototype of all there-is or is-available.

Now, a careful examination of the meaning of realism will prove sufficient for us to see that it is not a position characterized by radical indubitability. It signals that "being" is identical with "being-there" or "being *per se*," i.e., with what exists independently of me. But if somehow I were to play no role in the constitution of the presumptive being-there of things (say, by seeing or thinking of them), then the being-there of things would be devoid of sense, for I cannot think or say anything about it unless I do precisely that, namely, think or say something about it. In other words, I must be in some way *present*. If I close my eyes, this wall I am looking at disappears; it (literally) ceases to be-there. Accordingly, the realist's thesis cannot play the role of first principle, even though what it asserts, namely, that things continue being-there after I make an exit, is most probably the case. The reason for it is that such a thesis is insufficiently radical, if one takes "radical," to begin with, in the sense of firm. Or to put it equivalently: the thesis of realism implicates another, namely, that which consists in asserting that "the subject thinking the world is reality itself." In effect, this other thesis is seemingly firmer than the realist's, since it affirms, for example, that the reality of *my seeing* the wall is indubitable. "The thesis of realism is thus canceled and replaced by the thesis of idealism,"[46] which is characteristic of Descartes and modern philosophy.

In this context, Ortega again proceeded to characterize these two positions in terms of what I would refer to as the respective "psychological attitudes" from which they arise. He did so by mentioning the idealist's cautiousness, as opposed to the realist's naïveté, among other things. Furthermore, he pointed to the initial advantages and disadvantages of adopting one or another of the two theses in question, as when he argued that the idealist's position is "very hard to refute,"[47] and yet that living in terms of it is "paradoxical" or unnatural. Moreover, he indicated that, strictly speaking, the idealist's thesis must contain an acknowledgment of the partial truth of realism, even as it seems to cancel its claim. This is precisely the origin of the fact that the idealist's position is difficult to accept, since it must explain the apparent independence of the reality of things.[48] Now, the "objections levelled by the idealist at realism can be reduced to asserting that, upon affirming something universal about reality . . . , realism leaves itself out of account." Accordingly, the realist's thesis is not universal, for it leaves the very act of thinking it outside its scope. The idealist's thesis, by contrast, does not have this disadvantage, for, when it asserts that thinking is reality itself, it includes itself within the scope of its affirmation. And yet it exhibits another disadvantage all its own, since it eliminates the things and the world by means of a remarkable feat of sleight of hand.[49] But coming to this realization imposes on us the duty of exactly determining the nature of what is called thinking.

Once more, Ortega was underscoring the fact that thinking and what is thought about, taken as modalities of being, are essentially dissimilar and irreducibly opposite in kind. In effect, when the idealist attempts to reduce what is thought about to thinking, he stumbles upon the greatest difficulty he must specifically surmount in terms of his position. Apparently, the thesis advanced by the idealist may be characterized as sufficiently universal, but not as sufficiently indubitable. In view of this, Ortega proceeded to subject idealism to a relentless analysis or examination. He did so by trying to answer this question: "what is-there or is-available, when the only thing there-is or is-available is what-there-is or is-available to me?" In fact, he endeavored to do it "without recourse to evasion or subterfuge of any kind."[50] As the idealist's reply to this question is that "there-is only thinking or consciousness," Ortega resolved to concentrate his effort of analysis on the notion of thinking or consciousness. He thus proceeded to carry out a critical examination of this concept that succeeds in exposing the very heart of the fallacy involved in it, namely, that which is concealed in the meaning of those terms, insofar as the fallacy arises on the basis of their intrinsic ambiguity.

Let us turn to the idealist's favorite line of argument, namely, that concerned with hallucinatory experiences, which is the case most helpful to his position. If one carefully describes experiences of that sort, one will find that the situation presented therein is seen and lived as real. Accordingly, one would have to say that "what there-is or is-available in the universe" is, say, a "raging bull," [if that is what I am then experiencing]. Later on, when I come to see, upon reflection, that the prior event was a hallucination, the only thing there-would-be at that juncture is the totality consisting of me myself and the already elapsed hallucination which at that moment forms part of my past. In other words, I would then take the latter as a reality that, having once existed really and in fact, I now think of or interpret as a hallucination. In keeping with the example, I would at that point say that no bull would therefore form part of what there-is or there-was. And yet my hallucinatory act of thinking or living had once as much performative value as my present act of thinking or living, an event by which I am correcting my hallucination, but that would itself contain no warrant as to its own nonhallucinatory character.[51]

We have now become acquainted with the essentials of this part of Ortega's critical analysis. In fact, we have thereby gained access to something that is basic and of definitive value for Ortega's entire critical enterprise. I mean the distinction between "thought *qua* object" (or the "objective being of thought or consciousness") and "thought *qua* performance" (or the "*performative being* of thought or consciousness").[52] The latter "does not exist for itself; it is no object to itself; [strictly speaking,] it does not form part of what there-is or is-available. Accordingly, it is incongruous to consider it a thought. In order for a *thought* to be, it is necessary for it already to have been performed; therefore, I would have to come to regard it from without. In other words, I must have turned it into an object. It is then that I may refuse the conviction that it once was for me and say, 'it was just a hallucination'. Or to put it more generally: that which was thought about in that thought was merely a component of it, and thus had no effective reality. . . . [But] when thought is the only thing there-is or is-available, then there-is no such thing as that which is thought about thereby; it is-not-available in fact. . . . Consequently, a thought is a conviction no longer in force . . . it is an objective aspect donned by a conviction when it no longer convinces us. And yet . . . that aspect is only donned by it now, when I live by another conviction, i.e., the act I am performing at this moment, the conviction presently in force. Only an actual or actuating conviction is in force; only a conviction which as such does not yet exist for me can be in force."[53] Therefore, "it is not a thought, but an absolute positing. . . . Now, this is equivalent to saying that *there-is reality only when the act by which we think of it does not exist for us, when the act is not an object for us, but is only that which we are engaged in being or performing.*"[54] "Therefore, the condition subject to which a thesis may be considered firm is that which precisely makes it impossible for us to declare the idealist's thesis firm or true."[55] Hence, the idealist "commits the same error as the realist, albeit in a different direction."[56] In short, ". . . [t]*he very notion of thought or consciousness is* [merely] *a hypothesis, not a concept that was formulated abiding by what there-is, or precisely according to the manner in which what there-is is-available.* The genuine state of affairs is just the fact of the mere co-existence of ego and things, or the event in which things appear confronting an ego."[57]

My justification for having quoted so extensively from Ortega's text is that the passages in question are decisive for the critical examination of idealism, an analysis that rises therein to a new level. And yet I have excised considerable portions of what he said, although I have always kept in view what is essential to our task.

In these passages of his *Unas lecciones de metafísica*, Ortega has in effect attempted to bring about no less than the formal elimination of thought qua unmediated reality, if one understands "thought" in the broad Cartesian sense of the word, that is to say, as signifying "consciousness." Instead, he reduced thought to the status of a hypothesis. In other words, just as the idealists handled

the notion of thing or external world by showing its lack of immediacy and thus by rightly reducing it to the status of a hypothesis
(although they went, unwarrantedly, even further, by also reducing
it to the status of a thought or mental reality), so likewise did
Ortega with thought, or with that which the idealists had proposed as the radical reality. Accordingly, Ortega disqualified both
claimants to the title of radical reality, since neither the external
world nor thought can be considered to be unmediated and indubitable realities. Our minds had grown used, or "adjusted," to
disqualifying the external world from making any claim to the
title, but we were not yet prepared—and I doubt that we have
mentally advanced to a degree sufficient to be in a state of
readiness—to deny it to thought. Here lies the source of so many
misunderstandings and obstacles blocking a sound "initiation" in
Ortega's philosophical system. This is why I believe it is important
to insist upon this notion as a key concept in Ortega's critique of
idealism, for, in the absence of an adequate comprehension of it, it
is impossible to grasp the most genuine and creative aspects of his
metaphysical doctrine.

At this point, I would like to call the reader's attention to this
fact and invite him to take it seriously, however great the perplexity
may be that results, on a first hearing, when we come across someone formally denying the immediate reality of thought or consciousness. We are dealing here with nothing less than the very
principle on the basis of which Ortega's metaphysical system is
constructed. In other words, I am referring to the discovery or
insight that amounts, on his part, to recognizing the irreducible or
radical reality of human life, that is to say, of my life: such a
discovery consists in taking one's life as that which is genuinely
unmediated and indubitable, as that which is genuinely given, but
according to a new manner or level of *evidence* that Ortega described as "life's self-*presence.*" Mind you, this is the self-presence
of human life, of my life, not that of the ego or thought, which is
only a function of life and therefore presupposes it. It is thus that
Ortega abided by the postulate or imperative advanced in his *El
tema de nuestro tiempo,* namely, to turn human life into a principle. In other words, what is involved here is the effort to raise life to
a status allowing it to play the role assigned in modern philosophy
to the Cartesian *cogito* and any of its derivatives and modaliza-
tions, including Husserl's notion of *Bewusstsein* or pure conscious-

ness, inasmuch as the foundation of the argument line followed by
Ortega at this stage of his critical analysis of idealism is naturally
found to apply, as I will endeavor to show, to phenomenological
idealism as well.[58] But Ortega's attempt also implies the transformation of life into a "matter of right." This is the second component of his postulate, according to which one would be faced with
the task of intellectually justifying and "legitimating" life, in such a
fashion that its functioning as a principle of philosophical thought
would at the same time establish its entitlement to work as a
principle with regard to itself. This is what Ortega had in mind
when he spoke of "implanting reason in life," of "substituting the
rule of living reason for that of pure reason," of "reforming the
intellect," and so on. Everything depends on the following formulation: "thought *qua* performance . . . does not exist for itself; it is
no object to itself; it does not form part of what there-is or is-
available." "Thought *qua* object" is the only thing there-is or is-
available. But thought *qua* object is no reality; it is just an idea.
Only "thought *qua* performance" is genuine and primordial reality, but, strictly speaking, one has to deny it the status of a thought.
What is it, then? It is simply this: life, the "*act of living*," the one
act that living is, and which includes what is ambiguously called
"thought" as one of its "instrumental components." *Cogito quia
vivo* [I think because I live] is the formula proposed by Ortega to
replace the Cartesian *cogito, ergo sum*.[59]

Here I am leaving out of consideration Ortega's renewed attack
on the basic thesis of Cartesianism found in Lecture XIV of his
Unas lecciones de metafísica, except for the part already examined.
In a more ambitious study, however, it would be necessary to
analyze it in detail. Ortega pointed to the fact that the idealists
contradict and violate their own "inviolable" point of departure,[60]
and he wondered ". . . [h]ow it is that the idealists have been able
to behave . . . so inconsistently."[61] As he said, the reason for it is
found in the fact that idealism "has retained a realistic tendency
within itself," a tendency that consists in "believing that the real is
that which exists independently of subjectivity, instead of seeing it
as that which is and exists dependent on subjectivity."[62] The idealists commit the same error as the realists, but they do it in reverse.
Both idealists and realists commit the same offense against the
requirement of immediacy that the first principle of a metaphysical
system must fulfill; it is only Ortega's new position, which over-

comes both realism and idealism, that abides by it. The "character of immediacy" is not equivalent to transcendence, or to the pure and absolute externality that had been proposed by realism, but neither is it the same as the pure immanence propounded in idealism, for

> . . . [l]ife *qua* absolute reality is at once immanence and transcendence. . . . *I am not my life.* [My life] . . . *consists of myself and things. Things are irreducible to me, and I to them.* . . . [Things and I] *transcend one another, and yet things and I, both, are immanent in life* qua *absolute co-existence.* . . . The new thesis I am proposing retains the elements of truth in idealism [and] realism. . . . Transcendent is anything that is irreducible to subjectivity, that which cannot be identified with the ego. The wall facing me is once again, and without qualifications, what it self-evidently is, but it is not so *per se* and by itself, since it is only a component of a dual reality, the other side of which is myself: the wall that transcends me is immanent in my life. My life is no more my own than it is something belonging to the wall facing me. And here lies the difference between my life and that presumptive reality called thought. Thought is mine, it is a part of myself; my life, however, is not mine; on the contrary, I am a part of it. My co-existence with things is that comprehensive and vast reality called life.[63]

At this level of the argument, I hope nobody will easily misunderstand phrases like the one just employed, namely, that "my life . . . is not mine."

As you may remember, *Sobre la razón histórica* is the next text scheduled to fall under our scrutiny, among those listed as relevant to this stage or phase of Ortega's critique of idealism. This was a course given in 1940 in Buenos Aires, but it has only recently been published.[64] In the second lecture of this series, Ortega carried out an exposition of the two traditional theses, namely, realism and idealism. He thereby began with his critical analysis, which carries over into the third lecture, and in which realism is considered only briefly and idealism more extensively. Ortega developed his critical examination there in terms of four considerations, of which he wrote as follows: "I am going to make four points, on which, to begin with, I would focus my analysis of Cartesianism and, in general, of modern philosophy, which has never been able to transcend the magic circle drawn around it by the clear mind of Descartes, although it would be possible for me to include other matters as well."[65] After what we have learned so far, I may present these four considerations in just a few strokes, even though an assertion of this sort is not meant to signify that the text under scrutiny—as we have seen is also true of others—does not contain novel shades of meaning contributing to the further elaboration of Ortega's critique of realism and idealism, shades which are well deserving of examination and commentary. It is only that the manner of approach and the structure of this investigation force me to leave them out of account.

These points are:

1. Descartes sinned by omission, since he was insufficiently radical in his pursuit of the first principle for the construction of the universe. Indeed, he failed to take things just as they present themselves, having imposed on them a number of derivative theoretical interpretations; as a result, he distorted the way in which they in fact appear. What he should have done first was to *establish the foundations that would render any theory possible*. Now, an endeavor of this sort demands that "we accept what is self-evident and only what is self-evident. This would be consistent with an effort marked by intellectual care, precision, and courage—indeed, with an endeavor obligating us provisionally to invalidate any theoretical interpretation that may have been handed down to us."[66]

   Now then, when Descartes thought that he could doubt the reality of what he *was seeing*, what entitled him to do so, if anything? Isn't it perchance that he was still captive to the traditional realistic ontology he was striving to overcome? It is not possible for me to entertain doubts "concerning the reality of a horse I am seeing, as long as I am seeing it,"[67] unless the term *reality* signifies "a manner of being absolutely independent of myself." It is precisely in this context that Ortega returned to his decisive critical analysis of thought, upon which I have just insisted. But he did so by considering only a special case of thinking, namely, seeing, although he could have examined any other species of *cogitatio*. This is his analysis:

   > . . . [Expressions like] "I *am seeing* a horse", "a horse *is confronting me*", or "*there-is* a horse [or a horse is-available]" signify one and the same thing. But this is not all:

to employ the term "seeing" to refer to the event of experiencing a horse is a risky venture that fails to fulfill its intended purpose, namely, to describe what is actually taking place, since "seeing" is *but* the name of a psychological *hypothesis,* being entertained (to a point) in connection with a physiological hypothesis, and concomitantly with several hypotheses deriving from physics and other sources. . . .[68]

In other words, Descartes still retained the "notion of *being* or *reality* he had learned from an Aristotelian brand of Scholasticism." This is the reason why, according to him, only myself, and the doubt in which I live, constitute that which is indubitable and what there-is or is-available genuinely. As a consequence, the world is canceled. "For nearly three centuries, the fullness of the meaning of terms like *being, existence,* and *reality* is taken to be this: 'the ego is the only thing there-is or is-available'. To begin with, idealism means *solipsism.*"[69] Accordingly, if Descartes, as the standard bearer of idealism, was right in eliminating the "world of things" as a claimant to the title of radical reality, he erred in having believed that "we are entitled to doubt the things present to us."[70]

2.   We have already seen how Descartes was "still living on the grounds of the *belief* that the real must be that which exists absolutely independently of us." But, precisely because what was involved is a "belief" on his part, he did not make an avowal of it to us or, for that matter, to himself. Rather, he "admit[ted] . . . it without further ado"; he took it for granted; "he d[id] . . . not question it." Or to put it otherwise: if one regards idealism as a thesis concerning *being* or as an *ontological position,* one would have to say that it is still a manner of realism, albeit a novel one. Realism is thus the substrate of idealism. In effect, the idealists still abide by the ontological model of *res* or "thinghood," except that they substitute the thing "ego" or "thought" for the thing "world."

Descartes was entitled to cast doubt upon the reality of the world, because he believed it must be mediated in order to be referred to me. To this end, the reality of the world is in need of an intermediary, namely, the event of my seeing it, which is precisely an act of thinking. But he did not entertain doubts about this act, because it "is as immediately available to me as I myself am."[71] Therefore, it would have been absurd to cast doubt on it. (Actually, this version of Cartesianism is the highly refined formulation thereof to which Husserl had arrived in order to recapture it originarily in his *phenomenological* philosophy.) And yet the affirmation of the presumptive unmediated character of my thinking is sheer error. The reason is clear: "When I see a horse, there-is only a *horse* confronting me. . . . [One cannot say that] *my seeing* is present too. . . ."[72]

In this connection, Ortega again took up and developed the central thesis or premise of his argument, namely, that which asserts the "irreality" of thought, or the view that thought is a mere hypothesis, interpretation, or explanation concerning something else, which is the genuinely unmediated and originary fact. It is not convenient for me, however, to follow Ortega into this elaboration of his critique of idealism; I will not do so, despite the importance of the advancement, because at that juncture he proceeded from his critical examination of Cartesianism to that of phenomenology. Or to put it more exactly: at that point, he constructed his arguments concerning Cartesianism by keeping phenomenology in mind, since he considered the latter as the ultimate consequence of the former. Accordingly, the presentation of this amplification will have to keep for the moment when I am ready to undertake the exposition of that phase of Ortega's critique.

Now then, it is as the outcome of this development of his analysis that Ortega arrived at the formulation of his own position or thesis. And yet he did not do so without first insisting on the *"exceptional and decisive"* character of the view he was to propose as a result of his critical examination of idealism. This is how he put it:

> I contend, therefore, that no reality exists which consists in being an unmediated self-presence [as consciousness is claimed to be]. Accordingly, I contend too that we must eliminate terms like *cogitatio* or *consciousness* from the vocabulary employed to speak of the fundamentals of philosophy. This is unheard of; it is nothing short of a scandal, and yet this is what I contend. Let this point be clearly understood.[73]

Ortega then submitted several formulae in order to convey the thesis he was advancing. I will return to them later, but presently I wish to refer only to one, because it serves as the bridge to the third point he was to make in his critique. This is what he had to say:

> . . . one may succeed at the endeavor of carefully describing the radical fact of our relationship with things, only if one presents it as the naked co-existence of *ego* and *things*. The *ego* is as real as a *thing* is; *one* is as real as the *other*. But now the meaning of the term *reality* has changed; it no longer signifies *non-dependence*, but exactly the opposite: "reality" stands for the mutual *dependence* of ego and things, since they are inseparable and *are for one another* in reciprocity. Things are *for me*, and I belong *to* them. I am given to them; they surround me; they support me; they bring me harm; they are sweet to me. Between them and me, then, there-is none of that we call *consciousness, cogitatio* or *thought*. Man's primordial manner of establishing a relationship with things is not intellectual in nature; it does not consist in *becoming aware* of them or in contemplating them. Would that it were so! It is rather our dwelling in and with them, and their effective action upon us. . . . I assert that such things as a *non-dependent world* and a *non-dependent realm of thought* do not exist. They are just two hypothetical or theoretical constructs, never reality itself.[74]

Ortega proceeded immediately thereafter to refer again to his metaphor of the Dioscuri or Gemini, the "*dii consentes* or gods that exist in reciprocity." He had already employed it in 1916,[75] in order to present the new manner of reality to which his entire critical enterprise was leading. We are thus faced with a "third major metaphor" or third "radical thesis," the proposal of which implies a reformation of philosophy of such far-reaching consequences that it "obliges us to modify almost every concept belonging in the philosophical tradition, including the chief one, namely, that of *being* or *reality*."[76]

3. In effect, this modification is, among the subjects dealt within the exposition of Ortega's third point, the one that concerns us the most for the purposes of this investigation. It is also the matter therein that is most difficult to summarize and even to understand. Ortega was not there trying to present to us just one among many of his "novel concepts," but one of his fundamental notions, even that which, if rightly understood, proves to be the most fundamental one among those needed in order

to think of the new manner of reality discovered by him. I have in mind a concept that in fact we have come across repeatedly throughout the unfolding of Ortega's critique of idealism. Let us hear about it in Ortega's own words:

> Just as in the so-called act of *seeing, a horse* is present to me, or a horse becomes *real* to me, now, as I cast doubt on the reality of the world, the world, however, is not canceled. Against Descartes's opinion, . . . [the world] remains out there, about me. . . . It remains being other than I and outside me. At least, what has become dubitable [i.e., the world] remains precisely as dubitable.[77]

When I say that a flower is *a flower to me*, or that a horse is *a horse to me*, let me strive, following Ortega's urging, to endow the verb "to be" with an "active, performative sense." Let us hear about this in his own words too:

> . . . since language has been forged on the basis of a primitive philosophy, it lacks words capable of conveying, generally speaking, the sense of *being* or reality, when it is understood as *performance, execution*, pure *actuation*, or *operation*. . . . In keeping with this sense, the expression *"the flower's being-a-flower to me"* breaks down into [a manifold of meanings, among which I could mention] "its being-odorous to me by means of its odour", "its being-colored to me by means of its color", and so on. . . . [But] this is only part [of the total meaning] of the expression, *"the flower's being-a-flower to me"*. If we attempted to convey all those sense-components in terms of just one phrase, we would be in need of a general verbal locution signifying something like "the flower is enflowering me. . . ."[78]

In light of this, one would have to say, therefore, that when I cast doubt on the world, the world does nonetheless persist in being out there; it still continues to exercise its pressure on me and torment me by means of its one surviving quality, namely, its dubitability—or "equivalently stated by means of a hideously sounding formula: . . . if I cast doubt on the world, I nevertheless encounter an absolute reality, namely, the totality constituted by me doubting and by the world *rendering-me-dubitative* [*dudificándome*]. . . ."[79]

In these phrases, no great effort is required to recognize Ortega's attempt to display before us, in a different perspective, his most fundamental concept of performative being. Every new clarification of this difficult notion, every renewed endeavor to find its boundaries will prove useful, inasmuch as the concept involved is central to the adequate comprehension of Ortega's proposed reformation of philosophy, at least insofar as it implies the reformation or, more exactly, the "abolition" of ontology. Ortega's novel manner of understanding the concept of performative being, as it appears here, well deserves an extended exegesis, and even a step-by-step "genealogical" inquiry, carried out on the basis of his original glimpses into it which are already found in the writings of his first youth. Let us remember, for instance, the formulations employed in his "Ensayo a manera de prólogo," namely, "a thing *taken as ego*," "every thing is *ego* when it is regarded from within," and so on.[80] Now, by means of a vocabulary Ortega himself, so sensitive and creative in matters pertaining to linguistic expression, characterized as "extravagant," he endeavored to make us *see* how performative being dynamically involves both an ego (i.e., myself) and the world of things. In fact, he thereby established the existence of a radical bond of community between them, thus "fusing" them, without however con-fusing them. In short: performative being is but the *act of living*, in which I and those "things" forming part of my circum-stance at a given moment, both, play roles of equal standing. The act of living is therefore an act of reciprocity, i.e., an act I perform on things, and they on me.[81]

4. The last point made in Ortega's analysis also renders manifest a new level of discourse reached in his critique of idealism, a level at which Ortega tried to penetrate even further into the presuppositions of the Cartesian doubt. In effect, what is involved here is the attempt to find a way from the doubt to its living prerequisites or necessary conditions, conditions which must be understood if the doubt is to become intelligible. Strictly speaking, such prerequisites or conditions find themselves embodied in the doubt itself; in fact, they are "essential components" of it and factors involved in its genesis. Indeed, such prerequisites are the reasonings which, to begin with, provoked Descartes to doubt and, eventually, led him into a third phase in the process of reflection he was engaged in,

namely, that stage in which he "resolved" or "decided" to think about radical reality, or to seek a first truth on the basis of which to construct the universe. Taking into account Descartes' act of resolution would finally bring us to consider the situation preexisting it, namely, that setting in which a person would find himself living in a "state" of perplexity and non-methodical doubt. This is a "real and terrifying" manner of doubting, in which the person would live "prior to philosophizing," and which would move him precisely to engage in that activity. In short: Ortega substituted his formula, *cogito quia vivo*, or "I philosophize because I live," for Descartes's own, *cogito, ergo sum*. Or as he otherwise put it: "Theory finds its origin and essential foundations in life." Or again: "I cannot live my life, except on the basis of one or another form of philosophy." One may now see that Descartes' thesis, taken precisely as a first truth on the basis of which to construct the universe, is self-contradictory, "since it amounts to the unwitting incorporation, as part of its make-up, of an unnoticed back-ground consisting of . . . prior theses that function at a more radical level than Descartes's own."[82] Reduced to their simplest expression, such theses are:

A. People must find themselves already existing prior to their falling in the state of doubt and thus prior to their engaging in theorizing.

B. This prior manner of existence is a human being's genuine form of existence, i.e., his radical existence or reality.

C. Therein people find themselves surrounded by and subjected to the pressure of something obscure, confused, and enigmatic, namely, their circum-stance.

D. Life is the name given to that coexistence that is prior to everything else. Living consists in "having always to do something in order to bear oneself up" in the midst of the circum-stance.

E. People have to start themselves thinking in order to fashion for themselves "a schedule of undertakings [*quehaceres*]," for they are always in a more or less habitual condition of being at a loss, or in peril of being at a loss, in the midst of the circum-stance. Here we find the source out of which originate the activity of theorizing and what we call truth and reason. I am speaking of the genuine form of reason, that is to say, of *living reason,* which does not produce its concepts on the strength of its own resources, but has them imposed on itself as vital necessities, for *a human being's life is at stake* on getting something conceptually right.

F. Let me recapitulate by saying that, no matter which thesis one chooses as a basis to construct a philosophical system, it would nonetheless

> always presuppose human life *qua radical reality,* i.e., life taken as that within which, and in view of which, the proposed thesis would arise. Accordingly, the one genuine radical thesis would be tantamount to the affirmation of life *qua* primordial reality, i.e., as the reality in which every other reality is to make its appearance. Moreover, it would signify that the principles that constitute the foundation of theory and reason are not always rational, but just urgent needs felt in our lives.[83]

Actually, Ortega has claimed the idea or thesis concerning the *"irrationality of the* [first] *principles"* for his very own in several places, but especially in his book, *La idea de principio en Leibniz,* where he emphasized its importance and proceeded to expound it with utmost precision.

Now we are ready to enter the examination of the third phase of Ortega's critique of idealism.

CHAPTER 3

Ortega's Critique of Phenomenological Philosophy as the Most Recent Historical Form of Idealism

We have already had an opportunity to see how Ortega's early encounter with Husserl's phenomenology and his immediate response to it played a decisive role in the development of his thought.[1] At this point, I am not going to enter the examination of the problem of whether phenomenology is a kind of idealism or only another species of "realism," or whether perhaps it is neither, a discussion that would certainly take up the form of a disputed question. Naturally, I have in mind the sort of phenomenology Husserl himself called "transcendental." It is of little consequence that Husserl characterized it as a "new science," although, to be sure, it could not have been mistaken for "metaphysics." The fact of the matter is that for Ortega, as well as for many others (phenomenologists included), the new science proposed by Husserl undoubtedly was the most recent and refined species of idealism, indeed the most recent and subtle sequel of Cartesianism, its swan song, so to speak.

One finds Ortega's first exposition of phenomenology in his 1913 article, "Sobre el concepto de sensación," of which I have already availed myself.[2] There Ortega presented phenomenology according to its "classical" version, which appeared in [the first volume of Husserl's] *Ideen*,[3] a book that had then just come out. In fact, Ortega's piece was published the same year as that work, an event that allowed him to become immediately acquainted with the doctrine developed in that volume and to assimilate it. Ortega's writing is an expository presentation characterized by its brevity,[4] as well as by its being a clear and compact analysis of the subject in question. In his article, Ortega dealt with phenomenology as a descriptive but nonempirical science of essences and as a method of inquiry. First of all, he underscored the novelty of phenomenology in both respects, for neither is it to be identified with psychology (although there may be some danger of confusing the two disciplines), nor does it amount to the practice of inductive or deductive methods. Furthermore, Ortega emphasized the concept of *epokhé* particularly, for it is a key notion at the basis of phenomenology, regarded both as a science and as a method. Moreover, he stressed the importance of the concept of *pure consciousness,* or the notion of "consciousness of" (which is the expression used by Ortega), precisely as the residuum left after the performance of the "phenomenological reduction" (into which the phenomenological attitude is translated). Ortega insisted on the fact that phenomenology is not psychology, for consciousness, as Husserl understood it, is not to be identified with human consciousness, or with any other factual kind of consciousness for that matter, insofar as it is not subject to any spatiotemporal, biological, or psychobiological conditions. As he pointed to the difference existing between the "natural position" or attitude and the purely "contemplative" one adopted in phenomenological "reflection," which is conducted by means of a process of "abstention" or "parenthesizing," Ortega often employed his favorite expression *performative being* as a term needed in order to convey what is most characteristic of the natural attitude. I have in mind his concept of "performative capacity or value," which is, as we already know, a notion fundamental to the development of his critique of idealism.[5]

As was his practice whenever he expounded someone's theory, Ortega granted phenomenology, that "most novel school of thought, the headquarters of which are to be found in Göttingen," the highest degree of credibility. He thus endeavored to identify himself with the theory and its author, that is to say, he strove to understand it in depth and turn it into his own position, even if only provisionally. In his article, he attributed to it "an enviable ancestry, which endows it with historical significance without however depriving it of novelty."[6] He advisedly said "ancestry," for "every classical form of idealism . . . has adopted the phenomenological principle as its point of departure," but he also spoke of "novelty," because phenomenology "has transformed this concern with dwelling on the level of what is immediate and manifest as such, of what is *lived* . . . , of *intentive mental processes* [*vivencias*], into a scientific method."[7]

In passing, it is worth noting that the text under scrutiny is of some "historical" significance for the development of philosophical terminology in Spanish, above and beyond the general historical value it possesses as a piece of writing belonging in Ortega's corpus. It is there that the term *vivencia,* an irreplaceable expression coined by Ortega to translate the German word *Erlebnis* (then also of recent vintage and attributed to Dilthey by Ortega), made its first appearance. The Spanish locution met with such wide success and use that today it is not only universally employed in philosophical and scientific writing composed in the language, but in purely literary and even colloquial contexts as well. For the benefit of future historians of the Spanish language, Ortega has related, in a long footnote, the specific circumstances that motivated his invention of the term, his justification for its use, and the precise meaning he assigned to it.[8]

In his "Prólogo para alemanes," a 1934 text fundamental for the critical analysis of phenomenological idealism, Ortega again sounded his praises for phenomenology and reaffirmed his recognition of its great merits. In fact, whenever he referred to Husserl, he spoke of him as a great philosopher, even as the greatest one in our century, and on occasion he acknowledged him as his "teacher." And yet such words of praise were already geared to the critical evaluation of phenomenology; in fact, they were an introduction to it. Let us hear Ortega's own words:

> At the end of the last century, Husserl heroically resolved to endow idealism with the precision and careful formulation it lacked. In grand style, he proceeded to re-write the ledger of idealism and subjected it to the discipline of exactitude. The fruitfulness of this work has been of incalculable proportions.[9]

And then, a few pages later, he continued as follows:

> The invaluable advantage afforded to us by phenomenology was to render such questions so precise that one could catch idealism red-handed at the very moment and juncture in which it committed its crime and substituted consciousness for reality by sleight of hand.[10]

As the arduous inquiry concerning consciousness it was, Husserl's thought became the prerequisite permitting a genuine overcoming of idealism, and not just the waging of renewed battles fought against it from realistic positions of one kind or another. Or as Ortega himself put it:

> Accordingly, phenomenology was able, for the first time, to render the nature of consciousness and its components precise. . . . And yet when I seriously devoted myself to the study of phenomenology in 1912, I discovered that it apparently proceeded with the same degree of negligence in minute analyses as the old forms of idealism had done concerning larger questions.[11]

These words mark the beginning of Ortega's critique, for the purposes of which he focused on the notions of "consciousness" (*Bewusstsein*) and *epokhé* (or phenomenological reduction), that is to say, on the two concepts that are basic to phenomenological doctrine, the former belonging (despite itself) to "metaphysics," and the latter to the methodological order.

As we already know, Ortega's critique was directed against Husserl's position as formulated in the first volume of his *Ideas*. As an introduction to Ortega's analysis, I believe it will be useful first to expound Husserl's own understanding of his renowned concept of *epokhé*, and to do so in some detail. To that end, I will abide awhile by Husserl's own text.[12]

Following Husserl, one can say that the general *thesis* proper to what he called the "natural attitude" is the position (prior to any theoretical formulation) according to which I find reality "as a *factually existent actuality and also accept it as it presents itself to me as factually existing*. No doubt about or rejection of data belonging to the natural world alters in any respect the *general positing which characterizes the natural attitude*."[13] By contrast, Husserl proposed to "alter . . . [this 'thesis' or attitude] radically." It goes without saying that, strictly speaking, no thesis is here involved, for ". . . [this general positing] does *not consist of a particular act*, perchance an articulated judgment *about* existence."[14] Rather, it is a feature already exhibited ". . . before any thinking . . . [by] an . . . experiential consciousness . . . [of an object bearing] the characteristic 'there', 'on hand.'"[15] Such a feature may serve as the essential foundation for the formulation of "an explicit (predicative) judgment of existence agreeing with it."[16] But, as Husserl added, one "can . . . proceed with the potential . . . positing precisely as . . . one can with the explicit" judgment of existence.[17] But what is the nature of that procedure one *can* apply in both cases? To answer this question, Husserl underscored the aspect of *possibility:* he said that one "procedure, possible at any time, is the *attempt to doubt universally* which Descartes carried out. . . ."[18] And yet Descartes' goal, namely, "bringing out a sphere of absolutely indubitable being,"[19] was altogether different from Husserl's.

It is at this point that Husserl's troubles begin to take shape as he attempts to tell us what the *epokhé* consists in. In fact, he never succeeded in telling us what it actually is, but always just what it *is not.* Husserl's troubles are themselves of the greatest interest, amounting, as they do, not only to a struggle in definition, but to difficulties encountered even in "pointing" to the reductive act properly so called. In effect, the terms he employed to refer to it are metaphorical, the recognition of which fact is not however a serious objection in itself, if it can be shown that the metaphors in question are adequate to the task, and that he came eventually to translate them into precise conceptual formulations. But, above and beyond this problem, Husserl faced still another stumbling block in adopting such a procedure, for he availed himself of different expressions to denote what he meant, but none of them were sufficiently illuminating, whether they were taken by themselves or in conjunction with added explanations. To top it all, his terms were negative in character, if not by way of their grammatical form, at least in view of their meaning. All the locutions Husserl used to signify the matter in question are then negative, whether one takes into account the original names, such as *epokhé, Ausschaltung,* and *Einklammerung,* or their translations, namely, "parenthesizing," "putting out of action," "suspension," "exclusion," "making no use," or "abstention." "Reduction" is the only word employed by him that cannot be so characterized, but then it is meant to convey the result of the operation involved, or is an expression that keeps the outcome in sight.

At this juncture, Husserl proceeded to tell us that, like Descartes, he was to start from the *"attempt to doubt universally,"* but immediately thereafter he added the remark that "the attempt to doubt universally shall serve us only as a *methodic expedient* for picking out certain points which . . . can be brought to light and made evident by means of it."[20] Let us note the fact that Husserl speaks of the "attempt" to doubt and not of the doubt itself. The attempt involved is entirely a question of free choice. As he said, we "can *attempt to doubt* anything whatever, no matter how precisely convinced of it, even assured of it in an adequate evidence, we may be."[21] The attempt to doubt is the one thing that the *epokhé* resembles the most, and yet it cannot be identified with it, since the doubt, at least insofar as it is the end point of the attempt, forms part, in some way, of the attempt to doubt, while the "reduction" can in no way be construed as doubt. One could say that doubting something consists in oscillating between a *thesis* and an *antithesis*, but the *epokhé* is in no wise "thetical," whether it is taken affirmatively or negatively. In fact, it is characteristically "nonthetical"—and again we run across another negative expression. We are interested in the attempt to doubt to the extent, and only to the extent, that the "*attempt* to doubt anything intended to as something *on hand* necessarily *effects a certain annulment of positing.*"[22] The similarity between the attempt to doubt and the *epokhé* is limited to that.

But if the *epokhé* cannot be identified with the attempt to doubt (except to the degree indicated), less does it resemble the doubt itself, or the "transmutation of positing into counterpositing," or the transformation of "position into negation." Furthermore, it goes without saying that it is no form of "uncertain presumption" or "deeming possible," for such modalities of consciousness (like those of "undecidedness" or the doubt itself) have nothing in common with what lies "within the sphere of our free choice."[23] Moreover, it cannot be confused with mere *imagining*, although there is some affinity between these two modes of consciousness. (Later I will have the opportunity of showing that, in fact, the *epokhé* is precisely an act of imagining, just the view expressly denied by Husserl.)[24] Finally, it is even further from the truth to assert that it is "a matter of just thinking of something in the sense of '*assuming*' or *presupposing*."[25]

What is then the nature of the *epokhé*? Let us keep in mind the names employed by Husserl himself: they are all used by him as instruments of mere allusion, or of manifest avoidance, or of circumlocution. Let us appreciate this point by means of his own words: "*Rather it is something wholly peculiar.* We do not give up the positing we effected, we do not in any respect alter our conviction [emphasis removed]. . . . Nevertheless the positing undergoes a modification: while it in itself remains what it is, *we, so to speak,* 'put it out of action', we 'exclude it', we 'parenthesize it' [emphasis removed]. It is still there, like the parenthesized in the parentheses. . . ."[26] Again: "*We can also say* [emphasis added]: the positing is a mental process, but we make 'no use' of it [emphasis removed]."[27] Or again: "*rather* [emphasis added] . . . it is a matter of *indicative designations of a definite* [emphasis added] *specifically peculiar mode of* consciousness [emphasis removed] which is added to the original positing simpliciter . . . and, likewise in a *specifically peculiar manner* [emphasis added], changes its value."[28] But what is the nature of this "changing of value"? We are only told that this "changing of value is *a matter in which we are perfectly free* [emphasis added], and it stands over against all cogitative position-takings coordinate with the positing and incompatible with the positing in the unity of the 'simultaneous' . . . ."[29] And then, further down: "With regard to any [emphasis removed] positing we can quite freely exercise this peculiar *epokhé, a certain refraining from judgment which is compatible with the unshaken conviction of truth, even with the unshakeable conviction of evident truth* [emphasis removed]. . . ."[30]

Accordingly, the *epokhé* is not an act by which one would absolutely eliminate the thesis, but a performance by which one achieves only its "suspension," "modification," "neutralization," "invalidation," or "devaluation." In short, the *epokhé* "puts the thesis out of action."[31]

If at this time I were concerned with determining the scope of the *epokhé* or "reduction," despite the fact that it has only been insufficiently described, I would have to say that, generally speaking, it is an operation applicable to any thesis or object. The only exception is constituted by the "non-modified" judgments specifically belonging to the science of phenomenology. But this view is consistent with the goal pursued in employing the method of parenthesizing. Accordingly, the *epokhé* is applicable to the world of the natural attitude as a whole and to every empirical ego (the phenomenologist's included). In other words, the *epokhé* also applies to the ego, if by that term one understands man qua natural and social being.[32] But, then, what about the pure ego, that is to say, the residuum left after the performance of the reduction? Here one encounters a sui generis manner of "transcendency," what Husserl characterized as a "transcendency within immanency."[33] According to him, the pure ego cannot be "excluded," although this view is inapplicable to any of the doctrines advanced about it. The exclusion in question applies then to the natural (i.e., physical and psychophysical) world and, along with it, to every individual objectivity constituted by the evaluative and practical performances of consciousness. In other words, the *epokhé* is applicable as well to every cultural product, such as works of art and technology, the various sciences, every form of aesthetical and practical value, the State, every manner of social custom, the Law, religion, etc. Again, the natural sciences (which study the natural world) and the human sciences too, insofar as they are practiced according to the natural attitude, are subject to the *epokhé*.[34] And so is that special transcendency we call God, namely, the transcendency whose sense is exactly the polar opposite of the world's.[35]

Up to this point, I have been referring to reductions concerned with facts. But there are eidetic reductions as well, that is to say, those which apply to the formal and the material essences and to the respective sciences studying them, reductions which however leave behind a factual residuum. We have thus arrived at "the eidetic sphere pertaining to phenomenologically purified consciousness itself."[36]

When all is said and done, it is the well-known sphere of pure consciousness that remains as a phenomenological residuum, or is left as such after the performance of the reduction. In other words, the residuum in question is constituted by the pure mental processes [*vivencias puras*], a phrase in which the word *pure* means "having been purified of any manner of *factuality*," of any reference to any factual objects other than the mental processes themselves and to any essences outside the sphere of the mental processes. To be sure, here one is taking the mental processes in their entirety, i.e., as encompassing all their components, the "intentional" as well as the "non-intentional," namely, the *quality* and the *"matter"* constituting the full intentional essence, as well as the *"hyletic data"* (which are not "intentional") and the "intentional objects,"[37] provided, of course, that they all are regarded in terms of their reduced status, just as the mental processes themselves are. In other words, we are talking of the *noesis* and the *noema*. It is precisely by means of the *noema* that all objects eliminated by virtue of the various reductions reappear within the sphere of pure phenomenology, but, no doubt, only according to their "modified" status, that is to say, insofar as they have been parenthesized.

My consideration of these basic Husserlian concepts has been somewhat extensive, because they constitute the keystone of the entire doctrine that Ortega was to subject to a critical analysis. In my opinion, I need not go any further into an examination of them, since they are sufficiently well known. We are nonetheless entitled now to ask: have we learned, by virtue of this presentation, about the proper and peculiar nature of the *epokhé* and the "reduction"? I am afraid not, at least not to my complete satisfaction. In order to proceed any further, then, one would have to resort to interpretations of Husserl's text, which are always uncertain and therefore, insofar as they go beyond the literal sense of his formulations, make us run a serious risk of error. Naturally, I cannot dwell on this problem now, but let me at least refer to the essentials of Xavier Zubiri's answer to the question concerning the "nature of the reduction itself," before I turn to examine Ortega's own. Zubiri tells us that

> [the reduction] . . . is not an act by means of which I would purely and simply abandon the real world. In other words, it does not consist in believing in the *non*-existence of the world. On the contrary, the reduction is an act by means of which I would continue to live the world and in the world, but [only] by way of adopting a special attitude as I live it, namely, that which would consist in suspending the validity of my belief in the reality of the world. This suspension is not tantamount to denying that belief, for that would be the same as substituting one belief for another; rather it would be equivalent only to suspending the character of being-in-force exhibited by the belief, if by that one means abstaining from using it. This is precisely what the locution *epokhé* signifies—coming to a halt, abstaining. I am engaged in living my real life, in performing the acts of which it consists. If I were not, even the possibility of abstaining would vanish. But as I live, I can put my life in parentheses (*Einklammerung*). As I do, I would continue to live it, while abstaining at the same time from taking it according to its character of being-in-force. I do not therefore step out of real life; I remain in it [and have it] in all its wealth and detail, in terms of the full range of variation that every mental process [*vivencia*] may undergo. And yet I would not be living by the belief that holds my life to be real. Therefore, the *epokhé* is the act by which the real world in its entirety is reduced to something which is not real. By virtue of this performance, I have access to a reduced world. I lose nothing

of what is real, except its character of being-real. To what, then, is the world reduced? To being precisely that which makes its appearance before my consciousness, and to being just as it appears. In other words, it is reduced to the status of a pure phenomenon. The reduction is thus phenomenological in nature.[38]

Let this characterization suffice for now. I shall later attempt to exact its meaning and implications.[39]

Allow me at this point to present the part of Ortega's text which is pertinent to this investigation. There he said:

> Suppose now that, just as my consciousness had performed a perceptual act, so to speak, *in good faith* or naturally, it proceeded to turn [its attention] onto itself. Instead of *living* engaged in contemplating a sense-perceptible object [as before], now I would be busy with my own perceptual act. [As a result,] the latter would be left, so to speak, in a state of suspension encompassing each and every one of its performative consequences, including its attesting to the fact that there is something real before itself. It would no longer be effective or operative, for it would have been reduced to the status of a *phenomenon*. But it is to be noted, first of all, that the act of reflection, or the event in which consciousness turns about unto the acts it performs, does not disturb them. The perceptual act remains being what it was before the act of reflection took place, except that—to use that most graphic expression employed by Husserl—it is put in parentheses. Secondly, the acts of reflection are not attempts to explain the performances of consciousness, but only events by means of which to contemplate them, just as perceptual acts do not explain the objects perceived, but regard them in total passivity.
>
> Now, every act of consciousness and its [correlative] object can be put in parentheses. [Consistent with this] the whole "natural" world, and [the entire body of] science insofar as it is a system of judgments arrived at "naturally", are thereby reduced to the status of *phenomena*, except that this word does not signify, as it did, say, in Kant, something pointing to a sub-stance underlying them. Here "being a phenomenon" is merely a virtual status a performance would acquire when it is no longer lived according to its natural performative value, but has come to be regarded contemplatively and descriptively [by consciousness], an occur-

rence which would thus dispossess it of its finality.

Phenomenology is a pure description of this sort.[40]

One should bear in mind that Ortega, when he wrote this passage, had not yet had time significantly to reflect on the doctrines he was endeavoring to interpret. His remarks were composed in 1913, precisely the year of publication of the first volume of Husserl's *Ideas,* where such doctrines were expounded. When Ortega related the fact that he had devoted the preceding year of his life to the study of phenomenology, he was of course referring to Husserl's *Logical Investigations.*

According to Ortega, his critique of phenomenology was developed in 1914, that is to say, during the period in which he arrived at an adequate insight into the fact of human life. It was the year when his *Meditaciones del Quijote* came out. As he said, "since 1914 . . . the insight into the fact of 'human life' became the basis of my entire thought. On the occasion of expounding Husserl's phenomenology in various courses, I then formulated my thought by basically correcting the description of the phenomenon 'consciousness of', which, as is known, is the cornerstone of Husserl's own doctrine."[41] And further on: "Aside from the many passages where I gave expression to my interpretation of 'consciousness' in my writings of those years, one can find it in the text of the course I taught in 1916 at the School of Philosophy and Letters of the University of Buenos Aires. . . . Some select portions of the course were published in the [local] press, but an accurate shorthand transcription of it is extant and in the keeping of Dr. Coriolano Alberini, who later became Dean of that School."[42] Ortega did not therefore take a long time to come to a critical evaluation of phenomenology. Let me now proceed to a presentation of its essentials, as it appears in the text which is fundamental for this purpose, namely, his "Prólogo para alemanes" of 1934.

There Ortega began by acknowledging, as I have already indicated, the merits proper to Husserl, especially the one accorded to him by virtue of his being the first thinker to find a precise formula to express the nature of consciousness and its components. And yet Ortega proceeded to say, on that basis, that Husserl, as a philosopher, did not abide by what is given, that is to say, by that which im-poses itself on us and is not the result of being merely posed by the philosopher. Accordingly, one can say that Husserl was not faithful to the twofold requisite of radicalness and "non-intervention"—or equivalently stated, that he did not observe the requirements of seeking after "primordial, prototypical, and absolutely firm reality in order to have a basis to which to refer and on which to found any other reality," and of "abiding only by what is 'self-posing', 'self-imposed', or 'self-given,'" respectively. In effect, Husserl believed that he had found in pure consciousness a primordial reality of that sort, that is to say, he thought he had found it in "an ego that is aware of everything else" and is nothing but "awareness" or pure contemplation (i.e., *Bewusstsein von* or "consciousness of"). But an absolute reality like this would *bring about the "irrealization"* [*desrealiza*] of everything contained in it and would turn into a mere object, i.e., a "pure appearance," "spectacle," or meaning. Now, if "meaning" consists in being intelligible, reality would therefore become intelligibility pure and simple.

One may ask however whether any such affirmation or thesis is justified. Obviously not, I would contend, since the "candidate" chosen for the role of primordial reality is only a claimant to the status of being self-given or self-posed. In fact, it does not fulfill the requirements to which such a claim is conformed, inasmuch as the proposed "candidate" would come to play such a role only as a result of an act carried out by the philosopher, or as the "residuum" left after his performance, for the well-known reduction is just a "manipulation" executed by the phenomenologist. The phenomenologist, therefore, would have "*constructed*" reality, just as the physicist does when he claims to be "carrying out an observation inside the atom,"[43] but this procedure is the opposite of that which consists in *finding* the reality one is seeking after. "Primordial," "non-reflective," "naïve," or straightforward consciousness is however the only thing that any philosopher—the phenomenologist included—may in fact find, if he abides by what is given.

One must nevertheless say that the dimension of belief cannot be banished from primordial consciousness, if one understands "belief" according to the meaning assigned to it immediately and spontaneously in [everyday] life. With great discernment and insight, Ortega used that term precisely in this sense in his well-known doctrine concerning the nature of belief, for he found that "beliefs" have a fundamental "supportive function" to perform, namely, that of being the "ground" of life, or of providing it with something upon which to stand. This function is the opposite of the secondary or "subsidiary" role played by "ideas."[44] Accordingly, it is this primordial function of beliefs that makes them irreducible to anything else. Or to put it in Ortega's own words:

> Therefore, "primordial consciousness" is *essentially* characterized by the fact that nothing is for it a mere object. On the contrary, everything is real [which is given] to it. The manner of *becoming aware* proper to it is not contemplative, since it consists in [already] finding itself in the company of things, of the world. . . . [Consequently,] as long as the "primordial act of consciousness" is being performed, it remains unaware of itself, it does not exist for itself. But this signifies that "primordial consciousness" is not, strictly speaking, [a form of] consciousness.[45]

Prior to the occurrence of any act of reflection or [mental] operation directed upon "what is lived" by me, that is to say, while I live spontaneously and at the primordial level, the only thing there-is or is-available genuinely is the fact of the coexistence of "myself and things," i.e., precisely those things I have to cope with [*habérmelas*].[46] At that level, "however, there-is no 'consciousness'; no such thing is-available or found beside and along with the event of co-existence." What is it, then, that is required for consciousness to "be-available"? Nothing short of having stopped living primordially or "actively," which is what occurs when we turn our attention backwards in order to "remember that which we had just lived" or that which "had just happened to us." (Using words that are as plain as they are precise and to the point, Ortega asserts that life is "what we do and what befalls us.")[47] Let me underscore the fact that what there-is or is-available now is not my past life after having been "reduced." There-is such a thing, or it is-available, only as a "memory," never as my "actual" reality. As an *effective reality,* the only thing there-is (or is-available) now is the fact that I am doing something with this novel thing called consciousness: "*now* 'consciousness' *is-available,* or *there-is* 'consciousness', in the world, just as before were-available, or there-were, minerals, persons, or triangles."[48] But it is obvious that the present and effective reality, which at this point consists in my doing something with the thing called "consciousness," is not itself consciousness, for it is a manner of life "as naïve, primordial, and non-reflective"[49] as the originary one. In other words, it is apparent that it is as much of a performance as the latter.

Consciousness is accordingly barred from occupying the position of primordial reality, and it is thus reduced to the status of something with which I can do many things, as is the case with any other "thing," except presently to "modify," "correct," or "suspend" its reality insofar as it has been. The latter cannot, as such, be "revoked," even if, for any reasons whatever, I come to decide that the former reality was only a hallucination or an illusion.[50] The opinion that I have come to hold at this point in time is powerless with regard to the reality now past, inasmuch as "it does not *undo*, 'irrealize' [*desrealiza*], or suspend it. How could something be irrealized *now* when it is no longer real? How could the effecting of a reality be 'suspended' when it has already been effected and is no longer being effected, since there-is only the present effecting of an act by means of which I remember that the past act was effected once?"[51] The so-called "reflective consciousness" presupposes or implies the straightforward or primordial consciousness that would thus be its object. But the fact of the matter is that reflective consciousness itself "is a naïve and unreflective 'primordial consciousness' too." It is impossible to excise the dimension of naïveté from it, since that is precisely what there-is, or is-available, genuinely, namely, reality itself. "For idealism not to be devoid of sense, it is necessary that an 'act of consciousness' be capable of self-reflection, and not merely able to reflect on another 'act of consciousness.'"[52] Now, this is the point which is essential to Ortega's critique of idealism, a reason sufficient for us to dwell on it for a bit.

To begin with, let me say that, in Ortega's opinion, the above-mentioned condition that idealism would have to fulfill so as "not to be devoid of sense" (or equivalently stated, so as to make the "reduction" performable) is simply impossible. This conclusion is clearly implied in what I have already discussed, but Ortega himself did say so in so many words, when, in his book *Sobre la razón histórica,* he retraced his own thesis back to the 1916 course he had taught in Buenos Aires (and to which I have already referred). This is what he then had to say:

> [My thesis] . . . cancels the idealistic position taken in the broadest sense, since it refutes it in terms of the very context in which Descartes originally conceived it and in view of its most precise and purified source today, for it serves as the basis to demon-

strate that Husserl's renowned "phenomenological reduction" is simply and plainly impossible.[53]

But this is not all. Let me take this opportunity to expound my own position on the *epokhé* and the "reduction," for, in my opinion, it renders Ortega's own more explicit. I would say not only that a "self-reflecting act of consciousness" is impossible, but as well that an act of consciousness is incapable of reflecting on *another act* of consciousness. Indeed, if we bring to mind the interpretations of Husserl's notion of *epokhé* of which I spoke before (especially Zubiri's, for, in my judgment, his is the interpretation most favorable to Husserl), we will clearly note, by means of the expressions employed therein for the purpose of conveying it, how contradictory the presumptive operation of "reduction" or "suspension" is. Admirable as he was in his zeal to carry out a faithful exposition, Zubiri wanted nonetheless to arrive at an interpretation of Husserl's thought as coherent and intelligible as possible, despite the fact that he was well acquainted with the objection that the act of "abstention," or the "reductive operation," is itself a *living* act that includes, among other things, the component of believing in its own reality (and in that of its "object"). Now, this novel act too is therefore to be subjected to still another act of suspension or exclusion, and the resulting third act is to be reduced as well, and so on, ad infinitum. Or equivalently stated: "it is not possible to step out of life," as Ortega had already asserted in his first article devoted to phenomenology.[54] In other words, the "reduction," or the *epokhé*, is just an unfounded conception.

Now, if one carries a careful examination of this question to its ultimate consequences, one may wonder about the meaning of formulations like the following: "I would continue to live the world and in the world, but [only] by way of adopting a special attitude as I live it, namely, that which would consist in suspending the validity of my belief in the reality of the world."[55] Let us imagine a particular situation. Suppose that I wake up in the morning, and thus that I am about to begin my day. This would have been the meaning of saying "I would continue to live the world and in my world," if only we took the expression seriously. Suppose further that, as I perform any of the ordinary acts and concatenations of acts of daily living (e.g., washing up, getting dressed, or having breakfast), I were concurrently to engage, with each and every one of them, in an act of reflection amounting to this: "Mind you, even though I know nothing about the *validity* of believing that every object I handle, every act I execute to handle it, the locations in which I carry out such acts, and so on are real, I nonetheless *believe* that they are real. I must therefore renounce the validity of the belief." Now, it is evident that having to perform a reflective act of this sort would be an absurd proposition, no matter how accomplished the phenomenologist attempting to execute it is. At least, the act in question would be as devoid of sense as the endeavor to abstain is, insofar as such an endeavor would be an act [of living] seeking to "suspend life."

But Zubiri went on with his analysis and proceeded to say that ". . . I do not therefore step out of real life; I remain in it [and have it] in all its wealth and detail. . . . And yet I would not be living by the belief that holds my life to be real." The contradiction is manifest. Suppose I excised the validity of the spontaneous belief in reality, which accompanies every act of my life, from my real life taken "in all its wealth and detail." (I mean that excision also to encompass all "objective correlates," as Husserl called them, or every "thing" and the "world," as I have designated them.) If I did this, how could I then continue to refer to *what* is left by means of the expression "real life . . . in all its wealth and detail," assuming of course that such an operation were feasible (which it is not)? The "wealth" and "detail" of life, i.e., its "reality," are given to us precisely by the irrevocable and originary sense that our belief [in reality] is valid. Anything else is just an "idea."

Zubiri then moved on with his interpretation of Husserl and added: "I lose nothing of what is real, except its character of being-real." Now, I must say that I fail to understand how anything would remain, save a faded spectral presence "reflected" in the mirror of memory, were I to excise, from what I am living as real, its dimension of "lived" reality. (Incidentally, let me insist on the aptness of the ancient metaphor I have just employed: indeed, only and exclusively memory can serve as the "mirror" in which every act of "reflection" or every "reflective act of consciousness" is to be effected.) What could then be the meaning of saying that "I lose nothing of what is real," if what is lost is nothing less than the belief's most real dimension, which amounts to *believing in its own reality*? How can I "not . . . step out of real life," how would "I remain in it," if I excise my belief from it? The difficulty is not dissolved, mind you, by asserting that my belief in the reality of what is lived is also a component of my reduced "mental process [*vivencia*]," since that "belief," as excluded, bereft of validity, devoid of potency, or devalued, is anything but a belief—it is just an *idea* about a real and effective belief. Every genuine belief is effective, that is to say, it produces effects, or it has efficacy and actuality. Strictly speaking, a belief *is* effectiveness and actuality; it consists in being effective and actual, and immediate [or spontaneous] life is precisely the life of effectiveness and actuality. If the "reality-asserting power" that belongs to a belief were to vanish, so would the belief.

It is my contention that belief and reality are one and the same thing. Now then, this thesis is more radical than it would seem at first blush, or even if one were to take a second look. To appreciate this, let me state my view in a different but equivalent way by saying that reality is a function of belief (for reality *is given* in it), but only if belief, of which reality is a function, is not other than reality itself. Indeed, one of the central themes of Ortega's metaphysics is the problem of determining how this position is possible at all. The question may only be settled by means of a thorough analysis of Ortega's conception of reality, which I obviously cannot go into here. In any case, it is self-evident that I cannot *live* an act and at the same time "undo" it as an act of living, that is to say, eliminate or excise from it what precisely makes it a "mental process." (It goes without saying that here I am not using the term "mental process" [*vivencia*] in its usual psychological sense, but in that which Ortega proposed for it and which is prior to any psychological interpretation, namely, that of the *act of living*, a notion directly based on his idea of human *life*.) But to excise from a mental process its character of being a living act is precisely the same as to eliminate the dimension of "validity" from my belief in the reality of the mental process, i.e., in the reality of the act, and in that of the "objects" which it encompasses and in terms of which it is "constituted" for what it is. If I do that, or if I attempt to do it, it must be, as I pointed out above, that I do so by means of another act, namely, the "reductive" performance that would apply to the original act. But then the original act, taken just as an actually lived act,[56] would no longer exist, would have disappeared, or would have completely "elapsed." At that moment, there-would-be, or exist, an act other than the original, namely, the act of "reduction"

I would then be effectively living or, as Ortega says, performing. (In other words, the "reductive" act itself is not "reduced" at all, and is thus characterized by a belief at full in its own reality.) But this is the heart of the matter. Indeed, if one inquires into the nature of this "other *act*," and does so concretely and avoiding any subterfuges, one would come to discover that it involves a perfectly utopian and absurd claim, namely, that it is the attempt to "reduce," "exclude," or "parenthesize." (Call it what you will, if only the name signifies the "performance of an operation.") In other words, it amounts to claiming that one would be carrying out an operation, or doing something, with or on something which no longer exists, that is to say, with or on the act already lived or performed. (In this connection, let us again bring to mind Ortega's remarks, beginning with the words, "How could something be irrealized *now* when it is no longer real?")[57] The "reductive" act is therefore a performance that would not induce an effect on the original act itself (that is, on the act already carried out or lived), but on an *image* of it which would be given in memory, for, however clear, recent, and "immediate" the image in question may be, it would nonetheless continue to be, in the final analysis, a mere image of something nonexistent. But this quite simply signifies that the *reduction is impossible,* as Ortega categorically asserted. In my opinion, it was already evident to us that it is not possible for a reductive act to reduce itself, since that would mean meeting the threefold condition of being at once an act immediately lived, a reductive act, and a reduced act. But now it is also quite clear that it is equally impossible for the reductive act to have an effect on another act. In short: the "reduction" is absolutely impossible. In truth, the acts lived spontaneously and primordially are not reducible to anything else. (Among them, I mean to include the so-called acts of "reflection," which, as we now know, are, insofar as they are real, as performative in nature as any other act.) But such acts are not reducible to anything else, among other reasons, because they cannot be iterated: no act that has already been performed can ever become available again for us to carry out any "operation" on it. The uniqueness of each act is rooted in the radically irreversible nature of living time, as well as in other essential metaphysical features of human life. The act of "reduction" always applies to a memory of a prior act or, more exactly, to the object of a novel act which is a remembering. The original act is thus "objectivated," or transformed into the "object" of the subsequent act of remembering, but transforming an act into an object is like squaring the circle. Strictly speaking, there-would-be three acts: first of all, the act spontaneously lived; secondly, the act by means of which one retains the original act in the memory, once it has elapsed or been performed, so as to subject it to the "reduction" (here one can identify a first impossibility), and thirdly, the very act of "reducing it." The second and third acts could be simultaneous, even factually fuse into one act, even though it would still be analytically possible in principle to distinguish within it the above-mentioned mental operations, namely, that of retaining the original act in the memory and that of carrying out the reduction of what is thus retained.

Presently, at the conclusion of this excursus designed to elaborate on the foundations of Ortega's critique of phenomenological idealism, I believe we are better prepared to raise the essential question once more and to provide an answer to it. Again: what then is the specific nature of the "reduction" itself, of the presumptive "exclusionary operation"?

We have already been able to learn about the general character of the interpretations advanced concerning Husserl's reply to this question, and to appreciate how it would lead us to an impossible situation. And yet, in spite of being a resounding failure in achieving its goal, the elusive "act" of reduction may nevertheless amount to something.

Let me develop my own position about this. If one strictly abides by the sense of the question raised, then one would make the nearly surprising discovery that such a complex retentional-reductive act is just an instance of imagining, a fact the recognition of which would precisely fly in the face of what Husserl expressly denied. (And I say "nearly surprising," because the clear results obtained in my prior analyses should have allowed us to anticipate this "discovery.") In truth, the well-known "reduction" would amount, purely and simply, to imagining how the act spontaneously lived would be after excising form it its dimension of believing in its own reality (and, of course, in the reality of its "intentional contents"), or after eliminating the "validity" of the belief (which, as we know, is equivalent to the same thing). But an act of imagining like this comes to naught: it is fruitless, arbitrary and, in short, ineffective and utopian, given its constitutive *claim* to be the medium of givenness of reality itself (or to be, to use Ortega's own terms, the "radical datum"), for in fact the only thing given to us thereby is a mistaken and ambiguous manner of fiction, namely, the renowned notion of pure consciousness. We have already seen how strongly Ortega rebeled against this sort of "fiction," which indeed is the most dangerous of contemporary "utopian" conceptions to arise in the theoretical order, since it is the most subtle of them all, and is proposed concurrently with other philosophical insights of the highest caliber and, especially, is given expression concomitantly with the formulation of a genuinely fruitful method of inquiry, the practice of which has done away with some gross errors committed in the recent past. This is why Ortega turned that fiction into the main target of his "relentless struggle against *utopianism,*" a battle waged by him on the plane of metaphysical theory. The radical manifestation of utopianism, that is to say, its genuine root, is found, as is always the case when major human attitudes defining historical moments are involved, at the level of coming to terms conceptually with reality as such. And this is so, however removed such considerations may seem to be from the areas of thought and life in which utopianism—Ortega's bête noire and, according to him, the letter of marque authorizing all sorts of irresponsible conduct—makes apparent its most harmful aspects, among which I may cite epistemological "rationalism," ideological "progressivism," and political "revolutionarism." In Ortega's lifetime, Husserl's phenomenology was undoubtedly the highest expression of the effort to come to terms conceptually with reality as such. This is why Ortega reserved his most pointed critical attacks to level them against the notion of "pure consciousness," which is the fundamental concept of Husserl's philosophical doctrine, concerning which Ortega did not however spare his praise.

Ortega's judgment is that "pure consciousness" simply does not exist. Or to put it in his own words:

> If the notion of "consciousness", of which the idealist speaks, were in fact anything, it would be just one thing, namely, *weltsetzend,* i.e., world-positing, or the unmediated encounter with reality. Hence, it is, as such, a contradictory concept, since, according to the idealist's intent, consciousness signifies, precisely, the irreality of the world as posited and encountered by consciousness.

Phenomenology annihilates the fundamental nature of "consciousness", as it suspends the performative character constitutive of it, its *Weltsetzung,* or the reality of its "contents". But "consciousness" is just that which cannot be suspended; "consciousness" is irrevocable. Hence, it is reality itself, *not* consciousness.

The term "consciousness" should be confined in a leprosarium. It involved the claim to be the name for the positive or the given, the name for what is self-positing and not for what is just posited by thought. But the situation has turned out to be the other way around, for consciousness is a mere hypothesis, a venturesome explanation, a construction born in our divine fantasy.[58]

In his *Leibniz,* Ortega still insisted on the impossibility of suspending the "performative character (*vollziehender Character*) of consciousness," that is to say, of the so-called "consciousness," for in fact he meant thereby to speak of the primordial act of living and its "*positing power.*" This contention applies to "*any manner of consciousness,*" whether it is "primordial" or "reflective," "illusory" (i.e., hallucinatory), or "normal."[59] Or equivalently stated: ". . . *there-is no such phenomenon* called 'consciousness of' as the general form of the mind. . . . The attempt to describe the phenomenon of 'consciousness' [thus] becomes the description of the phenomenon of 'real life', [understood precisely] *as* the co-existence of the ego and the things surrounding it, namely, the circum-stance. . . . [Accordingly], *consciousness is a hypothesis, precisely the one we have inherited from Descartes.* This is why Husserl returned to Descartes."[60] Or again by availing ourselves of his "Prólogo para alemanes": "[In effect,] to believe that, by means of the *suspension* of the performative character of a primordial situation, of a naïve act of consciousness, one has side-stepped the positing aspect of naïve consciousness is tantamount to carrying out another naïve act of consciousness. . . . When I pretend to myself that I am *removing* the positing dimension of my prior act of 'primordial consciousness', I am only *positing* a novel reality of my own invention, namely, 'consciousness suspended', anesthetized."[61] Ortega then proceeded to re-assert that the method to be employed is just the opposite, if indeed one is seeking after "radical reality, or what there-is or is-available *genuinely.*" But this means that one ought to realize that "what there-is or is-available genuinely is this: someone engaged in seeking after reality pure and simple, or after what is given. . . . Accordingly, what there-is or is-available should include the present philosophical intent the person is living by, as well as those of his motivations that preceded it and forced him to be a philosopher—in short, *life* as unconstrainable, insurmountable spontaneity and naïveté." And then, insisting on the fact that, "as opposed to thought, reality displays the character of being out there beforehand, of *having precedence over thought*," Ortega came to the following conclusion:

> This was the path that led me to the formulation of the Idea of Life *qua* radical reality, that is to say, to an interpretation of phenomenology in a sense opposite to idealism. This meant fleeing from the prison constructed around the concept of "consciousness", by substituting for it the notion of the mere co-existence of "subject" and "object", i.e., the image of the *Dii consentes* [or gods in reciprocity]. . . .[62]

And further on:

> The analysis of consciousness allowed phenomenology to correct the position of idealism and bring it to perfection, that is to say, to a state that is the anticipation of its own demise, just as arriving at the top is proof positive that the mountain is lying beneath our feet. But pushing the analysis of consciousness beyond the point at which phenomenology had left it allowed me to find a loophole *e quindi uscimo a riveder le stelle* [and therefore we came out to regard the stars again].[63]

This is the substance of Ortega's critique of phenomenology. For some time now, especially since the publication of the volumes of *Husserliana,* it has been a subject of controversy whether Husserl, during the last years of his life, had not succeeded in overcoming his own brand of idealism. I am not going to broach this problem here. In any event, Ortega himself referred to the question, which had already been raised since the publication of Husserl's *Formal and Transcendental Logic.* In the "Anejo" to his "Apuntes sobre el pensamiento,"[64] Ortega quoted a sentence taken from that book, where Husserl seemed to acknowledge the dependence of "intellectual performance" on "pre-theoretical" or "living" conditions and, therefore, appeared to recognize the fact that knowledge characteristically presents itself as a "function of life." But, in Ortega's opinion, Husserl's acknowledgment certainly did not come to play the role of a principle, for it was not a matter seriously taken up by him and developed in a way consistent with the actual unfolding of his thought. The "radicalness" of phenomenology is thus hopelessly insufficient. This is how Ortega himself put it:

> The sphere of absolute reality, constituted—according to Husserl— by "pure mental processes" [*vivencias puras*], has nothing whatever to do with life [*vida*], despite the suggestiveness of the name [*vivencia*]. Strictly speaking, it is the opposite of life. The phenomenological attitude is the exact opposite of what I call "living reason."[65]

In Ortega's judgment, the concept of "genetic phenomenology," which, "by means of a last and maximal effort, Husserl expounded in his [*Formal and*] *Transcendental Logic*, . . . cannot have a retroactive effect on general phenomenology." In effect, as Ortega was correcting the proofs of his "Apuntes sobre el pensamiento," the fact came to his attention that "in 1935 Husserl had delivered in Prague a lecture entitled 'The Crisis of the European Sciences and Transcendental Phenomenology', the first part of which was published in *Philosophia*, I (1936) in Belgrade."[66] Again, in Ortega's opinion, this piece, containing an amplification of the ideas found in *Formal and Transcendental Logic*, which he had already discussed, was not actually written by Husserl but by his student Eugen Fink, although the ideas expounded therein are Husserl's and this version of them had met with Husserl's approval. The writing style was different; "in this work, phenomenology is elaborated in such a way that it leaps forward to a position that could have never been derived from it. This leaping forward of phenomenology has been an occasion of great satisfaction to me," added Ortega ironically, "for it is nothing short of resorting to . . . [what I call] 'historical reason.'"[67] But Ortega immediately thereafter proceeded to clarify what he had in mind, for he then said that ". . . [b]efore Husserl's article appeared in *Philosophia*, and long before its sequel was published in the *Revue internationale de philosophie* (Brussels, 1939)—the latter piece being where, in so many words, he resorted to *Vernunft in der Geschichte* [Reason in History]—a study of mine entitled, 'Historia como sistema' (1935) had been brought out in England."[68]

This seems to be the last tendency identifiable in Husserl's thought—or its last phase, as characterized by Eugen Fink, who found its inception in *Formal and Transcendental Logic*. [At that juncture, Husserl was apparently concerned] with the concept of "genetic phenomenology,"[69] and with the move consisting in resorting to primordial "historical becoming" and the *Lebenswelt*.[70] But, be all that as it may, it is unquestionable that he was not able to develop those ideas sufficiently. Moreover, as has been confirmed after the publication of the volumes of *Husserliana*, Ortega was, after all, quite right in saying that the last orientation adopted in Husserl's thought "cannot have a retroactive effect on general phenomenology." Indeed, today there is general agreement concerning the fact that, as Jean-F. Lyotard put it, the "radicalness of the transcendental *cogito*, as established in *Ideas*, I, is still the heart of his entire philosophy."[71]

PART II

Ortega's Overcoming of Idealism. Toward the System of Life Categories

We have become acquainted with Ortega's critique of metaphysical idealism by keeping only to the main texts in his corpus that are pertinent to this question. In that light, one may say, on the one hand, that such a critique presupposed that idealism had been overcome, insofar as Ortega did adopt his own metaphysical insight into life as the point of departure for his critical analysis, although his fundamental intuition was certainly subjected to various degrees of intellectual elaboration, depending on the stage reached by him in his critique. But, on the other hand, one can assert that Ortega's critical analysis also meant a development of the idea of life into which his overcoming of idealism is translated, and this occurred at least inchoatively, if not to a significant extent, as sometimes was the case. In effect, one may always find, in the basic texts devoted by Ortega to working out his critique of idealism, "further elaborations" of that idea (as, for instance, in *¿Qué es filosofía?*) or "anticipations" of such developments (as one can appreciate it in *Unas lecciones de metafísica*). At times, such expansions would take place simultaneously with the critical examination itself and intermingle with it. Passages of this nature are precisely the chief texts in which one ought to study the fundamental principles and concepts of Ortega's metaphysical system. In fact, more often than not, such texts deal with one or several "life *categories,*" to use Ortega's own name for them.

My purpose is to examine such categories, or at least some of them, in this concluding section of my investigation, which should complement or, if you will, serve as the "exemplification" of the first part. Before I attempt to do this, however, I believe it would be useful to say something about Ortega's understanding of the "cate-gorial sphere" in general. Since the times of Aristotle, the tradition-al approach has been to take the categories as fundamental "modes of being," insofar as they have been given expression by means of concepts or "forms," the universality of which can only be extensively "transcended" by that proper to the concept of "being" or "entity" itself, or by the universality of those notions that are convertible with it and which, for that reason, have been called "transcendentals." Such supreme "genera" would encom-pass, then, every thing, or would be the means to structure every-thing there-is or is-available. Accordingly, the categories would be the "inflections of being."

By means of his renowned "Copernican revolution," Kant in-verted the order prevailing in, but ultimately left intact the sense of, the categorial sphere itself, even though, when regarded from other points of view, the effecting of his inversion was tantamount to bringing about the most radical transformation undergone by metaphysical conceptualization since the times of Aristotle. Actu-ally, both thinkers took the categories to be "forms" of thought (or "concepts") which would strictly correspond to the forms of being, although, to be sure, the manner of such a correspondence, accord-ing to the tradition of realism, is determined by the fact that being would impress *lógos* or thought with its own forms, while, accord-ing to Kant, the case is just the opposite, for it is thought (or the "understanding") which would impress phenomenal reality (or, more exactly, the intuitive-sensible "matter" or the contents of experience) with its own forms.[1] This difference notwithstanding, such forms would amount approximately to the same thing in both traditions, since they would both perform a common function, namely, that of rendering "ontological" or epistemologico-ontological structures manifest. In other words, one may assert that, in any case, the idea of reality—which, understood as being or entity, traces its origins back to Parmenides—is the notion that would determine, by virtue of internal demands rooted in its own "logical" unfolding, the emergence and subsequent development of categorial thought. But let us hear the formulation of this point in Ortega's own words:

> Every theory of knowledge has been, without achieving a clear
> awareness of the fact, . . . an ontological theory, that is to say,
> first of all, a doctrinal position concerning the respective natures

of being and thinking (for the latter is, after all, a particular entity or thing), and only then a comparative analysis of the two. As a result, one either came to the conclusion that thinking was a consequence of being—this was the position known as realism— or to the opposite view, in which case it was shown that the structure of being derived from thinking itself—and that was the doctrine called idealism. In both cases, however, it was taken for granted, albeit without a clear awareness of the fact, that one had to establish the existence of a structural identity between the two termini involved, if one wished to provide a justification for knowledge.[2]

Accordingly, one ought to wonder about the limits of any attempt to continue talking, without further ado, about "categories" and "categorial thought," and even about one's entitlement to do so (i.e., to proceed along those lines with "logical legitimacy"), once one has entered a metaphysical system that does not allow the concept of "being" or "entity" to function as the basic idea of reality. The reason is that being has therein been replaced by living or life, a notion which exhibits—as we already know and will learn to appreciate even more closely—attributes quite different from those of being. Let us hear this point in Ortega's own words:

> . . . what is involved, then, is nothing less than the invalidation of the traditional connotation of the concept of "being". But, since in that notion one finds the very origin of philosophy, a reformation of the concept of being would imply a radical reformation of philosophy itself. For a long time now, a few other men and I have been devoted in Europe to this task. . . . You are hereby invited, then, no longer to show any deference to the most venerable, persistent, and established concept in our entire mental tradition, namely, the concept of being. Here I place the notion of being in checkmate, and I do so taking it in the sense in which it was understood by Plato, Aristotle, Leibniz, Kant and, no doubt, by Descartes too. What I am about to say, therefore, will not be understood by anyone stubbornly and blindly clinging to a connotation of the word "being" that I am precisely endeavoring to reform.[3]

Living, or "my life," is thus to replace being. Or as Ortega put it: "For me, 'to be' signifies 'to live'; it thus means being intimate with the self and with things."[4] Or further: "Static being has been dismissed (we will later see the subordinate role it would still play), and an actuating manner of being has been substituted for it."[5] Or again, "We will wring the neck of venerable locutions like 'existence', 'nature' [*consistir*], and 'being', so as to be able to say instead that 'my living' is the first thing there-is, or is-available, in the universe. Anything else would be-available, only if it is-available in my life, within the confines of my life."[6] We are thus in need of determining first of all "what 'living' specifically is, what this genuine and primordial manner of being amounts to. To this end, however, the concepts and categories of traditional philosophy—not even one among them—are of any use to us. What we are confronted with now is something entirely new; we have to make an effort to conceive what we see by means of fresh concepts. Gentlemen, it is our fortune to have to try on concepts for the first time."[7]

Now then, as is evident, Ortega continued to postulate—or at least to employ—the notion of category in connection with his conception of living. He contended that the "categories" are "the 'attributes' of the novel radical reality." Aristotle and traditional philosophy had taken the "categories" to be "the properties that any real being, simply because it is real, brings along and necessarily contains, above and beyond and apart from the fact that it has other distinguishing components." And yet, if this is so, it is evident that, once the idea of reality is subjected to such a drastic change, not only would the sense of the various categories articulating the idea of reality have to be modified, but so would the meaning itself of the "categorial sphere" as well. Indeed, Ortega argued this point as follows:

> This reality of ours that I call *living* consists of a set of categories or components, all of which would be necessary, co-originary, and inseparable from one another, inasmuch as living is a reality quite different from the cosmic reality of the Ancients. We are engaged in seeking after the categories of "our life". Now, our life is the life "belonging to each one of us"; mine is therefore different from yours. And yet your life or mine, each, is describable as "my living", and this means that one finds a set of ingredients common to both, namely, the categories spelling out the structure of "my life". In this connection, however, a radical difference is detectable between the reality called "my life" and the reality designated as "being" in established philosophy. "Being" is a general notion that cannot—by itself—express individuality. The Aristotelian categories are categories of being in general—*ón he ón* [being *qua* being]—but the name "my life",

whether it is applied in my case or yours, undoubtedly implies individuality. We have thus come across a most strange idea, combining as it does both "generality" and "individuality". The science of logic has until now been unaware of the fact that this kind of concept, which to all appearances is so affected by contradiction, is nonetheless possible.[8]

In effect, the essential difference pointed out by Ortega opens up a new categorial vista and thereby gives us access to novel logical possibilities still nearly unheard off, indeed to a well-nigh virginal field of investigation that is as difficult to grasp as it is promising, and which should become a challenge to young Spanish-speaking philosophers endowed with a genuine hunger for reality.

Let me, quite briefly, just indicate some of the most obvious characteristics exhibited by such concepts, precisely as they in fact perform their proper function in Ortega's thought. As Ortega himself did, I shall refer to the basic structural features of life as the "categories" of human life. I mean thereby those traits that are immediately accessible to us in a descriptive analysis of human life, an examination in which we are to live up to the rigorous application of the methodological rule forbidding us to "posit" as part of life anything that would transcend what is strictly and immediately given, that is to say, anything that would lie beyond what Ortega referred to as the "*radical* data." Hence, our manner of procedure would have to be descriptive, in accordance with the purest deictic attitude, by which we would be intent on expressing reality itself, in all its concreteness and immediacy. What is involved, therefore, is the exacting employment of a methodological rule that is already well-established and which has been accepted in modern and contemporary philosophical thought, to wit: that philosophers—by adopting an unmitigated spirit of radicalism in their primordial or fundamental inquiries concerning reality—should abide only by the facts, by the given. In other words, philosophers must remain true to the "unmediated data," in the pursuit of which contemporary philosophical thought (i.e., philosophical reflection as conducted in those quarters that still continue to accept this manner of quest as valid) has refined its critical acumen to the point of exhaustion. And yet this does not mean that the discoveries it has presumably made are not subject to precautionary measures and possible rectifications even to this day, in an attempt to arrive, by means of a maximal effort to "purify" the data obtained, at the most radical "point of departure" possible [for the construction of the universe]. In this context, Ortega's metaphysical thought would then signify the conquest of a new level of critical analysis, a level that we have grown to appreciate throughout this study. I have in mind Ortega's effort progressively to purify the process employed in establishing the data or, as he also put it, in discovering the radical fact, the "fact of all facts."

Indeed, the concepts by means of which one would strive to apprehend reality itself, as opposed to the notions proper to the science of metaphysics understood in a traditional or "ontological" sense, are characteristically synthetical and ambivalent. Actually, they display such features precisely insofar as they belong to the pure analytics of radical reality. Moreover, they show themselves to be "occasional,"[9] "scalar," and "multi-valued," whenever they are employed as "instrumentalities of concretization." Let me explain.

First of all, categorial concepts are "synthetical" in the sense that they are "originary syntheses," to use an expression I have sometimes employed. I mean that such notions are not synthetical as a result of the activity of some intellectual operation of synthesis, but that they instead show this character as their own originary endowment the moment they are subjected to analysis. This analysis is necessary for the purposes of formulating the theory of human life, and yet it proves to be "distortive" to some degree. Indeed, this is so much so that the resulting distortion must be methodically corrected by us time and again. Secondly, they are "ambivalent," inasmuch as the meaning they express always splits, to begin with, along two dimensions or "directionalities," that is to say, in terms of the primordial and dynamic duality that is constitutive of the radical fact or reality they are intended to describe or "depict" [trasumir]. Accordingly, they are not concepts one is supposed to employ in order to designate "things" or "entities"—whether they are taken to be "material" or "spiritual" in nature—but rather to signify "referential functions" lived along the twofoldness proper to a living ego. I have in mind the dual event in which the "ego" is "referred" to the "things" of its world or circum-stance, and the world or circum-stance is "referred" to the "ego," in whose life they are "actuating" or given. It is to be noted, let me say it again, that such a twofold referential function is, strictly speaking, constitutive of reality as such. Finally, these categorial notions must be characterized by a special "mobility" and involve a potentiality for development always open to new "aspects" and "levels," by reason of the fact that they designate a reality which is dynamic, always *in via* [becoming], and complex to the highest degree—indeed, this manner of complexity is, as we will have an occasion to see,[10] one of their "primordial determinations" [*primalidades*]. In passing, Ortega himself alluded to the mobility and potentiality for development of such concepts when he spoke of some of the notions that are meant to articulate the category of doing. This is how he formulated his point: "Each and every one of these words is a category, which, as such, would be open to an analysis without end."[11] Moreover, as we have already seen, such categorial concepts are "necessary, co-originary, and *inseparable from one another.*"[12]

Unfortunately, these brief remarks will have to do as aids in our efforts to make out the sense that the categorial sphere had for Ortega.

As I have already pointed out, I will now proceed to the exposition of a few select categories of human life, namely, those which are more directly connected with Ortega's critique of idealism. I hope that my explication of them will render more apparent the features I have just underscored as characteristic of such concepts. In this endeavor, however, I will follow a method different from the one I have practiced thus far, since, in attempting to unfold the *idea of life,* I cannot limit myself to the consideration of texts chosen because of their relevancy to the articulation of Ortega's critique of idealism, but must bear his entire work in mind. Accordingly, it will prove impossible, at least within the confines of a study having the structure and aims of the present investigation, to follow a number of texts organized according to a strict sequential order and to adopt a developmental approach to the subject matter. I will therefore make a presentation of such concepts—and even advance an interpretation of them—that shall be free, and which will not be restricted to the texts that may fall under my scrutiny, since I will be relying on the fruits of my personal reflection on Ortega's work, and upon the reading and study of his whole corpus (activities in which I have been engaged throughout my life).

My examination of these matters shall be focused on the notions of originary dynamic co-existence, absolute event (or the "fact of all facts"), and presence. Actually, Ortega characterized "absolute event" and "presence," both, as the "first category of human life," though he did so in different contexts. Strictly speaking, however, all these notions are interpretations of the one radical fact or datum when it is looked upon from various standpoints. Accordingly, one must say that they essentially implicate or "complicate" one another—or, as Ortega put it, that they are "inseparable" from each other. This "co-implication" does not therefore obtain only between those two categories, but affects them all. In point of fact, such a close and intimate "co-implication" corresponds to that existing among all real components of life itself, which is indeed marked by the highest degree of "complication" or complexity. This is the reason why, in my judgment, "complexity" itself should be regarded as a fundamental category or concept. Indeed, I will be adopting this view in my own exposition.[13]

CHAPTER 4

The Categories of Life

1. THE "ABSOLUTE EVENT"

We have seen how the discovery of life, which is both a presupposition and an outcome of Ortega's critique of realism and idealism, is for him tantamount to the overcoming of both these positions. It thus signifies having arrived at a new level in the posing of the metaphysical question and, no doubt, in the obtaining of a fitting "answer" thereto. This "answer" (and, of course, the special manner of "posing" the question that would render such an answer possible) are based—or grounded in the claim to be based—upon Ortega's decision to employ, with the utmost precision, the principle of never losing touch with reality itself in the process of elaborating his own theoretical account, a principle that is at once of simple and most difficult application. In other words, I am referring here to the principle that required him to resist any temptation to soar in a "flight of speculation," "constructivism," and the like, as well as any enticement to observe the inordinate "restrictiveness" of an inadequate empiricism and positivism. Indeed, such temptations have been responsible, by excess and defect respectively, for the fact that people had, to some extent or other, lost touch with reality when proceeding on the basis of any of the philosophical positions that prevailed before Ortega. The attitude Ortega proposed was, in his opinion, the most deeply and justifiedly rational one, since the "reason" of which he availed himself belongs to reality itself—it is the "*living* reason" by which reality "rules" the mind. But, by the same token, it is the most strictly positivistic attitude of all, in that one would thereby abide by the facts, that is to say, by the "radical fact" or "fact of all facts," inasmuch as it is the one in the context of which all other facts are constituted and endowed with their proper sense. Ortega's is an "absolute, not a deficient positivism." Furthermore, it is, in my judgment, an "empirical" stance in the broadest and most exact sense of the term, since it emerges on the grounds of, and is expressly based upon, the "integrity of experience" which life, in each and every one of its dimensions, intrinsically is.

One could spell out the principle in question by saying that it demands one be faithful, in the most exacting of fashions, to the immediacy and concreteness of reality itself. Actually, this principle specifies the fundamental requirement to be satisfied by anyone who advances a theoretical formulation the aim of which is in fact to be an account of reality, if he is not to be led astray from the outset. In the final analysis, it would depict the novel shape to be adopted by the injunction to abide by what is evident, which has always been—more or less explicitly—the tribunal of last resort where to settle matters philosophically. Indeed, one may give it expression as follows: the point of departure for an adequate theory of reality—and the source for the continual renewal thereof along the way of its development—must be reality itself, taken in its full immediacy and concreteness. Reality must be approached as it is immediately given, that is to say, by avoiding the recourse of "mediation" afforded by any idea one may have already accepted about it. In other words, one must keep from distorting reality by introducing "intellectual" interpretations between reality and one's originary view of it. Or equivalently stated: such a view is to be, or should arise from, my living grasp [*vivencia*] of, or my most direct contact with, reality itself. Moreover, reality must be approached in its concreteness, that is to say, one ought to take it without subjecting it to mutilations, simplifications, or "reductions" resulting from any conceivable sort of "abstractive" procedure or "restriction" that does not involve its own instrument for self-correction or self-rectification as an integral part of itself. Or to put it otherwise: one should abide by reality precisely as it is given, that is to say, just as it gives itself to me when I-encounter-myself-with-it.[1]

If we really come to the decision of complying, without exception, with such a methodological requirement, reality would accordingly display for us, to begin with, a number of features or characteristics that I will now attempt to describe in an elementary fashion.

We have already seen[2] how Ortega, by means of the exacting employment of this principle, came to discover the radical fact (or datum) which he called absolute event, and which is, according to him, the first category of human life. This concept, therefore, serves the purpose of characterizing the originary manner of there-being or availability. We are already cognizant of the fact that, when one says "there-is" or "it is-available," one means to banish the ancient notion of being and, further, that when one regards this manner of there-being or availability as originary, one has in mind something that is irreducible to any other. In other words, I contend that this manner of there-being or availability gives itself, or appears, originarily. Now then, the absolute event or primordial availability is just the fact of encountering myself living and striving in a world of "things" (let me speak of them by means of this name for the time being). In an event of this sort, I find that I cannot be reduced to the status enjoyed by "things" or they to mine, but I discover as well that neither am I without them nor they without me. In such an event, "things" and I, the world and myself, cannot be mistaken for one another, and yet, by the same token, neither can they be separated from each other, for "things" and I *co-exist* in terms of a bond of essential dependence, or of a constitutive and, therefore, indestructible relationship. Accordingly, any endeavor to think of things as if they were independent of me (this is the thesis called realism) would be, as such, a falsification of reality itself, but so would likewise be the attempt to think of myself as if I were independent of "things," that is to say, the effort to reduce the latter to my ideas or the "contents of my consciousness" (this is the thesis called idealism).

What we seek, then, is reality itself, precisely as it is genuinely given to us when we come to take notice of it, a goal that is not easy to achieve and which has required the prolonged series of intellectual experiences initiated in Greece and lasting up to the present. Reality, so considered, offers itself to us as being already involved in self-performance, that is, as being thus and so prior to any act by means of which one may think of it; in fact, it is in that fashion that it functions as a condition to be fulfilled if any act of thinking of it is to occur, and it does so in terms of the peculiar *dynamic duality* of reciprocity that living or my life is. I have in mind [the unity of] myself and what surrounds me, i.e., my circum-stance, between which permanent and unavoidable interaction and interfunctionality occur. Such a functional and dynamic character becomes specific by way of what we do and what befalls us. "Life is what we do and what befalls us,"[3] contended Ortega by means of a formula that is as perfectly simple as it is of the utmost precision. In my opinion, this is one of the clearest illustrations of the efficacy and exactitude characteristic of the "*lógos* of life," that is, of the fact that a wealth of significance can accrue to any straightforwardly everyday expression whenever it is assigned the role of "technical" term in the context of an authentic theory of human life.

Accordingly, the genuine, primordial reality of "things" is [a two-sided event, consisting of] my doing, like it or not, something with "things," and of "things" making themselves available to or withdrawing from me precisely in view of, or for the sake of, my doing. (Things then facilitate my doing or render it difficult, and thus they *urge* me to carry it out or avoid it, respectively). In other words, the primordial reality of "things" is to be characterized as a being-for, as the serviceable, pragmatic being they execute as they instance or urge us [to do this or that].[4] But this manner of being makes an essential reference to an ego, that is to say, to an "ego"'s doing, just as necessarily as an "ego" implicates or involves "things." Radical reality is not, then, anything attributable to an entity, substance, or static being: as Ortega put it, "any static remnant [we may find] is a sign that we no longer are at the level of reality," an assertion that one ought to take absolutely seriously and rigorously, that is to say, as a basic theorem belonging to metaphysics in the new style. Rather, radical reality is an event, that is to say, it ultimately is a living event; therefore, it is something consisting in being performed, something that is pure and primordial performativeness.

"Performativeness" and "event" are terms giving expression to complementary features. Performativeness, as an essential component of the "absolute event" that living is, underscores doing as an aspect of living, while event, or the fact of the occurrence of an event, seems to emphasize another side of living, namely, the fact of befalling, or that something "befalls us." But one should keep in mind that both dimensions of living are nonetheless inseparable, since they mirror the primordial functional duality of reciprocity into which living is resolved, namely, that consisting of myself doing and things befalling me.

Let me now insist upon some of the significant aspects that are constitutive of the notion of "absolute event," without however confining myself only to those that I have already mentioned.

2. ENCOUNTER

We have repeatedly come across this expression whenever we have begun to describe the radical fact or the unmediated datum, namely, my life. In effect, to live is to *encounter* or come upon *myself living*. But to say this means that I always and inevitably "encounter" or come upon "myself" *in connection with* one or another thing. In other words, I never encounter or come upon myself alone, since I always do it in terms of a bond of community or by virtue of the establishment of a nexus of communication with my circum-stance or, in the final analysis, with the world. Far from being a self-enclosed realm, as is presupposed in idealism, I am or live necessarily in a condition of "openness" to and reciprocation with "that which is other than I." But those dimensions of the fact of encountering myself which are signified by prepositions like "with" or "in" always exhibit a most concrete texture; they accordingly situate me in a definite here. The circum-stantiality [of life] is thus coextensive with a situation, which is comprised of many components, only some of which will I have the occasion to take a glance at here. Let me then begin considering the first one.

3. ACTUALITY

Encountering myself is something which is already taking place. I already find or encounter myself (that is to say, here and now) in the condition of being immersed beforehand in this dread-ful "world." I do not know how this has come to pass; I have not been consulted before the fact. In short, I encounter myself adrift in the world or, as Ortega preferred to say, in the condition of a "castaway" in its midst and, accordingly, as having no choice but to sink or swim. Elsewhere Ortega chose to convey the sense of this disconcerting primordial situation by saying that "I am shot with life at point-blank range."[5]

To encounter myself presupposes that I perceive [*percatarme*] or become aware [*darme cuenta*] of myself.[6] If understood in the broadest sense, this event constitutes the foundation of presence.

Now, both "presence" and "absolute event" are "categories" characterized by Ortega as "primordial." Strictly speaking, however, they are not two distinct categories, but only two different "dimensions" of one and the same primary fact. This notwithstanding, the concept of presence, given its major importance, deserves a separate and closer analysis.

4. PRESENCE

As Ortega said, ". . . [e]very life consists in experiencing itself living, in feeling itself engaged in living, in knowing itself as existing. This form of knowing does not however involve any kind of intellectual grasp or the possession of wisdom of any sort; it amounts only to the wondrous self-presence characterizing each individual life."[7] Or again: "Living is, to begin with, an event of disclosure: it is not merely the fact of existing, but also the performance by means of which I understand, perceive, or realize that I exist. Living is the ongoing discovery of myself and the surrounding world, a discovery that I am engaged in effecting."[8] And further: "Life is self-knowing; it is a [self-]evincing affair."[9] Or to put it otherwise: ". . . life . . . is what is manifest; actually it is, of all things, that which is most manifest. By reason of its sheer self-manifestness or transparency, it is difficult for us to take notice of it. We glance through it and beyond, in the direction of problematical forms of wisdom, only being able, by means of a special effort, to focus our attention on the immediate facts proper to life."[10] Life "is indubitable, and so is everything of which it consists, only by virtue of . . . [its self-transparency], and it is the radical reality solely because it is the only indubitable reality."[11] On this basis, one can gather why Ortega assigned first priority to this category. In effect, he identified it with the very fact of "encounter." This is how he put it:

> The first category of our lives is "self-encounter", "becoming self-aware", or "being self-transparent". But let me reiterate the point that we should never be oblivious of the fact that "self" does not designate subjectivity alone; it refers to the world as well. I become aware of myself in the world, that is to say, of myself and the world. Living, to begin with, is just that.[12]

But Ortega also turned presence into the origin of the self-possession characteristic of life: "This self-regard, this feeling I have of myself, this self-presence of my life hands it over to me, makes it 'mine'. This sense is precisely lacking in the madman. The madman's life is not his; strictly speaking, his is no longer life."[13]

The idea of "presence" is however much more complex than these citations might lead us to suspect. In his *Meditaciones del Quijote,* Ortega had already succeeded in giving a first version, indeed one marked by genius, of his theoretical account of presence.[14] Regarding it as fundamentally valid, he did nevertheless return to it in *El hombre y la gente,* so as to develop some of its aspects.[15] In that original formulation, he had made the complexity of the concept quite apparent, elaborating it as he did, on the one hand, in terms of the notions of "surface" and "depth," which would be the equivalents, respectively, of "actual presence" and "potential presence" (i.e., latency or copresence), and, on the other, as essentially connected with the concepts of circum-stance and perspective. There he was dealing with no less than the radical structure of life, wherein presence also shows up as a foundation for the primordial role played by truth in our lives. By means of that formulation, one can learn to appreciate as well the various senses assignable to presence, depending on what it may specifically designate, namely, the "world," the "ego," or "life" itself. Furthermore, one is to realize that there is a different mode of presence corresponding to each one of these areas. And yet this would hardly be sufficient to grasp the full range of essential relationships into which the concept of presence may enter, since it is also most directly connected, as is obvious, with the disquieting problem-set of time. Here I understand "time" in the sense of *living* time, as the "time of life," or, more exactly, as the time life *is,* inasmuch as "presence," along one of its fundamental dimensions, or perhaps along the most fundamental one, is the quality constitutive of what is present or of the present.[16]

As is only reasonable, here I am not going to enter into the formal examination of this complicated subject, since an effort of that sort would make it necessary for me to devote to it several times as much space as I am in fact assigning to it. But at least I would like to point to just a few of the implications of the concept of presence.

5. THE ACT OF BECOMING PRESENT

The constant self-presence of life is one of the aspects of its actuality. I mean, of course, the presence which, by virtue of its immediacy, is the warrant justifying the fact that life is characterizable as the "radical reality," as it is also the origin of life's [self-]possession and of its sense of "gravity" or burdensomeness (a side of life to which I will return).[17] Once again everyday language comes to our assistance here by means of a marvellous Spanish locution that, most insightfully, brings together the concepts of "actuality" and "presence." I have in mind the expression *acto de presencia* [i.e., the act of becoming present or of putting in an appearance]. I am availing myself of it in order exactly to formulate various theses belonging to the analytics of human life.

For the purposes of coming to an adequate understanding of the sense of the phrase "act of becoming present," one must clearly grasp the signification of the word *act,* that is to say, the connotation acquired by it when one has in mind the act-character proper to life (and to which I have referred by means of the abstract noun *actuality*). I am employing the terms "act" and "actuality" in a way that still preserves part of their original metaphysical import, which is, as is known, the sense assigned to their equivalents by Aristotle, although, to be sure, I have here essentially modified it. Let me explain.

Of the various components that form part of the connotation of the Aristotelian terms "being in act" and "being in potency," I would like to set aside the sense of "entity" or *ón* and preserve those of *enérgeia* and *dynamis,* which shall come together, in a special way, in the concept of act I am trying to develop. As I use it, "actuality" signifies, to put it concisely but with precision, the plenitude of reality itself. At first glance, the meaning of this expression seems to coincide with that of Aristotle's *enérgeia,* but in fact its sense is almost contrary to that of Aristotle's term. In effect, when I say "plenitude," I do not have in mind "[self-]sufficiency" or substantiality, but just the opposite. Furthermore, "actuality" is not to be regarded as antithetical to "potentiality" or "possibility." In my opinion, actuality must be taken as synonymous with "dynamism" and, therefore, as converging with possibility itself, as I have already pointed out. According to its intended use here, actuality is precisely the actuality of the possible. In other words, while I keep employing Aristotelian terminology, I do it by almost turning it on its head. The reason for this lies in the fact that, as is known, the formula "actuality of the possible"[18] is Aristotle's definition of motion, and motion is refused precisely the character of full "actuality" by Aristotle himself. If this were not enough, one would have, of course, to keep alive to the fact that the sense I assign here to "possibility" is not the same as Aristotle's own.[19] Moreover, I am taking the meaning of *act* to be identical with effective actuation, a contention that can be specified as follows: when applied to the ego, i.e., to me, "act" means acting in the sense of doing, understood in Ortega's sense of the word, which I will further elaborate below,[20] but, when it is applied to "things," it signifies in-stancing or urging (a notion that I will also explain later).[21] In short, as I use the term, "actuality" involves the constitutive or intrinsic temporality of human life, in the context of which "actuality" and "presence," properly speaking, are found to be identical, an identification given expression in what I would describe as "that which is *presently being in-stantaneous.*"

Accordingly, the act of becoming present, or of putting in an appearance, belongs to life itself, an assertion that has consequences affecting the two inseparable sides or components of life, namely, myself and things. When referred to the ego, that is, to me, the signification of such an act is not too difficult to grasp, at least at the first level of our coming to terms with it intellectually. Indeed, it seems most natural to say that an ego (i.e., a "person" or "someone") acts or performs acts, but, when somebody speaks of things in the same vein, it does not sound so convincing, however common it may be to find, in the philosophical tradition, statements about the *actiones* of things, where things, as in the formula, *actiones sunt suppositorum* ["acts or actions are the underlying subject's"], are understood as "sub-stances" or *supposita* [i.e., as the underlying subjects]. But, as we already know, the meaning of *act,* as I use the term here, has nothing to do with this. An explanation is therefore in order, if one wishes to understand the sense in which things perform their act of becoming present, or of putting in an appearance, in life. Let me now try to give such an account.

To begin with, I would say that there is no thing, that there is nothing of which one can speak or think that does not make its appearance in my life. I have in mind the much discussed but elementary fact that everything finds its roots in my life. This indubitable and primordial fact assigns, then, every reality, every particular "something" that has the power to stand out or is identifiable (and is, in short, perceptible, imaginable, or thinkable) to an equally primordial sphere to which it "belongs." My life is precisely this sphere. Every reality or thing, every particular something can of course find a place, and indeed does find it, in other "spheres," areas, or orders in which to belong—e.g., it can be an "individual member" of a "class," or again a part of any other "whole"; moreover, it can even be something that does not appear directly within the confines of my life but in another's, so as to become present to me by means of that other life, and so on. And yet, in any case, all such spheres are, on their own, implanted in my life (and in this sense presuppose it or are "reduced" thereto). But my life is the primordial sphere that is-available prior to any other sphere, and it is therefore irreducible to them. This basic way that any thinkable reality has of belonging to my life confers on any "rooted" reality the special and primordial kind of actuality of which I have been speaking. This manner of belonging means precisely that every such reality has to appear in my life somehow, if it is only by way of an allusion or a hypothesis or even a negation.[22]

The expression "*act of becoming present*" ought then to be understood in that manner whenever it is used with reference to things. I am employing the name to signify the "act" of belonging to the primordial manner of actuality, placing special emphasis on the most penetrating and far-reaching colloquial connotation of the phrase, namely, that of "putting in an appearance." Furthermore, it must be said that such a manner of actuality is taking place at a metaphysical level prior to that of being, even if one uses this term according to its traditional sense of existing. Anything has first to become present, if I am to be able to say of it that it is or exists, i.e., that it is, strictly speaking, capable of being or existing. I am hereby advancing a fundamental principle, the significance of which cannot yet be grasped, but about which one can nevertheless say that it is incontrovertibly true, provided one has understood it adequately. In point of fact, I am intellectually endeavoring to apprehend it in that manner by means of these remarks. Accordingly, one must say that every thing, every particular something must first make its appearance, or give-itself-to-me, within the sphere of my life. In other words, it has to become a datum, if it is to be something. This is true, even if one is dealing with the extreme situation in which one is faced with a datum that is just an "unknown": in the present context, as opposed to what happens in the science of mathematics, "unknowns" are also data, indeed they are among the most significant data of all.

For the time being, I shall limit the comprehension of the term "act of becoming present," whenever it is employed with reference to things, to the note "being a 'datum'." Naturally, just as the level of the nonmediated self-givenness of reality (i.e., of its giving-itself-to-me or of its mere appearing or becoming present to me) is prior to that of being (against the entire philosophical tradition, one can say here that appearing founds being), so is the manner of apprehension commensurate with it prior to "knowing," inasmuch as "knowledge," understood exactly, or according to the classical connotation of the word, has a role to perform [only] on the basis of the presupposition of being, or within the confines of the "order" established by it. This fundamental level of "apprehension," which could be characterized as the event of my being merely "notified," is comprised in or presupposed by all the modalities of consciousness (or of perceiving [*percatarse*] or becoming aware [*darse cuenta*],[23] to use Ortega's own terms), modalities which range from sense perception to "reception" of, or "reliance upon," something.

Naturally, the basic fact that every particular something is "rooted" in my life, or the primordial event of its being "implanted" in it, need not be taken to signify—as I think it should be evident by now—that "radical reality" is something other than the realities rooted therein. It goes without saying that, without the latter, there would be no "radical reality" (and vice versa). This is the reason why, when we speak of the immediate presence of things (or of the ego, for that matter), we are availing ourselves of a somewhat inappropriate manner of expression, since, if we wish to formulate matters accurately, we would have to assert that only life is immediately present to itself. This notwithstanding, it is permissible to say that the two essential components of life, namely, myself and things (or my circum-stance), share in the nonmediated self-presence of life and, therefore, in the act of which it consists, although each component does so in its own special way.

Let me now attempt to summarize this position by using a formula which, in my opinion, would do justice to the fact I am trying to describe. It reads as follows: "everything *makes its appearance* in life, and life *appears through* everything." The notions of "making an appearance" and "appearing through," as they have just been employed, must however be understood exactly. On the one hand, the expression "making an appearance" is meant to convey the way in which things, as I have been calling them, or, generally speaking, all realities "rooted in life," are present to me. (In a moment, we will have an opportunity to appreciate the fact that I have only insufficiently described the way in which "things" appear to me, since I still have to specify how it is they make their appearance.)[24] On the other hand, the concept of "appearing through" signifies the way in which life itself is present. Accordingly, one may say that life's presence consists in being transparent,[25] the "instrumentality" for which, of course, would always be myself. As we have already seen, Ortega often employs the term *transparency*. In fact, a genuinely nonmediated transparency, or the feature of being a "[self-]evincing affair" (as Ortega referred to it too),[26] is constitutive of life itself; in fact, it is one of its primordial metaphysical attributes and is found among the roots of the truth of life itself and of truth as such—or, in other words, of the truth of life and of thought.

It is by virtue of the transparency proper to the presence of life that it has been so difficult to notice or "see" life as the originary and "non-mediated" radical reality it is. It is just by reason of the fact that life "appears through" everything, through every reality "rooted in it" (for life is the universal "medium" in which we "live, move, and have our being"),[27] that life has always escaped our intellectual grasp, according to the principle that the more transparent a "medium," the more difficult it is to "see" it. The fact that life proper is "appearing through" is embodied, as a subtle "impregnation" so to speak, in the event itself in which every thing is making its appearance. This point is what the young Ortega already was gropingly trying to make when he wrote that "all things are alive." In view of this, one can now appreciate the fact that the appearing of things in life (or, more exactly, their act of becoming present) is thus coimplicated with the event in which life itself is appearing through. This should serve us as a preliminary confirmation of the fact, just alluded to, that my description of the way in which things appear to me has only been carried out in part. And yet this is not the only reason why the act of becoming present exhibits a complex nature, a fact that can be appreciated in other respects as well. Indeed, everything in life is complex, since life itself is characterized by the highest degree of complexity, and everything shares in this radical complexity.

In my opinion, this is the proper occasion to interrupt my examination of the act of becoming present—afterwards, I will resume my analysis of it—[28] and say something about another "primordial concept" or "category" of life. I have in mind the category of complexity to which I believe only insufficient attention has been paid. I wish to discuss it without further delay, since, if I do not keep it adequately in mind, my account of life would as a consequence lack the required intelligibility and at times may even sound ambiguous. I will attempt to do it now, even though my manner of presentation—its nature being that of a synthesis—will not unfortunately permit me to dwell on it either.

In effect, the final justification of the multivalued character exhibited by concepts referring to human life is to be found in the basic complexity of life. As you may remember, at the beginning of this [part of the] investigation[29] I took pains to underscore this multivaluation, which takes place in several registers. Actually, it corresponds to the various dimensions of which life's complexity consists, including above all that which has to do with the dynamism of life, or with its processing or "fashioning" character. It is by virtue of the latter that multivaluation is expressed in the fact that the concepts in question are occasional and mobile. It is just this multivaluation that may easily turn into equivocation, unless one adopts certain required methodical precautions.

A. Complexity

Radical reality is *complicatio omnium* [or the coimplication of everything]. I have already said that life is characterized by the highest degree of complexity, since it co-implicates everything. This is the reason why, in this connection, one can use the formula "*complicatio omnium*," which derives from Nicholas of Cusa,[30] but which is here endowed with a new sense, indeed with a twofold novel signification, which I wish to examine in what follows.

On the basis of all that has been thus far advanced, it would not be difficult to note—as in all probability the reader has already done—that the first sense or acceptation of the term *complexity*, in the phrase "life's complexity," is connected with the etymology of the word itself, as it is given expression in the Latin deponent verb *complector*, from whose participle *complexus* the locutions "complex" and, therefore, "complexity" derive. This first connotation is to "*comprise* or *encompass*." In effect, life "comprises" or "encompasses" everything, it "involves" or "envelops" all, since it is the radical reality. Or, in other words, it is that which consists of myself and what is other than I, namely, my circum-stance, taking this locution in the broadest sense, to mean the world and even the "background" of the world and the "horizon of the last things."[31]

Now then, it is most important to bear in mind that the event of encompassing or comprising is not to be taken as if it signified that life includes everything within itself, as the container holds its contents; moreover, neither is life to be understood as if it were everything or, even more subtly, as if everything could, "*in the final analysis*" [*en última instancia*], be reduced to life. Rather, as we will learn to appreciate, it is in the manner of a first, even of an absolutely first "*instancy*" that any particular something may belong to life.[32] No doubt, it is possible "somehow" to speak of "reducing" everything to life, in the sense that every thing, as I have been arguing, originarily belongs or is implanted in life, since such belongingness or implantation refers to the fact that things are given or appear in life. And yet, from another point of view, the opposite is the case, i.e., nothing is "reducible" to life as, for example, according to materialism, everything would be reduced to matter or, according to the general thesis of realism, everything would be reduced to "thinghood" or *res* or, again, according to idealism, everything would be reduced to ego, idea, mind, or consciousness. In effect, nothing that is given in life is life itself: life is no heavenly body, no stone, no plant; generally speaking, it is not even the world, whether one takes it as a whole or only in bits and pieces, i.e., in terms of any of its components or of any of the things that are parts of it. One cannot even say that a human being is his life, or that I am my life. Rather, life is, precisely, the *complicatio* of all that. It is not a question of whether life "has" a greater or lesser degree of "complication"; the fact of the matter is that life is, essentially and radically, *complicatio;* it consists in being *complicatio;* it is nothing but *complicatio maxima* [maximal coimplication] or *complicatio omnium*. Accordingly, one must say that complexity or coimplication is a genuine, primary metaphysical character of life. On this basis, I believe it is quite legitimate to regard it as a "primordial concept" or "category" of life. One may then assert that the event of encompassing or comprising, or the first sense of complexity, is just the specific structure exhibited by life qua radical fact, i.e., as the fact assigning everything the status of "being rooted" in life. Or, if you will, we may put it otherwise and say that it is the specific structure of the act of becoming present, provided, of course, that we take into account the various caveats with which we are already familiar.

This is another way of affirming what I have often stated, namely, that the radical reality cannot be identified with being. (Actually, I shall continue to insist on this thesis from different points of view, as required by the unfolding exposition.) In effect, the notions of "being" and "life" (always taking the latter in Ortega's sense) not only do not coincide, but are in fact polar opposites as well, if for no other reason—and there are many—that life is fundamentally marked by "maximal complexity," while "being," according to the teachings of traditional ontology, is characterized by "maximal simplicity." The concept of "life" (or, more exactly, of "my life") refers to the most concrete dimensions of reality, or to the most concrete reality of all, while the concept of "being" is the most abstract of all concepts, even to the point that its content is, properly speaking, nothing.[33] Furthermore, the concept of life is the dynamic and "occasional" notion par excellence, while the concept of being is the static and "intemporal" notion par excellence. And we could continue in this vein.

Let me now turn to the second sense of "complexity." The term also signifies intricacy, intertwinement, connection, or *complection* (the latter, again, in view of the etymology of the word). The meaning of such attributes, when they are predicated of life, likewise must undergo a maximization or an increase to the superlative degree. Not only is it true that life encompasses all by way of rootedness or presence, but it is also the case that the "all" in question is no *totum revolutum* or mere "aggregate" resulting from sheer "addition." In effect, the manner in which every ingredient or part of the *totum* or whole comes to "join" life, or to "be given" or "rooted" in life, is not that proper to an "element," which could exist independently of the rest on the basis of a sort of common and thereby "neutral" background. On the contrary, each and every one of those ingredients or parts makes its appearance as being essentially bound with the rest in various ways; in other words, it shows itself to be a member of the whole by means of a dense, intricate com-plection with the rest. Or equivalently stated: it does not come together with other ingredients to constitute a chaotic manifold, but finds its proper placement within a universal system of relations. Ortega did at one point use the image of an "intricate forest" in order to characterize the condition of life I have in mind, and he has even employed Dante's phrase, *selva selvaggia* [wild wood],[34] to that end. Now, if life is like a forest, it is one that is subject to continual transmutation and change, a fact that would only exacerbate its very complexity and intricacy, for, as it then turns out, the "universal" manifoldness of relations involved would also be undergoing transformations and would thereby continually "increase its manifold character" even further in the context of unfolding time. Life, then, as the major or universal context, is a dynamism that each "thing" joins by "performing a function", i.e., by "discharging a task" or "playing" a role in the originary *drama* life is.

Ortega clearly grasped this complective, connective, systematic, and totalizing character of life already in his oft-cited *Meditaciones del Quijote*. In that work, he gave it expression with the greatest possible acumen [and in terms of various formulations]. For example, he presented the idea of "universal connection," which is made manifest by the "disclosive" role of love that "ties one thing to another and all things to us within a firmly established structure." He also employed the image of the "countless reverberations" that the sun produces on something when it is placed in a favorable light, thus making the "dis-covery" (*alétheia*) that every thing is affected by repercussions, echoes, or reflections of each and every other thing. Furthermore, he gave currency to the notions of "surface" and "depth," to which I have already referred.[35] Moreover, he conceptualized a most fundamental insight by means of the clear idea that the structure of the "universal system" of relations in question is that of a perspective, a view implying that "life itself is a perspective," understanding this term, naturally, as signifying a dynamism subject to constant change. And he likewise advanced the notion of "profiling" or "foreshortening" [*escorzo*], which is intimately linked with that of perspective.[36] All of these theses most lucidly embody the second meaning of life's complexity, a sense that of course implies the first one.

Throughout his life, Ortega returned, time and again, to such concepts, and he came to regard them—according to the demands placed on him by his own method of inquiry—in terms of different "vistas" and precisely by means of various "profiles." Following Ortega's "dialectical" journey, in his own special sense of *Realdialektik*,[37] one arrives, with ever-increasing clarity, at the progressive realization that the fact that things make their appearance in my life is not a matter available to me in a purely ostensive manner, as if they merely showed themselves standing-there being this or that,[38] but in a way which is originarily conflictive. Let me insist on the fact that standing-there [*estar*], as well as being [*ser*], are pure abstractions, i.e., limiting concepts or abstractions with which one attempts to think the unthinkable, namely, that residual nothing that would "be left" were one to succeed in formally eliminating every determination and every circum-stantial concretion belonging to "what *there-is* or *is-available*." Strictly speaking, one cannot assert that there-is being or that there-is standing-there, or that they are-available, except perhaps as tendential modalities of what there-is or is-available, as Ferrater Mora, for one, has argued, although he has done so on different grounds and in terms of metaphysical perspectives other than my own.[39] Accordingly, to say that something is part of my life, or that it makes its appearance therein, is tantamount to asserting, of course, that it already is performing a function, actuating, or playing its role, that is to say, that it is doing so in conjunction with the role played by other "things" or particular "somethings" and with myself, in the context of the permanent dramatic conflict living is. But what has always been called the "universe," and what I call "life" [following Ortega], is the com-plection or dynamic intricacy binding all things together, the conflictive, dramatic, and totalizing (i.e., the all-comprehensive and all-coimplicating) structural unity characteristic of the act of becoming present effected by things. It is in this special sense that I contend that the system of relations in which all things are implanted is universal.

The "unity by co-implication" proper to life becomes actually manifest in any of the relationships one establishes with the "world" or "circum-stance." If one considers, say, the elementary way of relating to the world that one gives rise to in that special mode of becoming aware one calls "perception," and endeavors to arrive at a faithful description of it, one would make the discovery that one never perceives things in isolation, for one always grasps the world itself. In the science of psychology, it was learned long ago that there is no such thing as a "sensation," except as the product of an abstractive procedure to which perception would have been subjected. On a different theoretical plane, this point was later confirmed by philosophers like Jean-Paul Sartre, Maurice

Merleau-Ponty, and others.[40] Now, I contend that the same holds for perception itself, although only when it is regarded at a different level of abstraction. In other words, one must also assert that perception is just a "part" of a more "complex" act. Say one is perceiving a particular table. To be sure, this is what one is grasping, and yet one cannot perceive the table without at once becoming perceptually aware of the spatial location or "part of the world" it occupies, i.e., of its physical surroundings (for instance, this room), but neither can one perceive the room [as the environment of the table] without coperceiving, at the same time, the world of which it is a part. Almost at the beginning of our century, Gestalt psychologists already noted this fact, which they translated into their own specific theoretical formulations in terms of their "laws of totalization" (e.g., "figure and ground," "good form," and "constancy") and their basic concept of "perceptual field."[41] Therefore, when I say I am perceiving this table, what I really mean to say is that I am perceiving the table in the world or, to put it exactly, that I am perceiving the world but centered, of course, around a perceptual focal point now occupied by the table. This finding may be said to hold for every perception. (All of this is incorporated into Ortega's idea of perspective, in the organization or constitution of which attention and interest play a primordial role. This is a concept structured in terms of "planes"; indeed, it is a notion in the establishment of which the affective-volitional components of the personality decisively intervene.)[42] Accordingly, every perception has only one "object," namely, the world, in the midst of which, at every turn, one or another "part," of which we are used to say it is "present" to us, stands out as the "focal point [of the] perceptual [experience]."[43]

It is still possible to continue generalizing. In fact, we must do so, by applying to perception itself—as I indicated above—the principle of concreteness, if you would only excuse the apparent paradox, since what is involved here is not the "generalization" of the "concrete," but its "being extended" in order to have it coincide with its genuine boundaries, which, naturally, are not those corresponding to perception, as we shall see in what follows. No doubt, perception, understood as [a process essentially] referring to the world, is endowed with a sense that is more real than that corresponding to the term when it is taken in the usual way, and yet I contend that perception itself also is a mere product resulting from having abstracted from a much larger living and complex totality, namely, the living act being performed within every temporal component [of my life]. In my opinion, such an act should be called the *act of living*, for this name exactly conveys what it is, and this is precisely the option I have repeatedly exercised elsewhere. In effect, one is dealing here with one act, and not with a series of simultaneous acts (a state of affairs that would be nearly inconceivable), and yet, as I have argued, it is a most complex event, for it encompasses not merely perception, but also all other constituents which play a role in my manifold relationship with my circumstance and with myself, and which together constitute too a dense and intricate tissue. Or, to put it in familiar terminology, it would comprise rememberings, imaginings, desirings and avertings, expectings, emotings, fearings, lovings and hatings, forebodings, expressive and repressive feelings, preferrings and deferrings, thinkings, willings, projectings or projections, and so on.

At this point, one is certainly entitled to say that the correlate of my act of living is the act of becoming present, or of putting in an appearance, that things or the world perform, both acts "fusing" in the one act of becoming present belonging to life itself. But this is too the ultimate form taken by co-implication, namely, the event that involves the two "acts" or, to put it exactly, the two "sides" of a unique and unitary act in which I and the world, i.e., the two termini of the relationship in question, are constituted. It is this unique act which can, properly speaking, be characterized as life's act, or as the act that life is; it is the act of which life, really and effectively, consists, or, more exactly, it is the act in which life unfolds itself.

As it may be gathered, I am deliberately avoiding the employment of terms like "subject" and "object," or "subjective" and "objective," at least to the extent possible, in my effort to refer to the two sides of the act of living, since such terms are laden with significations—and are thereby affected by interpretations—which would only interfere with the understanding of the idea of reality being expounded here. I have in mind those interpretations deriving precisely from the twofold philosophical tradition that [Ortega] attempted to overcome by means of this [novel] idea of reality. In effect, there-are neither "subjects" nor "objects" in life, but, at best, only "pro-jective actions" and "circum-stantial *objections*,"[44] that is to say, only myself and my circum-stance as bound to one another by means of an indissoluble and reciprocal interaction, in the context of which both termini would be—if one were still to insist on using traditional terminology—at once "subjective-objective" and "objective-subjective." In the following discussion, what I intend to convey thereby will, I hope, become apparent.

As it turns out, actuality and presence (that is to say, the actuality of the act of becoming present and thereby the present of the world) entirely coincide, therefore, with my own, with the actuality and presence of my living, provided, of course, that one always takes "my" as the "occasional" concept it is. In other words, one is dealing here with a unique and unitary event (or with the absolute event, as Ortega referred to it), insofar as it exhibits two fundamental aspects, rather than with the simultaneous occurrence of two events. One is entitled to say, then, that I am as much present to things as they are to me, albeit in different ways, despite the fact that a formula of that sort may, on a first reading, sound odd. Moreover, one may say too that, in the absence of my presence to things, the presence of things to me would not be possible (and vice versa, naturally). Or equivalently stated: my presence to things implies (or co-implicates) their presence to me and that of myself to myself, albeit only in things and with things. I am-not-available, and there-are no things, except in terms of this radical bond of community. Indeed, many of the detours and mistakes observable in the history of philosophy derive from situations in which the philosopher was not cognizant, or was unable to be cognizant, of the elementary fact—a fact all the more imposing for its elementary character—that the present of the world is always and absolutely to coincide with my own present. Again, let us never lose sight of the "occasional" value of the concept "my own," for otherwise everything I am saying would ultimately be meaningless.

To be sure, somehow philosophers have always caught a glimpse or had an anticipation, however obscure, of this coincidence, but they have only advanced incorrect interpretations of it, be it because, as proponents of realism, they took the self to be a part of the world, be it by reason of the fact that, as idealists, they reduced the world to the status of one of my "representations" or "ideas." In both interpretations, an undue and ultimately unjustified assimilation has been effected, and consequently genuine presence has been overlooked. On the one hand, in the case of realism, this happened by virtue of the fact that, when I am no more or before I ever was, the present of the world could not coincide (that is, now or yet, respectively) with my own, for, under those conditions, I would have none. On the other hand, in the case of idealism, that occurred because there-is, in fact, no present other than mine, since, strictly speaking, there-is no world. With idealism, however, the difficulty responsible for the shipwreck of realism is obviated, for no proponent of that doctrine would advance a view resulting from referring to a present of the world that would take place either before or after me, since it is self-contradictory to relegate (or reduce) the present to a past (i.e., a before) or to a future (i.e., an after). Actually, the contradiction in question does become apparent by simply resorting to a question like this: how would the world look like "before" or "after" me, i.e., before or after any "me" or "conscious" life? The answer is obvious: the world would have no "looks," since the "looks" of something only become available to someone regarding it, or to someone's regard, that is to say, to a "perceiving" [*percatación*] or act of "becoming aware" [*darse cuenta*]. In other words, without the occurrence of an act of becoming present, there-would-be no "present" at all, and, strictly speaking, it would be meaningless to say that there-is anything, or that anything is-available. And yet the idealist avoids this difficulty by stumbling on another no less fraught with danger, for, upon transforming the present into something that would be exclusively his own, he formally eliminates the world as such, since he has reduced it to the status of that which is just one of his "ideas." The presence of his ideas would no doubt coincide with his own present, and yet, under further examination, this view would yield to the denial of [genuine] coincidence, for there is no presence of ideas, if presence is, as I contend, [intrinsically] effective or active, or a genuine act.[45] But, properly speaking, ideas, when taken as such, show themselves to be inherently inert or incapable of self-actuation. To be sure, ideas are capable, in some sense, of actuation, but only when they are no longer functioning as "*mere* ideas" and begin to play the role of "beliefs," and to the extent that they do. Whenever that happens, and insofar as it does, they are ideas no more, and they no longer function as such when their only role is that of "beliefs."[46] In point of fact, this is what lies at bottom of any doctrine that underscores the "force of ideas," as is the case with A. Fouillée's, in whose doctrine even the notion of idea-force is formulated.[47] Only a belief, never a mere idea, has performative value.[48]

In effect, when I say that things "*put*" in an appearance, I am not speaking figuratively but literally: things themselves are actuating in their process of "actualization." In other words, they perform the special act of putting in an appearance or of becoming present, an act which is more complex and nuanced than the sheer mention of such expressions may suggest, as I have already pointed out.[49] Locutions like "putting in an appearance" or "becoming present" usually denote an event in which things simply "become manifest," "show up," or "appear," words signifying modalities of presence corresponding to mere "being" [*ser*] or "standing-there" [*estar ahí*], i.e., modalities of presence that are derivative and which arise after one has adopted certain "ontological" interpretations of reality. If this were all that is involved here, the idealistic interpretation according to which things are "ideas" or "phantasms" would acquire plausibility. (I have in mind the view that things are just "projections" of my "consciousness," taking the word "projection" almost literally, as when we speak of the projection of motion pictures.) But what is involved is not just that, as I will attempt to show next.

B. Presence as Instancy

Things originarily become present by way of instancing.[50] This assertion is far removed from saying that they are projections of my consciousness (if one takes "projection" in the way I just alluded to). This is no objection, however, to arguing that they indeed have a "projective" value in some sense, although "projective" would now be used with a connotation that is not only different from, but even opposite to the signification just mentioned. I shall return to this point later.[51] It is on the basis of this preeminently real function of things that I am proposing the concept and name "*instancy*" to refer to them, thus replacing traditional terms such as "substance," "essence," even "existence," and the like.

Accordingly, I contend that, primordially regarded, things are instancies that force themselves on my attention and demand that I, willy-nilly, take them into account, or that I occupy myself and be pre-occupied with them. In short, I have to act by taking things and their instancing into consideration. In effect, the moment in which things are present is the present instant, as is said redundantly. Now, in this formula, "instant" is not a character deriving from the fact that things are present, if one understands "present" in the usual way, i.e., as signifying something like an "indivisible unit" of time. The actual state of affairs is just the opposite, assuming that, in the final analysis, the distinction between "instant" and "present" were to have any meaning at all. A present instant is present precisely because it is an instant, and it is an instant precisely because things effectively exercise their instancing therein and only therein. Or to formulate it more exactly: "present" just signifies "instant," and "presence," above and beyond being anything else and as the foundation of any other signification it may possess, is therefore the act, the actuation I have called instancing—or, to assert it once more, it is the primordial actuation of what is surrounding me. In view of this, it is justified and useful to refer to what is surrounding me by means of the name "instancy," or even by employing the term *circum-instancy*.[52] The latter word conveys what we are to understand henceforth by the locution "circum-stance." Indeed, it is in that sense that Ortega himself employed the word, but then this result is in keeping with the fact that that manner of using the expression is the way I have of interpretively coming to terms with his thought. And yet I will not avail myself of the name "circum-instancy," since it is so excessive and artificial.

Consequently, I contend that the circum-stance is no surrounding area that would comprise the things standing there about me; rather it is the action exercised by instancies, an action which consists in their genuinely encircling or "besieging" me. In point of fact, one cannot say about "things," when they are primordially regarded, that they are or stand, but only that they are carrying out their in-stancing. But instancing is the originary form adopted by the act of becoming present; indeed it is the real and effective way in which things or particular somethings present or offer themselves to me, before I come to handle them interpretively. In other words, what I have in mind is their way of producing effects, as it is only fitting in the case of any genuine actuation, or of anything that has performative value, to use Ortega's own terminology. This oblation[53] of things is to be understood, no doubt, generically, since it is meant to encompass both positive and negative cases of "offering."[54]

Now, the view that things "are merely standing there," as well as the thesis concerning their presumptive being, are already the outcome of the interpretive handling I have just mentioned. Indeed, they are the product of a prolonged and painstaking human interpretive manipulation. An enterprise of this sort is precisely a labor of abstraction, which can only be brought about by dint of sustained intellectual (i.e., "logical" or onto-logical) effort, intent on giving rise to a neutralizing effect. In other words, its purpose is the domination and elimination (or at least the "mitigation," to the extent possible) of the originary tameless instancing exercised by the so-called things. In principle, as is evident, "things" are not things at all, at least if one judges matters in terms of our contemporary understanding of the term, which derives from the "logifying" or "ontologizing" interpretive effort I just referred to. This is the reason why, if today we still desire to continue talking about things in a primordial or originary manner (that is, if we are to come to regard them as they themselves are, beneath the "layers" of interpretation covering them up), we would then have to look at them as *prágmata,* "affairs" [*asuntos*] or "occasions which matter to us" [*importancias*], "instrumentalities of service" [*serviciali-dades*], or "opportunities that facilitate or hinder" [*facilidades* or *dificultades*], to use Ortega's own words.[55] Or again, we must bring ourselves to take them as instancies, a term the connotation of which is meant to put together, in summary fashion, the senses of all those expressions, and which ultimately would refer us to a metaphysical signification that would be of equally originary value and would embody—without failing to link up with the traditional philosophical vocabulary—the essential relatedness of things to the ego, i.e., to myself.

In effect, an instancy "instances" or moves someone, that is to say, it "instances" or moves *me:* here one finds the reason why an instancy is prior to being, for it is in fact that which renders being possible. An instancy instances me to do or fashion something just in order for me to be something, namely, what I am going to be: as Ortega said, living is "having to decide at every turn what we are going to do, that is to say, *what we are going to be next.*"[56] But what we are going to be may have to do with many different things: its "content" is not preestablished; as Ortega asserted, it is something one has to decide at every turn, and the decision involved will depend—among various other "conditions"—upon the "situation" and, therefore, on the "circum-stance," that is to say, on the particular instancy that at every given turn besieges or encircles me. This is why Ortega contended that man is set on a "pilgrimage of being."[57] He had in mind the ever-changing and noniterative character of the "forms of being," which are numberless in principle and which humanity is engaged in taking on in the course of history. But it may very well be possible to translate this notion into the individual dimension of the life of every human being, and to do so without loss to its truth. Accordingly, I would say that an individual human being's life would be an unending and, in the final analysis, utopian "pilgrimage," for, to some degree or other, whatever human beings do is *utopian*. This is precisely the reason why Ortega was of the opinion that, instead of absurdly allowing "utopianism" to grow uncontrollably, we should struggle to reduce its active presence as much as possible.

In point of fact, the present is not being, but, strictly speaking, it precedes being—it is that which is pre-essent.[58] It is only when it is no longer present that it acquires the inflexible character of being or becomes an entity; in other words, this eventuates only when it has turned into a past, i.e., into what has been. These are the grounds for affirming that, strictly speaking, a human being properly so called only *is*—taking the word in its essential sense or insofar as it is in principle open to definition—what he *is-not* any longer (now using the word with an *existential* connotation). In other words, the only thing a human being properly is is his past.[59] Accordingly, a human being is what he has been: I am now what I have been; anything else I may be I am not "yet," being as I am what I am-going-to-be. And this includes that which I am to be "now," that is to say, that which I am going to be from "now" on. Therefore, the present is this going-to-be or going-into-being; in other words, it is a coming or making a departure from what has already been, naturally, but as a going towards where I am not yet standing, as is true of any case of going. Now then, this signifies that I never come to stand my ground in being, that is to say, in my being, inasmuch as I am always on my way towards it, except when all has turned into the past, at the point of death, i.e., when, contradictorily, I am no longer. But since we live in the present, it turns out that I consist in going to that place I can never reach, namely, being. I never reach being, precisely because I am always on my way towards it. A human being is thus *homo viator* [man the voyager].[60] I and, therefore, my life constitute a reality essentially characterizable as being *in via* [on its way], and being is thus the greatest utopia (and *uchronia*) belonging to a human being's essentially "utopian" reality.

To say it again: being—or that towards which we are always on the way—in fact can never be reached, since in death—the moment of its consummation—it is no longer within our reach. At that point, it would have become completely estranged from us and would have already turned into the sheer past. It is then, and only then, that one may speak, in a totally meaningful way, of the being of a human being; in other words, one may at that time, and never before, say what a human being has been or was, since—let me insist on this point—as long as I live, I am only and always on my way towards being, but the being towards which I am on my way can always be otherwise, for it is unpredictable, even from the point of view of the one who is on his way towards it. As long as I live, transforming the "shape" of my being is within my power; accordingly, I do not know, with absolute certainty, whether or not I am going to "make" it. By means of this formulation, I wish to convey the view that living consists just in bringing about drastic alterations in the "shape" of my being, for no doubt will I effect some such transformations. To be in a state of self-possession signifies that I have the power to govern my own life, taking "govern" in a sense related to that of a vessel's "governor" or "pilot." In other words, I can control its direction or shift its "course" at any moment. But the opposite is also true: to the extent that I lose that power, I can also speak of [self-]estrangement. Now then, such a power vanishes completely in death; therefore, in death coincide a human being's absolute self-estrangement and the consummation of his being. On the occasion of a human being's death, the shape of his life takes on rigidity and "*thickness*": one may then speak of rigor mortis, but with a signification in mind that is more far-reaching and radical than what is meant by the physical or somatic sense of the phrase. In death's *consummatum est* [it is finished],[61] every possibility of transforming the "shape" of someone's life has ben "consummated" or brought to a closure and an end.

This notwithstanding, a human life may be regarded by those confronting it, as it happens with any other thing, in many different ways and from many different "points of view." It may even be the case that it continues to actuate in and influence the lives of others in various fashions, albeit only as a component of their circum-stance, or as something "reified." Accordingly, only then would it be possible to refer to someone's life "objectively," i.e., as something which is, as something endowed with this or that manner of being that can be "identified," "determined," or "defined" to some degree or other. But the being it would possess at that moment would be entirely past; it would no longer be what life is, but necessarily what it has been. I asserted before that a human being's measure of being is his past, but, as long as he is living, even a human being's past, despite the fact that it is irreversible and, to that extent, "irrevocable," is, in some sense and to a certain point, modifiable, for, as long as a future is at his disposal, the transformation of the "shape" of his life—i.e., of its course or direction—is within his power.[62] This would result in accomplishments that have reverberations or repercussions on what has already been done, and this shall be true as long as possibilities are at his disposal. Accordingly, it will depend on what the human being comes to do. As long as a human being is living, everything belonging in his life (even the past, its most inflexible constituent) exhibits a certain degree of fluidity and is labile to some extent. Now, this is rooted in life's metaphysical condition, about which one would have to say that it *consists of possibilities*. Or equivalently stated: life is made up, to use Ortega's own expression, of futurity, of the primordial effect-producing power of the future. Although I will have to return to this topic,[63] let me now say that possibilities, insofar as they are "at our disposal," define one of the fundamental strata of life's self-possession. Hence, our lacking in them is tantamount to our life's [self-]estrangement. When any shimmer of possibility vanishes in death, self-estrangement is complete, since what then remains of us remains in the power of others; it is at that moment that we turn into somebody else's possession, that we bequeath ourselves to them, that we become a part of their assets [*haber*], or of what is-available to them.

A human being may be regarded, therefore, as a movement towards being in death, and not as a being-towards-death, as Heidegger would have it,[64] since it is death which bestows being on us. Naturally, this fact has many involved metaphysical implications, which this is not the moment to examine. Suffice it to say that, if space allowed, I would have to speak in some detail of the fact that we continue to "*live*" in others after we are dead, for this is one of the essential dimensions of history, of what I could call "historical life," as opposed to [my] personal life, however inseparable these two dimensions may be de facto (although they are never inseparable de jure or *formaliter*), for life is always one and the other, both aspects overlapping and existing for each other's sake. Actually, one can here identify one of the most far-reaching dimensions of the meaning of the expression, "life's *complexity*."

These findings should lead us to entertain the possibility of a basic reformation of the concept of being, which would have to be effected if this notion is to be of any use in the field of human realities, above all with respect to the radical reality. To begin with, "to be" here means having been and, at best, getting to be, albeit in a different sense of the word. What is in principle denied to it is the connotation *"making a stand in be-ing"* [estar siendo],[65] for it is impossible to bring being and standing to cohere in the present, that is to say, to make them coincide in the actual moment, in the now, since, as we know,[66] the present is never an act of making a stand, but only, if you will, an act of anticipating-being. Presence is precisely pre-essence. It is in this sense (and, to begin with, just in this sense, and then only after making the required distinctions) that it is possible to agree with the existentialists when they assert that *"existence* precedes essence."[67] No matter how good one is at "dialectical" acrobatics (as for instance Hegel was to the superlative degree), one shall never be able to drive away the presence of Parmenides and Spinoza from the foundations of any theory of reality that seeks to interpret it as being. Those two thinkers are the major standard-bearers of the mysticism of reason, and they have become, precisely because of it, the greatest personifications of *"ontological"* sincerity. There is no way out: the Eleatic heritage cannot be surrendered by anyone insisting on transmuting the theory of reality into "ontology."

As referred to a human being or life, one could then say that the verb to "be"—taken strictly and used exactingly—is to be regarded [as defective, that is to say, as a verb] which should only be conjugated in the past and future tenses, never in the present, precisely because it is only in the present, i.e., in that which anticipates being, that past and future acquire a measure of reality. But this is the polar opposite of the view held by Parmenides, the thinker who discovered "being," and for whom one of the essential attributes of be-ing [*ón*] is presence, or to be present (*parón*).[68]

In order to bring this brief but urgently needed commentary *perí tou óntos* ["on being"] to a close, let me underscore the fact that the being towards which a human being is on the way does not lie there [ready-made], not even as something "determined," "outlined," or "proposed" beforehand. Rather, a human being has to fashion it for himself; he even has to "invent" it. Our own being is not given to us; the only thing we are given is the necessity of fashioning it for ourselves. Or expressed in Ortega's own words: "... *life is given to us,* but it is not given to us done; it is something one has to do, a *task to be discharged* [*quehacer*]," "life gives [us] much to do," and so on.[69] But since we cannot do anything except with things, we are forced to bestow on them a certain manner of being, which of themselves they do not have. On the contrary, as I have argued, things, while performing their originary act of becoming present, function as instancies, not as entities. But, as we will have an occasion to learn,[70] one of the most characteristic specifications of the instancing exercised by things precisely belongs in a "pre-logical" or "logic-like" order. In other words, it is a specification deriving its cues from the fact that things are in need of having some kind or modality of being bestowed upon them.

Let me now proceed to present, in summary fashion, the most important dimensions of what I have called instancy. In what follows, my discussion will bear on those dimensions (of a functional order, naturally) which constitute this elemental, nonmediated, and primordial stratum of presence, dimensions that I have already considered, or at least alluded to. They are:

First, "in-stant"[71] literally means nonstanding. In other words, it signifies "in-stable," fleeting, transitional, fluid, mobile, and so on. By virtue of its character of in-stantaneousness, an in-stant is resistant to being grasped by any view that would present reality as static, and it is thus incompatible with doctrines like substantialism, ontologism, and the like. Or to put it otherwise: by means of the term "in-stant," I am referring to a "phenomenon" describable by phrases like "*going-to-be*" or "*going-into-being*," to use expressions I have already employed. This phenomenon is, in principle, of my own; it is something structurally belonging to my reality, and yet it is also something that belongs to things, insofar as things are instancies: it is of their own too, by virtue of the essential, close, and profound bond existing between myself and things or particular somethings. In short, it is a dimension of life. As such, it is therefore opposite to conceiving being as achieved, [to the thesis that a "thing" is] that which it already is, or is already what it is.[72]

Second, "instant" is here construed also in the sense of the present participle of the verb *instar*, as the word is usually understood in Spanish. Accordingly, it is meant to signify the actuation of that which "instances," i.e., that which solicits, invites, beckons, or moves (and often com-motes or e-motively touches) us, of that which makes its "appeals" to us, i.e., that which calls (*voca*) us and also, at times, becomes a pro-vocation to us, of that which turns into an obstacle for us and even, in extremis, urges, makes demands, or presses its point on us. (These various terms convey as many modal varieties of instancing, without however coming near to exhausting them.)

Third, "instant" and "that which is in-stantaneous" I take also in the sense of that which is in-tensive or intense: life acquires its special intensity in that which is in-stantaneous and by virtue of the instancing proper to it. In effect, every life and every moment thereof are marked by coefficients of intensity. I contend that intensity significantly depends on the instancy in question (as well as on the rest of the components of the given situation functionally correlated with it, naturally). In other words, intensity depends upon the measure of "in-stantaneousness" proper to each moment. But, by the same token, the *temper* of life, of each moment of it, depends upon the intensity or tension characteristic of it. (The notion of temper, or of *Stimmung*, as Heidegger referred to it,[73] having a direct bearing on "self-encounter,"[74] was also of fundamental importance for Ortega, although unfortunately I cannot dwell on the concept here.)[75] In fact, it is by virtue of this sense of instancing that it is possible interpretively to come to terms with certain forms of temper that are decisive for the global notion of life. Moreover, one may assert that a qualification in terms of temper essentially belongs to each "instant," if one now understands this word according to its temporal connotation.

Fourth, one also finds the pre-tentiveness characteristic of that which is in-stantaneous, a feature closely connected with that of intensity, indeed so much so that one could consider it as another aspect of the latter, although, in my opinion, it would be useful to devote to it a separate examination, given its significance. If regarded concretely in terms of its "directedness to the future," the "tension" [of living] is, in fact, a pre-tension.[76] No doubt, an instancy is that too, for things, upon exercising their instancing, "demand," "pretend," or "aspire" to something. To say it again: the pretensions of every instancy are manifold, given the concretion of every particular "instant," and yet it is possible to identify certain basic pre-tentive "directionalities," which I shall discuss later,[77] although I have already referred to one of them, namely, the fact that things demand to be endowed with being or to be logically interpreted or given a logical identity, in view of which any particular something may be taken as a logical instancy, at least inchoatively.

Fifth, one may regard the pre-tentive "component" of an instancy from the point of view of the ego upon whom its "instancing" is being exercised. If one does so, a new signification for the expression "that which is *in-stantaneous*" would become available. I have in mind the pro-jective character of an "instant." I am at this point, mind you, speaking of an "instant," and not of "*that which* is in-stantaneous," since here I would like to underscore the temporal dimension involved. Now, this dimension, as a constituent and attribute of life, equally encompasses things (i.e., my circum-stance) and myself, and yet emphasis is to be placed in this connection on the ego or myself. Accordingly, the projectiveness of an "instant" is to be regarded as just pre-tentiveness, that is, as a pre-tension taken insofar as it is mine. By shifting pre-tension from the plane of things to that of the ego, one is able to see it as an essential component of every "situation," as indeed it is, for it actually consists in my projecting myself with things, as I "keep them in view" or take their own "pretensions" into account. Or to put it more succinctly and exactly: pre-tension consists in projecting my life. In point of fact, my pretension—the one belonging to every moment or situation—is always conjoined with other pretensions in an "articulate" fashion. To the systematic "articulation" of pretensions Ortega referred by means of the expression "*living project*,"[78] in terms of which my whole life unfolds from "instant" to "instant." Later I shall speak of this aspect of pretension in greater detail.[79] Suffice it now to insist upon that dimension of pretension which is the function of a project, in terms of which I ultimately [*en última instancia*] engage in "projecting myself," although, no doubt, what I am particularly projecting, to say it again, is a sequence of doings with things or particular somethings, a sequence that is my response to the originary instancing they exercise upon me. To reiterate it: "projecting myself" is what I do always in the midst of that which is other than I, or in the world, if you will.

Therefore, I would say that an instancy, or that which is instantaneous about this "world" or "circum-stance," thus exercises its instancing upon me by urging me to project myself (and thereby to realize myself) in view of the instancy in question, as I have just pointed out. It is in terms of the fact that an instancy is kept "in view" in this fashion that the "apparent," "vision-allowing," "phenomena," and (in short) *noetic* character of instancies emerges. In other words, it is by means of it that an instancy is, strictly speaking, "present" (now taking the word in its usual sense). Indeed, the noetic effectiveness of an instancy contains a demand for, or necessitates, the resolution to which I referred above.[80] Or to put it otherwise: it amounts to demanding that the instancy be resolved into a particular *lógos* (i.e., a thought, concept, or word). Such a "logical resolution" would secure a foundation for my projection or project, that is, it would provide it with an "orientation." Moreover, it would supply me, by means of the project based thereupon, with a foundation or orientation for my ethical "resolve," or the "decision" proper to every moment of my life. But, by the same token, one would have to say—regarding my "ethical resolve" from another side—that it would, on its own, condition the "logical resolution" itself, and it would do so in several ways. In this connection, Ortega asserted—by turning a traditional maxim on its head—that *nihil cognitum quin praevolitum* [nothing comes to knowledge which is not willed beforehand]. I cannot enter now into an examination of this difficult question. Suffice it to say at this point that one can find, as part of this basic structure of instancies, the source of the ethical character of truth (a major theme for any reflective effort inspired by Ortega), or the "metaphysical roots of the mutuality or reciprocity existing between *éthos* and *lógos*," to use my own characterization of the matter.[81]

It is by virtue of all these reasons than an instancy does exercise its "instancing" upon me in the various senses indicated. Let us not lose sight of the fact that instancing is a metaphysical character meant to replace the concepts of being [*ser*] and standing [*estar*] (and their derivatives). Notions like "entity," "being," "essence," "substance," "thing," "object," and the like are so many interpretive devices employed to render "instancies" static; they are the fruits of a prolonged translational or reductive struggle with instancies, by means of which man has sought to dominate or "neutralize" their originary impelling force. But such attempts can succeed only to a very limited extent (in keeping with the precariousness of every intellectual interpretation), for an instancy is, I would say, "hopelessly" tameless. In other words, tamelessness is inherent to it and a constituent of "presence" itself. Actually, instancies are always being reborn and coming to "rally" again; they exert their reiterative influence on the interpretations people propose about them, with the result that they are renewed and become increasingly more complex as instancies. Most pointedly, the transformation of *ideas* into *beliefs*[82] belongs to the order of the reworking or reconstitution of instancies. This transformation is one of the radical aspects of "historicity," a name referring not so much to a human attribute (which is the usual way of understanding it) as it does to the radical tenor of life, namely, that fierce, dramatic dynamism responsible for the "fashioning" of human beings, who, in turn, are engaged in "fashioning" the dynamism of life. And this happens not because people are endowed with a suitable "faculty" (for no substrate is involved here), but by reason of the fact that they are being instanced or urged to do that at every turn; in fact, a human being is in need of doing so each instant. As we already know, the term *instant,* when understood in a temporal sense, is but a collective (and thus "abstract") noun referring to instancies, to the system or nexus consisting of the "instancies" actuating every moment or "now." Moreover, as I have already pointed out, an "instant" is the sheer temporal dimension of that which is in-stantaneous at every particular "now."[83] That which is in-stantaneous thus "fills" in the presumptive temporal void of an "instant"; it indwells and qualifies it, for, in fact, "indwelling" and "qualification" are two essential features of every situation, in terms of both its here and now.

As we have seen,[84] people have, every instant, to engage in doing, that is to say, they have to fashion themselves or fashion their own life. Their life is given to them, but it is not given to them done; rather, it is given to them precisely as the radical problem of having to fashion it for themselves. (This is a point to which I will have to return.)[85] Now, one can appreciate the fact that this is not just a situation that "originally" prevailed in our lives, but rather a state of affairs being verified throughout, or at every particular instant of our lives, as I have already indicated.[86] In effect, people are "instanced" to do this as long as they are living, provided that they want to live, that is to say, as long as they want to live. To begin with, and radically, an instancy thus urges me to want to live (or it exercises its "instancing" upon my will, to express it in everyday language). Indeed, everyone's will is rendered specific by means of the "volitions" it performs, for every particular volition is, so to speak, lodged within one's will to live, which would be the *permanent volition,* the volition being permanently reenacted in every particular act of will one effects. In point of fact, every particular volition has sense only in terms of one's will to live. Therefore, an instancy exercises its "instancing" upon me, insofar as I can be characterized as volitional. And yet this is not necessarily so in order to "favor" or "facilitate" my wanting to live, but, rather, to "obstruct" or "hinder" it, as is always happening to some extent, and in some sense or other. Naturally, one can also discover that an instancy "facilitates" living, for, if that did not occur, no life would be possible at all, but that is verifiable only to a much lesser degree and especially in a different sense. Moreover, I would say that such "facilitations" would always come upon the ob-jection originarily exercised by an instancy.

As it turns out, the will is then a sort of counter-instancy, for it is that by means of which I counter an instancy. Indeed, it is a co-originary force in terms of which I respond to the force to "ob-ject" proper to the "instancing." My wanting to live—that primordial force of my will which underlies every particular volition, as I have just pointed out—thus affirms itself by confronting and opposing every instancy that would, as part and parcel of reality, exhibit hostility or present its "objection" to it. But, in order to do that, it must also admit the hostile "instancing" exercised by the instancy in question. As Ortega has said, anyone wanting to live wants thereby everything life affords; anyone who accepts life accepts everything implied and coimplicated by life. Accordingly, "everything happening to us happens to us because *we want it to.*" In other words, the voluntary acceptance of life is the sine qua non of life itself, for, in order to live, one must want to live. Now, this metaphysical character, like any other having its foundation in one and the same basic structure, turns human life into something unique and thus irreducible to any form of "life" belonging merely in the "biological" order. To counter this view by means of the assertion that such a character is nothing but the manifestation of the "self-preservation instinct" in people, or in terms of any other equivalent thesis deriving from a "scientific" or "naturalistic" conception of life, would be clear evidence that one has no idea at all about the essence of what is usually called a "voluntary act." Moreover, to argue in this fashion would be tantamount, generally speaking, to absurdly ignoring the fact that science (and consequently biology) are themselves "creations" effected by human life, or interpretations it advances concerning certain facts, all of which do, therefore, intrinsically presuppose the radical "fact" of life qua origin, to which those facts and any subsequent "scientific" interpretations thereof would refer and be subordinated.

All contrasts and tensions would "emerge" from the originary contrast and tension between instancies and the "will" qua counter-instancy, of which the ultimate structure or "form" of life consists. Furthermore, the Protean "morphology" of life, or the varieties thereof (which are numberless in principle), would arise in conjunction with those contrasts and tensions during the ongoing course and succession of history. In other words, the apparently endless unfolding of the social and individual "historical forms" of human life would find its origin there. One is here face to face with the primordial and radical dramatic conflict, the perennial "drama" human life is, namely, the dramatic conflict between the "world" (taken as "abiding *instancy*" and deliberately understood in the broadest sense possible, i.e., in terms of its own force of reality) and the no less real and originary force of my "*will*." I have in mind the unremitting traumatic "en-counter" or clash between these two *primitive forces,* to use the Leibnizian formula (though assigning to it a sense quite removed from Leibniz's own).[87] On the one hand, the force of reality proper to the world would actually tend to limit, "compel," "determine," and accordingly *negate me.* In this context, the validity of the Spinozistic principle, "*omnis determinatio negatio est*" [every determination is a negation],[88] would still be preserved, albeit solely to the extent that it fits a perspective that is not only remote from, but indeed opposed as well to, the original sense of the formula. On the other hand, the force of my will would tend to "build me up" precisely as freedom and "indetermination," i.e., as a spring, inexhaustible in principle,

of possibilities. But again one comes here face to face with paradox, which is always lurking in matters human, for that which
tends to negate me is that which would affirm me, or allow me to
affirm myself, as freedom, since the "possibilities," in the midst of
which freedom can and has to be exercised, are afforded me precisely by instancies, i.e., by those things (or components of my
particular world or circum-stance) that are exercising their "instancing" upon me every moment. But the reverse is true too, for
that which tends to affirm me would negate me, in the sense that, if
my force of will (or the originary impulse of my freedom) were to
be extended without hindrance, so as to encompass an "infinity"
of possibilities, it would be automatically annihilated, for it would
lack any foothold on the basis of which to achieve any self-
specification or self-realization, having become incapable of carrying itself out by means of the act of "choice" that constitutes it.

Accordingly, what is involved in all this is a conflict between
powers that are ultimately "positive," no matter if they imply negative intentionalities, and yet the "positivity" characterizing them
would be sui generis, for the conflict in question would take place
between the compelling, limiting, determining power of what is
unremittingly given to me in that which is in-stantaneous (i.e., on
the occasion of every "instant") and the liberating, affirming, con-
structive, confirming power of my will to live. (Nietzsche's expression "will to power" is a redundancy, for every will is not merely a
will to power, but an effective power, i.e., the originary human
power that is the source of every other form of human power, as the
proverb puts it across with profound "living" wisdom: "where
there's a will, there's a way" [*querer es poder*].) In short: what is
involved is a conflict between destiny and freedom. One must
always bear in mind, however, that both forces, powers, or poten-
cies need one another and function in perfect reciprocity; that is to
say, they are, as I have already pointed out, "reciprocating forces"
within the unique reality that my life is.[89] (One can never insist too
strongly on the primordial fact that life is a "dual unity": one must
reiterate it on every occasion one comes across any new manifestation of it.)

As I have indicated,[90] my circum-stance, as the manifold instancy it is, is that which opens up precisely the field of my possibilities, to the extent that it forces me to "project myself" *in view*
of it, that is to say, insofar as it "instances" me to take up a definite

future for myself. But, naturally, my circum-stance simultaneously limits the field of my possibilities, and it succeeds in doing so to the extent that it *"becomes present* or *makes its appearance"* here and now. In effect, the simultaneous interplay between those two dimensions of an instancy (namely, that taking place between the opening and closing or *stopping up* effected by an instancy) sets itself as the very condition that *"renders"* the exercise of my freedom *"possible."* Indeed, it accomplishes that by means of the determinate act in which, on the occasion of every instant, I choose or decide. But, in operating in this fashion, a condition such as that becomes the primordial and abiding possibility which is the origin of every other possibility.

6. POSSIBILITY AND FREEDOM

As Ortega has said somewhere, "life consists of possibilities." This simple statement already discloses the importance he attached to the concept of possibility, or the "categorial" character it exhibits in his doctrine. Accordingly, this notion deserves a more extensive treatment than the briefest of outlines that I am about to offer. The reasons for this decision are, however, too involved to be developed here.

The concept of possibility, the lasting presence of which has been central to the metaphysical tradition, underwent a "Copernican revolution" in Ortega, as did the rest of the basic notions of "first philosophy." This is, I believe, an implication of the present study. In the classical tradition, this concept, in effect, had always been understood primarily with reference to being, no matter what particular interpretation was assigned to the latter notion. In one way or another, "possibility" has always meant, therefore, the possibility of being, whether one takes being in the sense of essence or in that of existence. In fact, as Hartmann has pointed out,[91] essence and existence are acceptations or "moments" of being that, for such purposes, are indistinguishable from one another. In other words, the possibility of existence indeed belongs to some essences which are not only *"intrinsically* or *absolutely* possible," but also *"extrinsically* or *relatively* so." Extrinsic or relative possibility involves the collaboration between intrinsic or absolute possibility and a cause *in actu* capable of bringing the essence into existence. At best, possibility is spoken about with reference to some process understood also in terms of both being and non-being, that is to say, as a "coming-into-being" or a "ceasing-to-exist" or, more exactly, as a passage from one modality of being to another, as is the case in Aristotle's doctrine. In our context, however, possibility is not primarily related to being, but to doing. The notion of possibility has thus been translated from one metaphysical plane or level to another, a change that has resulted in the reduction of this concept to the novel standpoint of life qua radical reality. Such an eventuality, to say it again, has been the fate not only of this notion, but also of all the other concepts belonging to any formulation of the science of ontology that has been elaborated in more or less traditional terms. Consequently, one should not speak of possibility any longer, except in view of a determinate relationship to one or another particular life and taking into account one or another given situation. Possibility is now to be understood as belonging to life, that is to say, as a possibility of living, not of being.

Strictly speaking, however, one ought to refer not to possibility but, essentially and necessarily, to possibilities. But this is not all: not only has this concept been essentially pluralized, but it has been rendered essentially dynamic as well, even though in a sense quite different indeed from Leibniz's own.[92] One is now to regard no possibility as effective, unless it is capable of producing effects; any such possibility is always an actual possibility of action or of choice, although, properly speaking, the possibilities of choice are also reducible to those of action. In this connection, let me bring to mind the descriptive formula that presents life as the "actuality of the possible,"[93] the sense of which is quite remote from Aristotle's understanding of such matters.[94] Or equivalently stated: possibilities are to "actuate" or "function" precisely as instancies, if they are to be effective. The notion of a static world consisting of pure possibilities is a concept belonging to a bygone idealizing and perfectionistic metaphysics characterized by the sufficiency and "purity" of being and reason. (And here I mean to include as well the notion of [possible] "worlds" as expounded by Leibniz, despite the fact that he made the concept of "*conatus*" part and parcel of what he understood by possibility.)[95] But this judgment also applies to any "naturalistic" metaphysics of becoming, taken as a passage from being-in-potency to being-in-act (wherein possibility is seen in connection with process). Moreover, it is applicable to a position in which, as one attempts to break loose from such binding ontological and logical ties, one ends up eliminating possibility itself for the sake of a unique (and irrational) dynamic and "creative" actuality, as it happened in Bergson.[96]

None of these points of view may now be espoused validly, since each and every one the them sidesteps reality itself, which Ortega's thought, on the contrary, is after. They substitute for it interpretations that are products of "abstractive" procedures which cannot be justified at this level or stage of a "search" now lasting millenia. Moreover, as we know,[97] this critique applies to the modal aspects of being belonging to the metaphysical tradition, since the formal expulsion of being from the premises where it occupied the position of *radical* reality makes such modal aspects undergo an equally "radical" change of signification. Just as the meaning of "necessity" is translated into its polar opposite, as it comes to be identified precisely with the first principle of "freedom" (or, in a different sense, with the neediness and direst poverty of life, or with the contrary of self-sufficiency), and just as "contingency" is likewise transformed so as to have it refer now to the most positive dimension of happening [*acontecer*], so does possibility immediately acquire significance and importance as a "primordial function" of reality. This is so, inasmuch as possibility, like necessity, is connected with freedom in an essential way. In other words, it has become "pluralized" insofar as it is the metaphysical horizon corresponding to choice or decision, wherein freedom time and again turns specific or is exercised. Possibility thus turns into the nonmediated actuality of life, to the extent that life is a concrete, finite, and organic whole consisting of possibilities. Ortega has adopted terms like "stock" or "keyboard" precisely in order to refer to such a totality. "Possibility" and "necessity" constitute the basic structure of reality, since they are indissolubly linked, by essential implication, to the primordial and irreducible freedom which living is, to freedom as our unrelinquishable source.

Now, the connections existing within this structure, and therefore those arising on the basis of the essential bond of implication obtaining between necessity, possibility, and freedom, will be clarified by means of the following elementary and concise description of human life. This description will involve, in part, the recapitulation of points I have already made, although, for our purposes at present, such points will be articulated in a different fashion.

As we have already seen,[98] what is given to me, or the radical and absolute datum or fact prior to any other, is my life itself, my act of living, or the event of encountering myself living (or of finding myself already living here and now). But what is given to me, i.e., my actual living, is most especially characterized by the feature of not being *ready-made* or already constituted. My life is no entity; it does not have a nature [*consistencia*], which one could use as a tribunal of "last resort" [*última instancia*], or as that which, in the final analysis, one could employ as a support [to stand upon], or as that by which, when all is said and done, one can abide. What is given to me is just something that is yet to be done, precisely that which I have to do, that which I have need to do. It is a task [*quehacer*] of mine that I cannot avoid, being that which I have to do. And yet what I have to do, or that task which is mine, is not given to me either; it is not something [pre-]established; on the contrary, I myself have to decide what it is. Now then, a set ("keyboard," "stock," "cast," or "horizon") of possibilities is indeed given to me, but only in conjunction with the need of having absolutely to do something: it is among such possibilities that I can and have to choose; it is about them that I can and have to decide. This however means that such a primordial need would exhibit the traits of the necessary, this term being understood in its traditional sense, that is to say, as referring [both] to the fact of having to be and to that of having to be thus and so and not otherwise (i.e., to "existential" and "essential" necessity, respectively). This notwithstanding, it should be characterizable as well as that which is necessitating or, equivalently, as that which is needed because one does not have or is lacking it (which is a formulation that gives expression to one's neediness or condition of direst poverty), and yet as something one cannot bear to do or "be" without. Now then, the fact that possibility is plural signifies, in turn, that no single possibility can—by itself—be imposed on us. If this were not so, a "possibility" would ipso facto cease being a possibility and become a necessity (in the first acceptation of the word "necessary" alluded to above), an event which would automatically result in the annihilation of all other possibilities. On the contrary, every possibility offers itself to me; it "*urges*" [*insta*] me to choose and realize it; therefore, it is, in this sense, a genuine instancy. But if no possibility, insofar as it is an instancy, can impose itself on me, and if, further, I have no choice but to do something, it is then self-evident that what I ought to do will be *one* among those possible doings. Let me state it again: the fact that no possibility can impose itself on me is just the reason why it is a possibility, that is to say, "something" I can do, a possible doing which, insofar as it is possible, is of course not necessary, but, to the extent that it is not necessary, it is contingent as well, again taking this term in its traditional sense.[99]

To be sure, one among such possible doings ought to be realized by me, and yet a problem is involved in saying this, for the particular possibility in question has at every turn to be decided upon. It shall be no other than the possibility which I come to make prominent out of the various ones ["available" to me], that is to say, the one I come to choose or will, and this is self-evidently, unavoidably, and necessarily so, since none of such possible doings may be imposed of itself on me. Therefore, I have no choice but to choose among the possibilities proper to each moment or instant. Or to put it equivalently: I have need to choose among them, a formula in which "need" is understood with reference to the two senses of the word "necessary," albeit placing special emphasis on the first one.

By means of this acknowledgment, we have gained access to the second "moment" of necessity. In fact, I would say we have thereby obtained our third datum about it. Let me recapitulate our findings. First, I have need to do; I have to do something. Second, I have need to choose; I have to choose, like it or not, that which I have to do from among all possible doings. Therefore, [my] possibilities are, so to speak, flanked by these two needs or necessities. In fact, [my] possibilities are implanted between them. Now then, decision is the name we employ to refer to the act of choosing one possible doing out of many. But [thirdly] it is my contention that a decision of this sort, taking place as it does at every moment, cannot be refused, avoided, or subrogated. By virtue of this fact, it is grave or heavy. Here we find the origin of what Ortega called the "burdensomeness" of life.[100]

"In every instant of our lives we have to decide what we are going to do, that is to say, what we are going to do next,"[101] reiterated Ortega, using all registers and keeping every context in view. Humanly speaking, living is thus a constant reenactment of my decision, by virtue of which process life decides itself: I decide my own being, i.e., what I am-going-to-be, and no one is ever able to substitute himself for me in the process of decision. Therefore, life is a self-deciding affair, and this is the source of its burdensomeness, of its gravity, of the "gravitative pull" it exerts on every one of my acts. Ortega has also expressed this point otherwise by saying elsewhere that we "feel the weight" of life or "restlessly bear up under" it, that is to say, that we carry the "burden" of our lives "in the four corners of the earth." No other reality, no "physical" or merely "biological" entity, no mineral, no plant, no animal faces this possibility, this terrible and (at once) magnificent possibility, if you will, of deciding, much less of deciding for itself. This is an exclusive prerogative of human life that characterizes it essentially and distinguishes it from any other reality, to say it again. But the possibility of deciding conditions every other possibility (a formulation in which "conditions" is meant strictly to refer to a sine qua non). In fact, it is the first and primordial possibility, inasmuch as it is a formal constituent of every other possibility. Now, such a possibility is lived by us as a most primordial and absolute necessity.[102] Here we are dealing with the necessity of the non-necessary, that is to say, with the necessity of freedom. In consequence, one ought to assert that freedom is not only the "possibility of choosing" (as it is usually defined), but as well the necessity of choosing. In effect, freedom is the most profound metaphysical necessity of human beings, indeed their radical necessity. But, by virtue of this very fact, it communicates part of its "essence," so to speak, to the other human necessities, which therefore—once more in a paradoxical way—can be called free necessities. They are so characterized because anything that can be accepted or rejected is free. Actually, we can accept or reject our own necessities, since, so far as they are concerned, an ultimate option can always be exercised by us, namely, that of ceasing to live.

Accordingly, human necessities are freely accepted upon our acceptance of life. In this connection, let us bring to mind again Ortega's own formula, to the effect that "everything happening to us happens to us because we want it to."[103] Free are, then, all human necessities except one, namely, that of freedom itself, since, even if we arrive at the decision of renouncing it too, thus renouncing life, in that very decision we would be affirming and exercising it, we would be "enacting" it. Therefore, freedom is the need most properly human, the only one about which there is no choice. In effect, I can choose any doing save one, to wit: the "doing" called "choosing." Indeed, no one can choose between the alternatives of "choosing" and "not choosing"—just putting this choice into words is a most flagrant contradiction in terms. But neither the idea of the "unavoidability of freedom"[104] nor the concept of "free necessity," which is properly bound up with it, can be reduced to a play on words. On the contrary, the formula, "unavoidability of freedom," gives expression to the most radical metaphysical structure of human life, namely, the one that allows us to speak, in a totally meaningful way, of the "*a priori* character" of freedom. Freedom is therefore the "absolute *a priori*" of life, indeed the presupposition already operative in any of its other dimensions and the absolute condition of them all. Freedom is then the only absolute necessity, a view that perhaps conveys the most fundamental signification of the "Copernican revolution" that Ortega brought about in his metaphysical doctrine.

But, next to the absolute unremittingness or "unavoidability" of freedom, one must underscore, no less emphatically, another manner of "unavoidability" or necessity, namely, that of the limited character of freedom. Or to put it otherwise: next to the unremitting or, if you will, "fated" fact[105] of the plural character of possibility, one finds another no less so, to wit: the limited character of our possibilities. This is the first sense assignable to the "finitude of life." But the limited character of our possibilities (and, consequently, the existence of a stock thereof, for the two imply one another) can be determined by the following four fundamental factors: a. circum-stance, b. situation, c. vocation, and d. "pro-jection" or project. Once again, I wish to point out that these components are inherently inseparable, as are other "moments" of the act of living. As such, these four factors "co-implicate" both myself and that which is other than I, i.e., the two termini involved in such an act, although one or the other side would appropriately be "stressed" depending on the factor in question. "Circum-stance" is thus the "technical" name of one of the termini, and "situation" is meant to encompass both termini "on an equal footing," while "vocation" and "project" are denominations which underscore the dimension of the "*ego*." Let me at this point turn to an examination of these factors, which I will consider by speaking of the first three in summary fashion and by dwelling on the last.

7. THE CIRCUM-STANCE

Taking it in the broadest sense possible (as it appears in Ortega's famous dictum, "I am I and my circum-stance"),[106] the locution "circum-stance" signifies everything that surrounds me or with which I encounter myself. In other words, it refers to the bodily or "physical" world (including my own body and its particularities) and the mental "world" (including my own "soul" and its individual characteristics). In effect, I am neither my body nor my "soul"; rather, I encounter myself with them, although, to be sure, they constitute that part of my circum-stance which, more regularly than anything else, accompanies me. But it refers to the social and cultural world as well, including therein other human beings, and to everything encompassed by the terms "society" and "culture," namely, opinions, beliefs, ideas, institutions, artifacts, instruments, and so on. In short, it signifies everything we find which is a product of human doing or action, everything social and historical in which—as in a vast ocean—I am immersed. Finally, Ortega also referred thereby to what he called the "background" of the world [*el trasmundo*] and the "horizon of the last things" [*el plano de las ultimidades*]. He dealt with such questions especially by way of extensive descriptive developments of his doctrine, as they are found in *El hombre y la gente*,[107] developments that complement his first statement of these matters—a statement of genius, indeed—which appeared in his *Meditaciones del Quijote*.[108] In brief: the term "circum-stance" signifies everything there-is, or that is-available, insofar as I encounter myself with it, save one thing, namely, I myself.

To employ the term in question in order to refer to all that means that everything there-is, or is-available, is found to be "organized" around a center that is myself, and according to an order which is articulated by way of "planes" or, if you will, of [concentric] circles, ranging from those that are closest to me to those that are most remote, i.e., the horizon of the "last things."[109] If I avail myself of the locution "world" to signify all that,[110] I could restate what I have just said by asserting that the structure of this world is that of a perspective, as Ortega himself already put it in his *Meditaciones* and has reiterated in a thousand ways throughout his work. Let us hear it in his own words: "When shall we become receptive to the conviction that the *definitive being of the world* is neither matter nor soul, that it is no special thing in particular but only a *perspective?*"[111] This most fundamental concept of perspective has provided us with the expression "perspectivism," one of the better known and most significant names that have been used to refer to Ortega's philosophy. [Given its importance,] I should therefore make at this point a comprehensive presentation of the concept, and yet I will dispense with this task in the present context, since there is a book in Spanish devoted to it, and to which I would refer anyone, if need be.[112]

As Ortega himself did, I shall employ the locution "circum-stance" in a narrower sense. Accordingly, let me now use it to refer to the area of the "world" that surrounds me closely, or more or less proximately. This I am allowed to do by virtue of the "perspec-tival" structure of the "world." Now then, my circum-stance, espe-cially if we understand the term in this narrower sense, always exhibits a most concrete character: in every case or at any moment, it is this or that circum-stance, that is to say, the given one, which is as it is and cannot be otherwise. It is in the midst of these particular circum-stances that I have to engage in all those doings which my life consists of, or in which it unfolds. In every case or at any moment, I have to live with the "things"[113] I find in these particu-lar circum-stances, or in view of those which I miss in them, both formulations being equivalent for our purposes at present.

No doubt, I can modify my circum-stance, and I can do so in various ways. As a matter of fact, we are always engaged, in some measure or other, in this work of transformation. To illustrate the point, just consider an elementary case: I can, for instance, change my circum-stance by simply moving to a different place. To be sure, I am capable of bringing about such transformations, and yet, taking all things into consideration, I may only say that I can do so to a very limited extent. In any event, even to do that, or to arrive at such a "decision," I must rely on the particular circum-stance existing here and now, and I have to do what I do unavoidably on its basis and in view of it. Therefore, *every* doing is, like it or not, circum-stantial (and I underscore the word "every," so as to in-clude any manner of doing, even those forms of it which, like thinking, appear to be most remote from a conditioning of this sort). In his continual "struggle against utopianism," Ortega pro-ceeded on the basis of the postulate amounting to the requirement that we take up the inevitable "circum-stantiality" of our living in every one of its dimensions, and that we do so in a fully conscious, "deliberate," and responsible way. This postulate is meant to apply to the dimension of thought as well, a fact that endows Ortega's philosophical doctrine with one of its most pronounced, original, and fruitful determinations. The demand in question also serves as the foundation for his theory of truth as a whole. The notion of truth is another fundamental concept forming part of Ortega's teaching, one which would also require a more extensive development than the treatment I can devote to it here, at least so far as its metaphysical dimension is concerned, for it too is a "primordial concept" about human life. I will however not treat of it any further, by virtue of the same reasons why I did not deal with the notion of perspective, with which it is essentially connected.

Now then, when I employ the term "circum-stance" in this narrower sense, I am already alluding to the second one of the four factors enumerated above, to wit: the situation. Let me then to turn to it at this juncture.

8. THE SITUATION

Again, I shall not be able to dwell here upon this concept, which has profited from having been of central interest to contemporary existential or existentialist philosophy. No doubt, I would have had to examine it in detail had this study been of larger proportions, or had it been a comparative analysis of the major philosophers belonging to that current of thought (especially J.-P. Sartre, Gabriel Marcel, and, above all, Karl Jaspers), an examination that would have been intent on establishing the main differences between Ortega's doctrine and the positions held by each of them. Julián Marías too has dealt with this concept in his two basic works entitled *Introducción a la filosofía*[114] and *Antropología metafísica*.[115] In the former, he regarded it in terms of the concept of pre-tension, and in the latter he analyzed it as a function of the notion of installation. Both texts are of great importance for the purposes of giving an account of the concept of situation. I cannot, however, go into any such discussion for obvious reasons. I will content myself with indicating, almost in outline form, the essential points to be developed in a presentation of the concept.

First of all, let me bring up the word *situs*,[116] from which "situation" derives. It refers to the "brute" and most elementary fact that human life is inextricably located somewhere, provided we understand "human life" at the level of its *empirical structure,* to use a conception elaborated by Marías, as indeed we must.[117] Actually, we are always living in a given here. Furthermore, the "localization" of human life refers as well to the equally "brute" fact that can be enunciated by saying that we are always living in a given now. Accordingly, the two first features of a situation would be "hereness" [*hicceidad*] and "nowness" [*nuncceidad*].[118] These are two different aspects, and yet two aspects of only one fact, namely, the situational *"fact."* I mean to say thereby that every here is a here-now and, vice versa, that every now is a now-here. To this I would add that both dimensions, of course, are always qualified by an inevitable possessive, which is the foundation of any real concretion, for it is always a matter of a here-now (or vice versa) which is mine.

Being-located here is a necessary consequence or expression of the "bodiliness" and "sensibility" proper to our living. "My body," said Ortega, *"nails* me down to a *here."*[119] The greatly significant avatar of "sensibility" is, in turn, a consequence of the avatar of "bodiliness." My body is encountered—I encounter-myself-with it—always at and among other bodies. This fact condemns us—without recourse and for life—to being at a here, or to being "nailed down" to it, to employ Ortega's turn of phrase. But "here" is a thoroughly occasional concept, for the fullness of its meaning varies, for each person, from moment to moment—it is always an individual and nontransferable determination.[120] In other words, a here does not exist at all, being just an abstraction, as anything is which is taken in its pure or unalloyed condition, as when one understands "here" in a "purely" spatial or "physical" sense. On the contrary, a real here is always concretely "filled" and "qualified," and one can say exactly the same thing of any now, for it can never be severed from its correlative here.[121] Hence, a real here actually constitutes a certain "sphere" or "region," and our consciousness of it is always the consciousness of a world. This fact signifies that a here coimplicates an entire perceptual, imaginative, and projective nexus. In short, a here is lived as my "immediate" circum-stance, which is, in turn, circum-scribed or surrounded, "perspectivally" speaking, by the mediate sector of the circum-stance, that is to say, by the great encompasser the world is, and yet the "horizon"[122] or boundary line between the "immediate" and "mediate" zones of the circum-stance is not fixed, carrying out its function as it does with a high degree of flexibility.

But where is the horizon? A first acceptation of the word is "bound of the *visible*." In this light, one can appreciate that the horizon should vary as a function of my own "localization."[123] Therefore, one ought to say that, at every turn, there-is always a perceptible area about me. In other words, there-is a region containing what is not actually perceived but is nevertheless capable of being actualized as such from the location in which I happen to find myself. Beyond this zone, there-is another, of vast proportions, which is not perceptible from here but would be perceived were I gradually to displace myself by means of future successive and appropriate placements. Let me refer to this vast hinterland by means of [the descriptive formula], "a *zone* of the world or circum-stance constituted by *what could be perceived [percepturible]*."[124] (Again, the boundaries delimiting this particular area are flexible, and this is true from various points of view. I would say, for instance, that they are flexible, as is obvious, in view of the time at our disposal for such displacements, even concerning—"in principle" and in the broadest sense of the words—not only what "can be brought about," but also that which is merely possible or thinkable.) Finally, even beyond the zone of what could be perceived, there still lies another region that I shall call, following Ortega, the "background" of the world, of which the ultimate dimension would be the horizon of the "last things."

"Here," understood as referring to a "sphere" or "region," is a notion that should be examined in terms of the following conditioning factors, as a function of which it varies:

First, [the locations designated as] there, over there, and the beyond.

Second, the intrinsic qualification of the now (of which I will speak below),[125] and therefore the determinations called "before" and "after."

Third, the situated who, namely, I, you (singular and plural), he or she, we, they (men or women), and He.

Fourth, the pure and simple fact consisting in abiding somewhere [*estar*]; living (e.g., "dwelling," "residing," etc.); "*working*", and so on, that is to say, "doing" something (in general).

Fifth, the magnitude of the field or space opened up by the question "where?," a magnitude that is dependent on the perspective or the standpoint in terms of which, or on the presupposition on the basis of which one poses the question, that is to say, on the dimension or dimensions along which one's expectation for an answer is moving.

Were I to develop these points, I would be able to show that, within the sphere or region I have called "here," there-are "sub-spheres" or "sub-regions" that are different from one another in terms of their "scope." They would extend from the exact and unextended localization of a mathematical point (within a given space of n-dimensions) to the entire world. In fact, the entire world would turn into a here at the moment the there should become the beyond, and the situated who "humanity" or "humankind": we humans would then be inhabiting this here, this world, or "this vale of tears." Furthermore, I would also find "trans-real" or "imaginary" spheres, about which I could undoubtedly speak as metaphorical or "analogical" modalities of the here, and yet I would have most emphatically to underscore the fact that my abiding [*estar instalado*] in any of them is indeed to find myself in a most real situation. And I could continue even further along these lines. In any case, I would always be dealing with derivative forms of "hereness," that is to say, with those which are founded upon and referred to the originary, most individual, and personal here, namely, the concrete and untransferable here corresponding to my every now. It is about this primordial here that I say it is "filled" or "qualified," these two features strictly determining its concreteness. Let me refer by means of the formula "condition of being filled" to the determinate totality of "things" or instancies in, among, and confronting which I encounter and move myself and act at every particular moment. In other words, it signifies that my surroundings or immediate circum-stance, i.e., the sphere constituted by every here, is "full." Moreover, the feature I have referred to by the name "qualification" has to do not so much with things, as it does with the "functional aspects" they exhibit at the given moment. In other words, it designates those aspects of things that become ostensive by virtue of the function now being performed by them in my life. Consequently, "qualification" has to do with the effective instancing exercised by things on me, with the possibilities they afford or refuse me. In short: [the phenomenon of] qualification is related to the "pragmatic" and "dramatic" reality displayed by things at every determinate instant [of my life]. I would say that the now, i.e., the nowness of a situation, is to be defined, strictly speaking, in terms of qualification, an assertion which does not imply that the latter ever comes to be detached from here or hereness. Qualification is the means by which one is inadvertently translated from the "spatial" to the "temporal" dimension of a situation, both dimensions being, as I have said, inseparable from one another.

In the present context, I am unable to dwell upon the concept of now or nowness, the examination of which would be even harder and more complex than that of the notion of here or hereness. Indeed, all the problems concerning the structure and "temporal" nature of human life are connected with the concept of now or nowness. I will not, however, devote to that analysis even a cursory presentation, as I have just done with hereness. This is not to say that I have not already dealt with various fundamental aspects of the now in several sections of this study, especially when I had the occasion of considering the notions of presence and instancy in this part of the investigation.[126] At this point, I will limit myself to indicating what ought to be developed in this connection with regard to the concept of situation, and I will attempt to do it just by means of a mere outline, consisting of the following points:[127]

First, I would contend that the "temporal" is a priori with respect to the "spatial." The a priori character in question is evinced by the fact that the "temporal," though it belongs as well to the "empirical structure" of life, is already an essential feature identifiable in the "analytics" of life. By contrast, the "spatial" is squarely a part of the "empirical structure" of life, as I have argued above.[128] A human life that would be free from any metaphysical reference to the "spatial" is thinkable, but an intemporal life is inconceivable, since "temporality" is an absolutely inherent and necessarily constitutive characteristic of human life, even to the point of being the fundamental stratum of its "essential structure," which is the subject of study of the analytics of human life, to formulate it in terms of the pertinent distinction made by Marías.[129]

Second, every now, as is the case with every here, is filled and qualified. Qualification and the condition of being filled are determinations common to both now and here. In fact, it is by means of them that every here and every now communicate with each other or, more exactly, "fuse" with one another.

Third, every now is a synthesis. The fact that the now is filled gives expression to a twofold synthesis, namely, the synthesis of "coexistence" and "succession," as it used to be said.[130] Besides, the qualification of a now unfolds over its "qualitative" moment, which is a component of every now and consists of the synthesis of that which has-just-been-in-stantaneous[131] and that which is newly-being contingent. But these syntheses are characterized by being originary, in the sense I have given this term and explained elsewhere in this study.[132] I may add that the synthesis operative in the now exhibits other aspects as well, aspects that are likewise "syntheses" essentially connected with the former. Let me explain.

Fourth, every now involves what Heidegger called the "three *ectases* of temporality,"[133] which overlap one another in a peculiar fashion, namely, in the manner of retrotentive projectiveness, that is to say, in the way of a before-in-the-now, a later-in-the-now, and a present-in-the-now (the latter bringing the other two to "synthesis"). But this all implies that:

1. Every now, as is the case with every here, is itself a particular "sphere" or "region" too.

2. Every now is a structure, but this is to say that the sphere or region of the now is endowed with a particular dynamic "*structure.*"

3. Such a structure, within which coexist the three dimensions of temporality (namely, "*present-past-future*"), is characterized by the fact that protentiveness is essentially a priori with respect to retrotentiveness: as Ortega used to say, "life is futurity" [*futurición*] or, again, ". . . [l]ife is an operation directed toward the future."[134] Accordingly, one may say that, within such a structure, the present-in-the-now or "instant" is the moving point of "convergence" at which the solidary continuity that is our very living finds itself subject to a process of "unfolding." But the notion of instancy may be of help to our understanding of the fact that the dimensions of temporality overlap or interpenetrate: a given now projects itself into the future [*se futuriza*] precisely in the instancy, or by virtue of it. Or employing a term coined by Marías, I could say that a now is future-tending [*futurizo*].[135] One may thus assert that "we are living in the future," a statement that is meant non-

figuratively, and which is characterized by the utmost precision.

Fifth, every now is antinomic in character.[136] Among the antinomies involved, one ought to underscore, first of all, the maximal one, which is operative in the everyday use of "now," insofar as it always designates something future or past. This becomes evident, if one only pays careful attention to the expressions in which the locution plays a role: when one says "right now," for instance, one never means the now proper to the utterance or thought involved, but always a now which, to some extent or other, has just elapsed or is about to arrive. This acknowledgment by no means invalidates the futurity essential to living to which I have referred, a futurity that is "present" in every mental process [*vivencia*] directed upon the past. I could formulate this antinomy by asserting that the express consciousness of the now is always characterized by being referential and figurative [*traslaticia*]. There are, no doubt, many other antinomies affecting every now, some of which will make their appearance in the considerations that follow.

Sixth, every now is projective. This trait exhibited by nowness, by means of which one may corroborate, complement, and even "found" (in some respects) the features already listed, will be the subject of a separate analysis.[137]

Seventh, every now is a meaning structure in which the global meaning structure of my life is "profiled" or "foreshortened," that is to say, it is therein condensed, compressed, or implicated. One finds a twofold process of profiling taking place in every now, insofar as it is directed toward both the past and the future. My entire life exercises its gravitational pull on the minimal sphere or region every now is, thus endowing it with sense. Such a gravitational pull is exercised by means of the duality characteristic of the weightiness or "burdensomeness" of responsibility, namely, that which belongs to my entire past (to the extent that it is irrevocable) and that which is proper to my future (insofar as I can decide it), both dimensions of the duality being interconnected, naturally, by means of an indissoluble system of reciprocal relations. By way of this dual "gravitational pull" or "gravity" (which, as we know, presupposes our originary freedom),[138] life can "unfold" from now to now along the "solidary continuity" of presence. In effect, this is the definite way in which one can speak with absolute exactitude of the genuine "self-presence of life." On this basis, one may say that every now is the metaphysical locus where the act of becoming present belonging to the world, or to life itself, takes place, inasmuch as I encounter myself in the now. This is, therefore, the most genuine dimension of the actuality constituting every now.

Eighth, every now is "perspectival," "advertent," or "perceptional." All of this we already saw when presence was analyzed,[139] but it would at this time be useful to clarify the character of the plenitude of presence proper to the now and to give it a precise formulation, for such a plenitude is not so much perceptual in kind as it is originally *apperceptive*. To be sure, I am using a classical term here, but I am endowing it nonetheless with a new signification, which does not coincide either with Leibniz's "monadological" sense or with Kant's "transcendental" understanding of the word.[140] The manner of apperception characteristic of the living act is, strictly speaking, empirical in nature; one could even say that it is the radical and primordial "experience," or at least that it is one of its founding and constitutive moments. Furthermore, it is not transcendental at all, but transcendent proper, being the originary manifestation of transcendence itself. This is what I meant to convey by the formula according to which all things become present in the act of living, so that both the act of becoming present belonging to things and the act of living itself constitute the one act that the actuality of every now is.[141] Moreover, it is also by virtue of this fact that I contend that every now exhibits a logical or logic-like structure,[142] or that every present "presents" a logical "demeanor" (whether the manner of presentation involved be positive or negative), and that the world, insofar as it is a participant in the act of becoming present, is thereby the "horizon of *logicality*." From this standpoint, "meaning structure" and "logical structure" are equivalent expressions. Therefore, every "nexus of sense" encompassed by *living reason* would essentially belong to such a structure. But no less primordially (strictly speaking, even more so) belong to it any connections or proto-structures forming part of the ethical or dramatic dimension of life, among the most important instances of which I could mention those that, by virtue of their essential reference to the structures already listed, I would—for lack of a better word—characterize as ethological. I take this locution exactly in the sense fitting the present context, that is to say, as denoting the basic "meaning" connections at work in those ways of understanding I would refer to by means of the expressions "justification," "rendering evident by recourse to motivation" (or to *"motives"*), "problematization," and "verification." I am employing these terms according to their originary or living signification, that is to say, as connoting a process of "authentication" or "falsification" affecting—it goes without saying—life itself.[143]

Ninth, every now is dialectical. And this is so:

A. insofar as it is set in contraposition between an instancy and a counter-instancy (or "will");

B. in that it involves a "dialectic" of temporality (past-future), to which it is intrinsically conformed in different respects, as we have already seen;[144]

C. to the extent that every now is set in opposition to destiny and freedom—therefore, it is, if you will, a "compromise," "dialectical moment," or point of un-stable (i.e., of in-stantaneous or in-stantial) equilibrium between the two;

D. inasmuch as every now is also set, in the heart of freedom itself, in opposition to an exultant-depressive "temperamental" rhythm,[145] depending on the way one lives one's freedom, to wit: either in terms of its unavoidable necessity, by bearing up under the burdensomeness of the unremitting responsibility characteristic of it (that is, by taking it as one's "destiny," in the sense of doom or fate), or as a function of its force, power, or capacity for self-determination (that is, understanding it as one's "destiny," in the sense of a freely adopted mission);

E. [insofar as it is located] between myself and my circum-stance (by means of thinking, or the "dialogue" I conduct with the latter), and

F. [in that it is placed] among various *lógoi* [or thoughts] properly so called, a group including, for example, those belonging both to me and "others" and those which are solely my own (as it happens in the inner speech of thinking).[146]

At this point, I bring my analysis of the notion of situation to a close, an examination that has been long enough, despite the fact that I have confined myself to just pointing to certain themes or aspects that are implicit in the concept in question.

Let me at this juncture turn to the idea of vocation, the third among the "factors" already mentioned, and attempt to make the most summary presentation of it.

9. VOCATION

Like "projection" or "project," vocation plays its role within a given situation. In light of this, I would say that these categories could have been included in the section I just devoted to "situation," in which case they would have been regarded as components thereof. And yet I chose not to do so, for they are, properly speaking, not so much components of a situation as they are the most essential conditions it is to meet. Indeed, one of the chief modalities or aspects of the instancing exercised by an instancy—let us recall this fact—consists in being the soliciting, urging, or beckoning it puts into action.[147] Now, an instancy does not perform this function without rhyme or reason, so to speak. On the contrary, it does so in terms of a given course and direction. The "beckoning" or "call" proper to an instancy is perceived or sensed by me as vocation.[148] Vocation, therefore, is a kind of radical "sensibility" and "orientation" characterizing a person's life. The forms of sensibility and orientation also are—like the circum-stance (which no one has chosen for himself) and freedom proper—"brute," "ultimate," or "fated" data. Such forms do not fall within the "purview" of freedom, and yet they are "operative" by interacting with it, thus essentially contributing to the inherent limitation of the possibilities to which both the circum-stance and freedom are open. I mean to say by this that neither my circum-stance nor my vocation, taken in terms of their respective manners of concretion, can be chosen by me. On the contrary, they are imposed on me as something fated, as being just my destiny (understood in the sense of doom). Strictly speaking, circum-stance and vocation, regarded in terms of their situational concreteness, are the primordial reasons [*primalidades*] on the basis of which the field of possibilities proper to every now comes to be limited, although one should not lose sight of the fact that they are also responsible for the opening up of the field in question. This is why I contend that they render freedom metaphysically possible, and that they do so precisely as they limit it.

In point of fact, I would also encounter myself with my vocation, but not in the way I would with the "circum-stance." Rather, I would encounter myself with it as being the most intimate center of myself, a kernel that Ortega has sometimes referred to as one's "incorruptible depths,"[149] namely, as just that "*for the sake* of which one has been born." In everyday language, one often finds phrases that signify this fact—for example, "you have not been born *for* that," "he has been born *to* command," and the like. Apparently, we have been born, or encounter ourselves living, for the sake of something definite; it seems as if we had been "consigned" beforehand to arrive at certain "ports of destiny," without however having been consulted about the particular "voyage" involved. Or to put it otherwise: "Someone has 'born' me," as Miguel de Unamuno said somewhere, in an act of eschatological effrontery. Vocation is the particular being-for-the-sake of which my life, mysteriously and "already before the fact," has been apparently consigned to; it is that sort of chief "orientation" guiding my every step in living. In short: it is that grave and transcendental calling no one can fail to hear for himself, no matter how hard he may try to turn a deaf ear to it, since it arises from his heart of hearts. As I have already said, vocation belongs to our fate or destiny, but in a manner more far-reaching than that of any other component thereof, since it is precisely that to which our life is destined. And yet this fact does not infringe or violate the absolute law governing our freedom. Like anything else forming part of our destiny, vocation is, strictly speaking, not so much something that is im-posed on us as it is a pro-posal presented to us. In other words, it is another form of what I have called free necessity. I contend that it is something with which we encounter ourselves, even something with which at times we clash, with which we often struggle, but it is as well something that we pursue (joyfully or valiantly, depending on the "circumstances"), or something to which—enthusiastically and even heroically—we deliver ourselves. This is why our vocation unavoidably qualifies our doings. Every single one of them is vocational in character, whether positively or negatively. In other words, it either favors or counters our vocation, the consequences of one or the other alternative being for us of the utmost importance, transcendence, and gravity. Whatever we do about our respective vocations contains the final key to the polar and "permanent possibilities" of life, namely, plenitude or emptiness, happiness or wretchedness, moral consistency or demoralization, authentication or falsification—in short, salvation or perdition. Every such qualification affects the reality of life at the level of its metaphysical "nature," if you would excuse the expression. They are the grounds on the basis of which a life is more or less of a life, or a reality is more or less of a reality. But acknowledging this fact corroborates once more that Ortega's notion of reality is far removed from any traditional conception.[150]

Now, one's vocation directly manifests itself in, or translates itself into, the projective character of life; it gains expression in the "project" within which life unfailingly unfolds itself. Let us now see whether this is the case.

10. PROJECT AND PROJECTIVENESS

Life is "projective" or "programmatic" in character. I have to fashion it for myself, and yet I am not to do this just as I please, but always in terms of a project or program to which, naturally, my doings are to be conformed. If instead of preferentially directing my attention toward things (taken as termini of my possible doings), or even toward the possible doings themselves, I were to advert to the reality of my ego (or of myself qua possibility), I would discover that my reality is always reducible to the functional relationship existing between what has already been done (i.e., my past or the resultant of those doings that I have already carried out) and my present project (i.e., my future doings or the projective or programmatic resultant of what I am going to do). In short: it is always reducible to a project and its ongoing realization by means of one or another determinate doing. Life amounts to the fact that I am at a world or circum-stance by way of my self-projection and self-realization, which are being accomplished in terms of the world in question and of its inherent pre-tension. Both self-projection and self-realization are manners of doing, or are factors continually overlapping each other in every doing. Besides, these forms of doing essentially depend on one another or exist interdependently. The action of projecting is, to begin with, subordinated to that of realization, and yet the latter depends on the projective function, albeit in a sense different from that of the dependence of projecting on realization. In other words, no human being can, strictly speaking, realize anything that has not been previously projected to some extent or other.

Now then, realization—or its function—also depends on normative structures, the role of which is to guide and qualify it in relation to goals, if one wishes to make this point employing traditional terminology. Therefore, realization depends, again and in a different sense or way, on the project itself, insofar as the latter is fashioned by already having taken into account such goals and norms. In consequence, the overlapping and reciprocal relatedness of both functions is so intimate that they "livingly" balance and complement one another, even if every projective action is subordinated to the realization of what has been projected, that is to say, even if one's projects are only designed in view of their realization. To show that this is the case in a clearer way, let me first enumerate the various essential "moments" of self-projection and then proceed to give a brief account of each of them. Those moments are:

A. anticipating my actions or doings (the roles of the imagination and the intellect);
B. the valuing or gauging of them;
C. deciding which project, among those that are possible, I shall take up as mine;
D. inventing, in some measure or other, my own project; and
E. taking into account my circum-stance and vocation, or the factors at work in my personal destiny, for the sake of the "invention" in question.

A. Anticipating My Actions

First of all, let me point out that one can anticipate only those doings that are—or are deemed to be—possible. In other words, one can anticipate only those doings that are capable of functioning as "concrete possibilities." Now, this thesis implies that possibilities may function as if they were concrete when in fact they are not "realizable" [for one has taken them to be thus and so], and vice versa, namely, that some concrete possibilities may not function in that capacity, since one does not deem them to be "realizable." The character by virtue of which a possibility is concrete (to wit: that it is thus and so only if it is deemed to be such) is the mark that most clearly distinguishes the notion of possibility in-

spired by Ortega from the traditional concept thereof. To anticipate, then, is not merely to imagine or conceive just any action
judged to lie in the future. One can form representations of the
most varied, fantastic, and even impossible actions, lines of comportment, or enterprises (just as one would do in a certain kind of
"fiction"), but they would be capable, if at all, to turn into anticipations, to the extent that they are regarded as "feasible" by someone. This may in fact eventuate, even when the most fantastic
representations are in question, as is the case when the persons
involved are madmen or "illuminati." In other words, such representations may function as anticipations only if they become part
of an effective horizon of possibilities.

As we already know,[151] the actions or doings I can anticipate
in terms of my project are mine (if not absolutely, at least straightforwardly), and they are mine not just by virtue of the obvious fact
that what I am projecting is my life, but also because I cannot
project another's. To be sure, in my project there are components
that are "anticipations" of the doings of others, but only in the
sense that the anticipations of the comportment of other human
beings are part and parcel of the totality of my anticipations concerning the conduct of any component of my circum-stance, insofar as I have to take into account those anticipated comportments
in order to be able to fashion my own project. But it is also true
that at times I project the life of others in a way similar to my own
when I project mine—say, in the case of my progeny, at least
during their childhood. This notwithstanding, it is to be noted that
projecting somebody else's life is an activity endowed only with a
limited scope (for in that eventuality I would be projecting only
special components or "aspects" thereof), but, above all, it is to be
remarked that my engaging in projecting them would be an extrinsic affair, since I would be projecting only particular actions or just
the general lineaments of the conduct of another as they would
appear to me when regarded from without. It is not possible to
project the details belonging to what is intimate, qualitative, and,
in the final analysis, of a personal nature, and to do so precisely in
the definite manner with which someone in particular would take
up a project and realize it, whether the person in question is to do
it willingly or against the grain.

Nowadays, the endeavors directed to bringing about an ever-
greater intervention in the innermost lives of persons and the at-

tempts to manipulate their minds which we observe occurring in mass societies, politicized and subject to the constraints of technology as they are, are ominous signs of the fact that forms of approximating and planning social conduct are about to arrive, or may have arrived, which would serve the purpose of reaching layers of the human personality located at ever-increasingly profound levels. In fact, to the extent that the personality is so penetrated, it is destroyed, bringing the average individual living in those societies—the mass man of whom Ortega spoke—[152] to a sorry condition that resembles—more and more—that of a living robot. The techniques developed to destroy people by means of the progressive elimination of their capacities or "possibilities" of self-projection are being "perfected" every day—in other words, they are becoming efficient to a degree beyond compare. A few authors, among whom I should list Aldous Huxley and George Orwell, have striven to draw the horrifying picture of a future but proximate world in which tendencies of this sort would have achieved their final victory. In my judgment, however, no such somber prophecies will ever be fulfilled, since, before their realization, humankind would have disappeared. The latter indeed is an effective "possibility."

Anticipation, then, has to be the anticipation of my own doings, an affair that consists, to begin with, in imagining or conceiving them in view of their eventual realization. Now, this ideative or imagining activity too is a form of doing, or even a series of doings. Therefore, one must say that living is doing something at every juncture, whether what is being fashioned at the moment is a project, a decision or choice, or the realization of that which has been projected, i.e., of the project I would have already taken up, or the part thereof befitting the given situation. In fact, always and at every turn, three things are being done, all of which form part, according to a special manner of articulation, of the structure of human doing as such. Those components are the "performative,"[153] the "elective," and the "projective." Sometimes, however, one or another prevails, or stands out, or is at work with greater emphasis. As we know, every human doing is in fact what it is by virtue of a *why* and a *what-for,* which endow it with sense and justification.[154] Actually, it is only in terms of its "why" and its "what-for" that a human doing is intelligible. Now then, the projection or project, the election and the realization always mediate between the why and the what-for. Finally, let us note the fact that what is being projected in the project is, in the final analysis, my entire life and, therefore, myself. Again, as we know, what I am going to do is what I am going to be, just as what has already been done is what I now "am," provided that one understands that the project already carried out is part and parcel of what has already been done.[155] I am then what has already been carried out, as well as the project of what I am going to be, which I am now living. The project, taken as such, is still to be realized or "carried out."

Usually, what has been carried out or done by me is part of the same global project that consists also of components that have not yet been carried out. The latter are, therefore, the only parts of it that now are in fact functioning as a project. And yet exceptionally (though not relatively infrequently) a peculiar nexus is verified, in which what has been done and what is to be done belong to two different projects, for a living project may have been abandoned or given up, at whatever phase of its process of fulfillment, to be replaced by another. Such occurrences may range from simple passing "fluctuations" affecting the project in question (events that are quite normal) to the final replacement of the project itself, or from differences between one project and another at a more or less "superficial" level (which would thus leave our personal depths untouched) to those extreme situations, of which an extreme example would be the truly exceptional experience called conversion. Even if none of that is detectable, a project would nevertheless constantly undergo modifications, since, belonging to life, it would share in its metaphysical properties and would thus participate in its originary and constitutive flux-character. In other words, a project too is a living affair.

B. *The Valuing of a Project or of the Doings Pertinent Thereto*

The mere imaginary anticipation of [a series of] doings could never amount to a genuine project, even if it proposed an organic and sufficient totality that would be constituted by them, thus providing a shape for my entire life. In that case, it would only establish a neutral image of a possible life, even if it is an image of a possible life of mine. To begin to be a project (that is to say, to begin to be capable of being one), what is so designed must become part of a positive valuative or estimative horizon or perspective. In other words, it would have to offer me incentives of some sort, so as to be capable of appearing to me as one of the "possible shapes of life" containing a promise of *personal happiness*.[156] Now, it is evident that such a positive valuation or gauging of the shapes of life would transform them into as many complex possibilities, since a "living project" is, in fact, just a constellation of possibilities organized as a structural totality. Taken all together, such totalities would constitute as many complex and "sufficient" possibilities, which [consequently] should be referred to as *life possibilities*. It is precisely as being such possibilities that they are given to me as options among which to choose. If this were not so, they could never become my genuine projects. But this acknowledgment already leads me to the next point.

C. Deciding About, or Choosing, a Particular Project as "My Own" Among Those That Are Possible

Among the many acts of choosing or deciding of which my life consists, the one involving my living project is crucial, since it constitutes the major crossroads of my life. (Nowhere is the worn-out adjective "crucial" better employed.) In effect, the event in question corresponds to the moment that, sooner or later, always arrives, and in which one comes face to face with the terrible problem posed in the question, *quod vitae sectabor iter* [which path shall I follow in my life]?[157] And I say this is a terrible problem, because its importance and gravity cannot be compared to those connected with any other decision. To some degree, all my future decisions depend on the "crucial" one, since, in fact, all of them are particular ways I have of realizing the major life-project I have taken up as my own.[158] They are, therefore, the "modulations" of my major project.

Now then, a project of this sort cannot be merely imposed on me, or even proposed or given to me as the one project in which I already would have encountered myself before I took my own life or destiny "in hand" (or before I arrived at the "crucial" situation). Rather, I must take up or choose this project, if indeed it is to be truly my own. But, if this is to be so, then my project must be personal, individual, and, in consequence, of such a character that no one could ever say that it had been plotted beforehand. On the contrary, I always have—in some measure—to fashion it; that is to say, I must mold it to my own measure, or else I have to re-fashion it. But this requirement will be examined in the context of the next point.

D. *Inventing, "in Some Measure or Other," My Own Project*

At first sight, the requirement in question seems to run counter to the fact that the projects among which I choose are possibilities that appear to be already available, or to be given precisely as possibilities, as though I only had to take up one among the many that are kindred to my system of pre-dilections. Indeed, in a certain sense and in principle, this is the way in which things happen. Let me explain.

During the initial stage of the process involved, that is how matters do work out, since at that point I would be living at a deliberative phase that may turn out to be quite long. When I want to plot out the shape of *my* possible life or lives, the first thing I do is look round me and see about those possible life-shapes that are already given and pro-posed, inasmuch as others have by this time invented and lived them. And I find them there, whether in the abstract and communal way of living which is proper to a "social mold" or "role" (i.e., what is called a "profession" or a "career"), or in the more concrete form (or, if you will, in the less abstract way) characteristic of a "living model."

In the next stage of the process, that is to say, in the phase beginning once I have already decided to *be* this or that [sort of human being], things will proceed, however, along different lines, for the need to translate the abstract project into a concrete one would immediately arise. In other words, I would then experience the want to transform someone else's project—i.e., a project that would be merely "appropriate" but without belonging to anyone in particular—into a personal one. Now, this is equivalent to saying that it is then I realize that every living project I would merely "take up" is generic in character and thus not yet done, except so far as its "general" outline is concerned. I would thus become aware of the fact that I have to carry it out for myself or that, at least, I have to make it my own. In other words, I would have then realized that I have to invent it in some measure or other.

Accordingly, what I have to invent is the "plot" or "novel" of my own life, to use Ortega's own words,[159] but that plot or novel could never coincide with that which is proper to any other *who*. To be sure, when we forge or "invent" our "own" projects of living (even when the project involved belongs to a most "original" man), parts of it would have been taken from, or imposed upon us by, more or less generic "situational" necessities. I have in mind those constituents of a project that would be characteristic of life as such, or those that would derive from its "empirical structure" (as is the case, for example, with the forms of "communal" living or those pertaining to social and historical life). As opposed to the magnitude and importance of these components of a project, the magnitude and importance of my personal contributions thereto always pale into insignificance. Or to put it in Ortega's own words: a human being is certainly the "novelist engaged in composing the novel of his own life,"[160] and yet the novels he invents—the novels about himself—are usually, in most instances, in the "great majority" of cases, quite unoriginal. But, naturally, one finds as well the "large minority" consisting of "eminent individuals" or "novelists" of genius engaged in composing "their own" novels, namely, those who, even though they are subject to such conditionings too, manage nonetheless to make innovative, fruitful, and most meaningful forms of living part and parcel of their own selves, even to the point of turning such forms into "paradigms" and into agents and molders of history. Ortega has greatly insisted on the importance of this "creative" factor for the purposes of historical development, a position of his which is intrinsically linked to his conception of society as involving an essential interplay between a mass and a minority.[161]

To the components deriving from the projects of others or from given situational necessities, I must now add those irrepressible factors originating in the constant intervention of chance and contingency in life. An intervention of this kind is equivalent here to the perpetual happening or "coming about" that life is; in other words, it is taken to mean the "taking place," "occurring," or "coming to pass" that—in conjunction with doing—so primordially defines life, and which constitutes itself as a decisive "moment" of presence. I am of course aware of the fact that none of these factors functions with complete independence of the rest, for all of them, more or less, "imply or co-implicate my pre-tension and project," and yet it is no less certain that they also intimately condition my pre-tension and project and, therefore, also unceasingly, essentially, and decisively condition the "field of my possibilities." In short, there is no "self-projection" except in the world or circumstance, but the latter always is, as we already know, a circumstance and a circum-possibility, and "doing" (including therein the fashioning of projects) what takes place in terms of it.[162]

No matter how imitative the "plot" or project of a life may be, or however conditioned it may turn out to be by the factors listed above, it is nevertheless true to say that at least its inner "modulation," its every detail, and each particularity belonging to its development would differ to a considerable degree from those proper to the model imitated. In fact, these would acquire, by contrast with the "conditioning" factors at play, an organization that would be, to a point, "personal" in character. But this is all as it should be, for it is "in the very nature of things," as the phrase goes. In other words, this is the case by virtue of the strange sort of reality human life genuinely is. Essentially speaking, life is, on the one hand, circum-stantial and contingent, and, on the other, situational, individual, untransferable, and, above all, unavoidably free. Accordingly, to assert that the "novels" a man composes for "his own" life are, generally speaking, quite unoriginal does not run counter to the view that a man also has, willy-nilly, to exercise his freedom within the channel, set of lineaments, or given rhyme and foot that, in every case, is the equivalent of the "limitation of possibilities" in which he must carry out his "self-projection." In fact, he will do so—again, willy-nilly—in a manner individual or personal, within a broad margin of flexibility, no doubt, as defined by the variable bounds of his limited "originality." Or as I have already put it: I have to invent my living project in some measure or other, since no common project—or project belonging to someone else—is completely fashioned to *"my own measure."*[163] But an invention of this sort must take into account the factors at work in my personal destiny, as I have often pointed out and now will proceed expressly to consider.

E. My Having to Take into Account My Circum-stance and Vocation, or the Factors at Work in My Personal Destiny, for the Sake of Inventing My Project

We are thus brought to the last point to be subjected to analysis. At this level we come into contact with the deepest reaches—with the abyssal depths, if you will—of the matter under scrutiny. But at the same time we are confronted with the most paradoxical aspect of it, as well as with the undoubtedly most revealing dimension of the sui generis, incomparable, and remarkably strange condition of the reality I have been referring to by means of the name "human life."

What I have in fact asserted is that I must invent and decide my life project or program (i.e., the series or sequence of my doings), but this is tantamount to saying that I must invent my own being. It would already be exceedingly strange to find a reality (and not just any reality, mind you, but the "radical" one), the "being" of which would involve not only not being yet (whatever it would eventually come to be), but also having to fashion itself by way of choosing itself. But it would be even stranger and more astounding to discover that the actions of inventing and choosing (or deciding) one's own "being" (i.e., one's life project or program) should be unavoidably free, and yet at the same time unavoidably conditioned by the two constituent dimensions of one's fate. I mean, on the one hand, that most concrete circum-stance or world in which, like it or not, I have to live, and which, like it or not, I have therefore to take into account in order to "project myself." On the other hand, I have likewise in mind that strangest and most para-doxical dimension of my fate, namely, the "*project*" I already am beforehand—again, whether I like it or not, inevitably. This project is my deepest and most intimate "necessity," indeed the source and spring of any other necessity belonging to my life. My project is not, however, a necessity in a generic sense, as I have said my freedom is.[164] Here I am not advancing the contention—let me mark this well—that the project I am is an absolute necessity, but only that it is my "*deepest* and *innermost* necessity." It is not, then, a necessity absolutely speaking, as my freedom assuredly is, but it is certainly a necessity in a most definite sense, namely, in that it constitutes the most personal stratum of myself. In effect, such a project is identical with the very depths of a given person taken as such. Consequently, it is *on this stratum* that human freedom exercises its pressure in the most decisive and radical of ways. I am thinking, then, of what Ortega called our "incorruptible depths":[165] in this sense, my project coincides, therefore, with vocation itself. Accordingly, what I have asserted about the latter[166] also applies to it: my project cannot be altered or alienated;

on the contrary, were I to attempt to do that, I would end up "alienating" or "falsifying" myself, without however completely succeeding in eliminating my project. Hence, it constitutes my ultimate and deepest sense of *identity*. Let me avail myself of this occasion to quote a passage from Ortega's "Pidiendo un Goethe desde dentro," which describes the project one is with remarkable precision. This is what he had to say in that context:

> Life means the inexorable necessity of realizing the project of existence that each one of us is. This project, which the "ego" intrinsically is, is no idea or plan a human being has conceived and freely chosen. It is prior to every single idea our mind may fashion, to every decision arrived at by our will. I mean to say that it is independent of them. But this is not all. Usually, we have about it the vaguest of notions, and yet it constitutes our genuine *being,* our destiny. Our will is free to *realize* or to *refuse* the living project we ultimately are, but we cannot alter, correct, disregard, or replace it. We indelibly are that unique programmatic personage who must be realized, and yet the world about us or our own character renders self-realization easier or more difficult, to some degree or other. Life is inherently dramatic, for it amounts to engaging in a frenzied struggle with things, and even with our own character, in order to attain in fact the one person we already are in terms of our project.[167]

But if indeed the project we are beforehand is handed to us in conjunction with life, someone may argue that expressions like "having to invent our project" are difficult to understand. What would then be the use of inventing other projects? The answer, however, is already contained in the passage I have just quoted from Ortega's "Goethe." First of all, one hears that the "project" in question is no "idea or plan a human being has conceived. . . . It is prior to every single idea our mind may fashion . . . we have about it the vaguest of notions. . . ." In other words, we are dealing with a non-formulated project. Our project only makes its appearance as such when, upon forging, inventing, or imagining a project (that is to say, upon "formulating" one), we have the sense that the "line" we are plotting coincides with or diverges from our project, thus "bringing it out" or "developing" it for us (employing the word "developing" here as is done in photography). Secondly, a project is not given to me by means of an act of im-position, but is offered to me as a pro-position, as Ortega has put it elsewhere.[168] In other words, it is given to me in the manner in which, as we already know, every life necessity is given, namely, as a free necessity (the only exception to this being the absolute necessity of freedom itself).[169] Accordingly, I am not free to substitute another project for the nonformulated and originary one I am, but I can accept or refuse it. I am not free to alter my vocation, my destiny, but I can be faithful or unfaithful to it, since the project is the ultimate stratum of my being, namely, that which I have to be. This is why the young Ortega already made Pindar's imperative his own, for he then adopted, as the fundamental moral norm, the maxim, "Be faithful to yourself," or "Be who you are."[170]

Therefore, I would argue that there are three "projects," or three ways in which my "living project" functions. First, we have the project in which I am already placed when I encounter myself living: this project is not "mine" in any sense of the word, since I have neither fashioned nor "invented" it, but neither can it be equated with what I am *a radice* [radically or from the root up], for I have been lodged in it by others (e.g., my parents, my teachers, or society at large). Second, we may also speak of the project I forge, invent, or choose: this is my project, in the sense that I fashion it. And, finally, we may point to the "project" I am, which may be assigned various names, such as personal destiny, vocation, "*incorruptible depths*," individual mission, and the like.

Now then, these three "projects" may or may not coincide with one another. This is especially relevant in the case of the second and third senses of the word, since they are the ones which really matter, inasmuch as the original "project" is usually forsaken soon enough—if not, it will be taken up or appropriated personally, thus turning it into the second sort of project. As we already know, life is affected by the consequences that grow out of such coincidences or divergences, and those consequences, which I have already discussed under the rubric of vocation,[171] are of the utmost gravity and transcendence for human life.

Conclusions

My presentation of the categories of human life has thus come to an end, and yet I have dealt only with those concepts which, in my opinion, are the major ones when they are looked at in the light of Ortega's "critique of idealism." In other words, I have examined those notions which, in terms of the results arrived at in the critical analysis of idealism, have a more direct bearing on the task of overcoming it. I am not oblivious to the fact that my presentation of the categories of life is incomplete. I would have liked, above all, to elaborate the concepts of "perspective" and "contingency," with which I have in fact dealt elsewhere.[1] Such concepts are, no doubt, categories, and yet subjecting them to an examination would have taken me too far afield, since, to engage in an analysis of them, I would have had to go into Ortega's metaphysical system to a degree inconsistent with the purpose and structure of this study and the merely "introductory" character I had intended for it. In other words, I believe I have sufficiently served my purpose and not belied my intent.

Now I would like to offer a summary, presented in the most succinct of fashions, of the conclusions that are derivable from this survey. They are the following:

First, the critical analysis of idealism appears to be an essential component of Ortega's thought, if one judges it in terms of various philosophical objectives, but fundamentally in view of the goal of determining the character of the *new metaphysical plane* on which his thought was moving.

Second, a novel idea of reality took shape[2] as the strict or "literal" outcome of Ortega's critique of idealism. This idea, on the basis of which he was to overcome idealism, was connected with the unusual, indeed the radically paradoxical, claim that it is no "idea" at all, or at least that it is the minimal expression that an "idea" could find. In effect, it was meant to be just the mental instrumentality necessary for us to be able to establish immediate intellectual contact with reality itself, or to reduce the mediation needed to do so to the lowest possible level. The purpose here was no other than coming to terms with reality "in person," precisely as it gives itself and just as it is prior to the application of any ideative or cogitative operation to it. The justification of this position lies in Ortega's opinion that every intellectual performance, upon being applied to reality, "deforms" it in principle and to some degree. Here we find the major *aporia* [difficulty] and challenge to be met by the immense "thirst for reality" characteristic of Ortega's mind and life. Such a challenge was all the greater the deeper Ortega's conviction (and even painful sense) was that the idealistic doctrine to which modern thought had conformed itself had finally resulted in the "intellectualization" of all things. Now, [in Ortega's judgment,] an outcome of that sort was exceedingly dangerous to the proximate future of mankind, thus urgently requiring us to counter it by means of a dynamic and far-reaching effort of intellectual "detoxification." The response to the challenge in question—and to the terrifying *aporia* it harbors within— is found not just in the method practiced by Ortega in his work, but as well in his philosophical teaching as a whole. What is here involved is nothing but the genuine theme of our times, including all of its dimensions, even those that are nontheoretical in character, namely, the moral, social, cultural, political, and (ultimately) historical aspects of it.

Third, this is the true meaning of the "re-implantation" of reason in life, which is its befitting and originary dwelling-place. And yet life is the home from which reason has continually evaded itself ever since it began to be employed in Greece. Reason's endeavor has even turned into an attempt to substitute itself for life, especially by means of the doctrine known as "idealism." In fact, reason has, from its very beginnings, striven to move away from life, to the extent that it has amounted to the historical effort to achieve its own autonomy, an experiment of vast proportions that Western humanity has conducted under the name of philosophy.[3]

Fourth, Ortega has proposed—in order to effect such a "re-implantation"—that an idea should operate, to be sure, as what it necessarily is, namely, an intellectual instrumentality, and yet that it should do so by harboring within itself a mechanism, so to speak, for its own undoing as an idea, or for its own self-correction, insofar as it is an "idea." Or equivalently put: a "tool" of this sort should preserve its originary ties to life, from which it derives and which it seeks to bring to knowledge. This approach would apply to every idea, but above all to the idea of radical reality, or of reality itself: it is from this application that the entire metaphysical orientation and signification of Ortega's thought derive. But this goal of his does not have the status of a mere proposal, for he has in fact striven to act on it with exemplary courage. The vitalization of ideas, then, is what is involved here, a process that would allow them to be living ideas, views, or reasons, without however losing their character of "ideas" or "views." In other words, the validity of an idea should be seen as stemming more from its *living function* than from its "logical" significance proper. Or, if you will, the "logical" or "cognitive" value of an idea is to be understood as being strictly dependent upon its living sense, which, I should say, is primodially a moral one.

Fifth, all of this implies a profound reformation of our understanding of the structures of "rationality," a reformation that is to be carried out in conjunction with, or in terms of, the reformation of our understanding of the structures of reality itself, inasmuch as "rationality" is inherent in the latter. But this novel understanding should bring metaphysics to a new level, thus rendering accessible a philosophical horizon that we have hardly begun to explore by virtue of very definite but also quite complex historical circumstances proper to our century, especially those that have prevailed during its concluding half.

Sixth, I would have to say that a few basic categories determine the shape adopted by the radical reality or primordial instancy of there-being or availability arising from Ortega's "critique of idealism" (to which I have confined myself). Among such categories, I would have, above all, to point to the fundamental concepts I have called "absolute event" and "presence." In fact, I have tried to focus my presentation on them, although this way of proceeding did inevitably lead me to consider other related categories, such as "instancy," "complexity," "situation," "circum-stance," "vocation," and "projectiveness." Such a categorial elaboration could have been pursued even further, by means of the network of strict interconnections existing among the concepts involved, eventually to encompass Ortega's thought in its entirety. But the fact that the subject of this investigation, which I have barely outlined, has brought me face to face with the whole of Ortega's philosophy (as would have also come to pass had I analyzed any other of its themes) forces me, finally, to arrive at a further conclusion, namely, that the view that Ortega's philosophical doctrine is strongly systematic in character has been confirmed. This contention, which runs counter to an opinion espoused by quite a few commentators, is advanced by assigning a novel signification to the word "systematic," one which [indeed] is commensurate with Ortega's novel idea of reason.

NOTES

PREFACE

1. José Ortega y Gasset, *Obras Completas* (Madrid: Alianza Editorial / Revista de Occidente, 1983), III. Translation: *The Modern Theme*, trans. J. Cleugh (New York: Harper & Row, 1961).

2. Ibid. Translation: *The Dehumanization of Art and Other Writings on Art and Culture* (Garden City, N.Y.: Doubleday & Co., 1956).

3. Ibid., IV. Translation: *The Revolt of the Masses* (New York: W. W. Norton & Co., 1932).

4. Ibid., IX. Translation: *An Interpretation of Universal History*, trans. M. Adams (New York: W. W. Norton & Co., 1973).

5. Ibid. For the essential rootedness of Ortega's critical evaluations of historical and cultural phenomena in metaphysical analyses proper, cf., e.g., infra, Part I, chap. 3, p. 70.

6. Cf. "Guillermo Dilthey y la Idea de la Vida" (1933–34), ibid., VI, pp. 166ff. Translation: "A Chapter from the History of Ideas—Wilhelm Dilthey and the Idea of Life," *Concord and Liberty*, trans. H. Weyl (New York: W. W. Norton & Co., 1946), pp. 132ff.

7. Ibid., I. Translation: *Meditations on Quixote*, trans. E. Rugg et al. (New York: W. W. Norton & Co., 1961). Cf. Julián Marías's edition of this work, published together with his "Commentary" (Madrid: Universidad de Puerto Rico / Revista de Occidente, 1957), as well as the first volume of his *Ortega*, 2d ed. (Madrid: Alianza Editorial, 1983). Translation: *José Ortega y Gasset. Circumstance and Vocation*, trans. F. M. López-Morillas (Norman: University of Oklahoma Press, 1970).

8. J. Ortega y Gasset, *Meditaciones del Quijote* in *Obras Completas*, I, p. 322. Cf. J. Marías's "Commentary," pp. 266ff.

9. For Ortega's critique of classical idealism, cf. infra, Part I, chap. 2, pp. 21ff.

10. E. Husserl, *Ideen zu einer reinen Phänomenologie und phänomenologischen Philosophie. Erstes Buch: Allgemeine Einführung in die reine Phänomenologie*, ed. K. Schuhmann, 3d ed. (The Hague: Martinus Nijhoff, 1976) in, *Husserliana*, III, 1–2. Translation: *Ideas Pertaining to a Pure Phenomenology and to a Phenomenological Philosophy. First Book: General Introduction to a Pure Phenomenology*, trans.

F. Kersten (The Hague: Martinus Nijhoff, 1982). For Ortega's critique of phenomenological idealism, cf. infra, Part I, chap. 3, pp. 51ff.

11.   E. Husserl, *Logische Untersuchungen* (The Hague: Martinus Nijhoff) in *Husserliana*, XVII (i, 1975, ed. E. Holenstein) and XIX, 1–2 (ii, 1984, ed. U. Panzer). Translation: *Logical Investigations*, trans. J. N. Findlay (New York: Humanities Press, 1970), 2 vols.

12.   Jan Patočka, *Platon et l'Europe*, trans. E. Abrams (La Grasse: Éditions Verdier, 1983), iii, p. 49.

13.   J. Ortega y Gasset, *¿Qué es filosofía?* in *Obras Completas*, VII, chap. 7. Translation: *What Is Philosophy?*, trans. M. Adams (New York: W. W. Norton & Co., 1960).

14.   J. Ortega y Gasset, "Prólogo para alemanes" (1934) in *Obras Completas*, VIII, p. 43. Translation: "Preface for Germans," *Phenomenology and Art*, trans. Ph. W. Silver (New York: W. W. Norton & Co., 1975), p. 55.

15.   Ibid., p. 47. Translation: p. 60. Cf. *¿Qué es conocimiento?*, 1929–30; 1930–31 (Madrid: Revista de Occidente en Alianza Editorial, 1984), i, 8, p. 61. Vide infra, Part II, chap. 4, §§ 1–2, pp. 83ff.

16.   J. Ortega y Gasset, "En el centenario de una universidad" (1932), *Obras Completas*, V, p. 472. Cf. *¿Qué es conocimiento?*, iii, 5, pp. 107ff. Vide Martin Heidegger's concept of *Geworfenheit* in his *Sein und Zeit*, 10th ed. (Tübingen: Max Niemeyer, 1963), §§ 29 and 38, pp. 135 and 175ff. Translation: *Being and Time*, trans. J. Macquarrie et al. (New York: Harper & Row, 1962), pp. 174 and 219ff.

17.   J. Ortega y Gasset, *¿Qué es conocimiento?*, i, "1929–30 Course," no. 8, p. 58.

18.   Ibid., i, "Problems," § 7, p. 15.

19.   Ibid.

20.   Ibid., i, "1929–30 Course," no. 6, p. 44.

21.   Ibid., pp. 46ff.

22.   In fact, there is, in Ortega's axiom, a third term referring to the self. I have in mind the word "my," which has immediately to do with the relationship between what is signified by the second "I" of his formula and the circum-stance it is faced with. In the present context, I have chosen, for simplicity's sake, to leave out of consideration what that locution stands for. This does not mean that it is in any way inconsequential. Quite the contrary: it is only that it is grounded in the other two which I am here focusing upon, and that is a sufficient reason, I believe, not to insist upon it in this introductory presentation. Moreover, the complexity of the matter it represents is too great to be dealt with in a few strokes, involving as it does a plexus of categories, such as freedom, project, and vocation. Cf. infra, Part II, chap. 4, §§ 6ff., pp. 119ff.

23.   J. Ortega y Gasset, *¿Qué es conocimiento?*, i, "Problems," § 9, p. 20.

24. Ibid.

25. That is to say, *el ser ejecutivo* (or *la presencia ejecutiva*). Cf., e.g., ibid., pp. 17–18, and "1929–30 Course", § 5, pp. 37–38 and ii, pp. 91–92. Vide "Ensayo de estética a manera de prólogo" (1914), *Obras Completas,* VI. Translation: "An Essay in Esthetics by Way of a Preface," *Phenomenology and Art.*

26. J. Patočka, *Platon et l'Europe.,* p. 50.

27. Ibid.

28. Ibid.

29. Cf. ibid. One must say, on the one hand, that my life, taken as an individual whole, is the subject par excellence, and that therefore the categorial analysis thereof need not be an "asubjective phenome-nology" (as J. Patočka's attempt to go beyond Husserl's transcendental turn seems to have required. Vide Erazim Kohák, "Jan Patočka: A Philosophical Biography" in *Jan Patočka. Philosophy and Selected Writings,* ed. and trans. E. Kohák [Chicago: The University of Chicago Press, 1989], pp. 91ff.). This is so because my life is a being-for-itself spontaneously, *not* as the result of its being contemplated and objecti-vated by me in a grounded act of reflection. But it is also true, on the other hand, that my life is *not* to be identified with subjectivity (i.e., with the ego or any of its acts or ingredients), for subjectivity is just "one component or part of the most fundamental structure" of the subject-life, namely, ". . . this or that one before whom that which ap-pears (a being) makes its appearance. . ." (J. Patočka, *Platon et l'Eu-rope,* p. 50). It is no wonder, then, that it is so difficult not to commit the error of mistaking the rational distinction between the subject-life and subjectivity for a separation.

30. J. Ortega y Gasset, *¿Qué es conocimiento?,* i, "Problemas," §8, p. 16.

31. Cf. J. Ortega y Gasset, *¿Qué es filosofía?* in *Obras Completas,* VII, especially chaps. 5 and 7–9.

32. Cf. J. Ortega y Gasset, "Pidiendo un Goethe desde dentro" (1932), *Obras Completas,* IV, pp. 403–4, n. (Translation: "In Search of a Goethe from Within," trans. W. R. Trask in *The Dehumanization of Art and Other Writings on Art and Culture,* n. 3, pp. 135–37) and *La idea del principio en Leibniz y la evolución de la teoría deductiva* (1947), *Obras Completas,* VIII, chap. 29 (Translation: *The Idea of Principle in Leibniz and the Evolution of Deductive Theory,* trans. M. Adams [New York: W. W. Norton & Co., 1971], pp. 276ff.).

33. Cf. J. Ortega y Gasset, *¿Qué es conocimiento?,* iii, 8, pp. 143–44. This passage is most interesting, because Ortega's basic objection to Hartmann's position is that in it he failed to make use of the distinction, also found in Heidegger, between "Being" and "entity."

34. Cf. Jean-Paul Sartre, *L'être et le néant* (Paris: Gallimard, 1943).
Vide J. Ortega y Gasset, *Una interpretación de la historia universal* in
Obras Completas, IX, p. 216 (Translation: p. 285).

35. Cf. Maurice Merleau-Ponty, *Phénoménologie de la perception*
(Paris: Gallimard, 1945).

36. Cf. Max Scheler, *Formalism in Ethics and Non-Formal Ethics
of Values,* trans. M. S. Frings et al. (Evanston: Northwestern University
Press, 1973), pp. 143–44 (n. 32), 377–78, 404ff., 412–13, and 417ff.,
and *The Nature of Sympathy,* trans. P. Heath (London: Routledge &
Kegan Paul, 1954), pp. 10 and 75. Vide J. Ortega y Gasset, "Sobre la
expresión fenómeno cósmico" (1925), *Obras Completas,* II, pp. 577ff.;
"La percepción del prójimo" (1929), *Obras Completas,* VI, pp. 153ff., *El
hombre y la gente* (1949–50), *Obras Completas,* VII, chap. 4, pp. 138ff.
and chap. 6, pp. 160ff., "Algunos temas del 'Weltverkehr,'" *Obras Completas,* IX, p. 339, and *¿Qué es conocimiento?,* ii, no. 4, pp. 91–92, and
iii, no. 6, p. 124.

37. Cf. infra, pp. 23ff.

38. He was born in Fuenllana (Ciudad Real, La Mancha, Castille)
in 1912 and died in Madrid on Sunday, April 29, 1990.

39. J. de Salas, "Muere el filósofo Rodríguez Huéscar, discípulo de
Ortega," *ABC* (Madrid), May 2, 1990, p. 50.

40. J. Ortega y Gasset, "Ideas sobre Pío Baroja" (1916), v, *Obras
Completas,* II, p. 75.

41. Cf. Plato, *Republic,* 429a–430c.

42. Cf. infra, p. 153.

43. J. de Salas, "Muere el filósofo Rodríguez Huéscar, discípulo de
Ortega," p. 50. The posthumous edition of Prof. Rodríguez Huéscar's
book on *lógos* and *éthos* is being readied for publication. It is expected to
appear in Spain in 1995.

44. It might be of interest to the reader to know that this work was
awarded first prize at the National Professorial Competition which, on
the occasion of the twenty-fifth anniversary of Ortega's death, had been
sponsored by the Ministry of Education and Science of Spain. Ortega's
death occurred on October 18, 1955.

PROLOGUE

1. Translator's Note: Cf. A. Rodríguez Huéscar, *Perspectiva y verdad,* 2d ed. (Madrid: Alianza Editorial, 1985).

2. Translator's Note: Since composing this prologue, Marías has
already published this book. Cf. J. Marías, *Ortega: las trayectorias* in
Ortega (Madrid: Alianza Editorial, 1983), II.

3. Translator's Note: This prologue was composed in July 1982 in Washington, D.C.

INTRODUCTION

1. Translator's Note: Cf. J. Ortega y Gasset, "Nada moderno y muy siglo XX," *El Espectador,* i in *Obras Completas* (Madrid: Revista de Occidente/Alianza Editorial, 1983), II, pp. 22–24.

2. Cf. "Glosas" [*Obras Completas,* I, pp. 13ff.].

3. Translator's Note: *Ataraxia,* a term used by Democritus and later by the Greek Epicureans, Stoics, and Skeptics, signifies "tranquility or peace of mind." The word "halcyonism" is derived from "halcyon," the name for a mythical bird supposed to have a calming influence on the sea during the winter solstice, a time in which it hatched its young in a nest floating on the waters; hence one can understand the expression "halcyon days" as meaning "days of tranquility." Cf. Julián Marías, "A-taraxia y alcionismo," *El oficio del pensamiento* in *Obras Completas* (Madrid: Revista de Occidente, 1961), VI, pp. 423ff.

4. Translator's Note: "State of mind" or "mood." Cf. Martin Heidegger, *Sein und Zeit,* 10th ed. (Tübingen: Max Niemeyer, 1963), §§ 29, 30, 40, and 68b. Translation: *Being and Time,* trans. J. Macquarrie and E. Robinson (New York: Harper & Row, 1962), pp. 172ff., 179ff., 228ff., and 389ff.

5. Translator's Note: Cf. J. Ortega y Gasset, *Meditaciones del Quijote,* with a "Commentary" by Julián Marías (Madrid: Universidad de Puerto Rico/Revista de Occidente, 1957), pp. 43f.; "Commentary," pp. 266f. (Translation: *Meditations on Quixote,* trans. E. Rugg and D. Marín [New York: W. W. Norton & Co., 1961], pp. 45f.); A. Rodríguez Huéscar, *Perspectiva y verdad,* pp. 71–74.

6. Translator's Note: "Philosophies have their own fate."

7. Translator's Note: The Spanish verb *hacer* connotes two different ideas, which are expressed in English by means of two distinct locutions, namely, *do* and *make.* Ortega takes full advantage of this "ambiguity" of the language, which must always be dissolved in English. *Hacer* derives from the Latin *facere,* which means "to make," and yet it takes over the sense of "to do" as well, for the Latin verb *agere* (which has the meaning of "to do") has disappeared in Spanish, except for some of its derivative forms.

8. Translator's Note: "Fact" derives from the Latin *factum,* which is the neutral form of the perfect passive participle of *facere,* and it signifies "something which has been made"; *faciendum,* on the other hand, is

the neutral form of the future passive participle of the same verb, and it means "something to be made."

9.   Translator's Note: Cf. J. Ortega y Gasset, "Historia como sistema," *Obras Completas,* VI, pp. 35–36 (Translation: "History as a System" in *History as a System and Other Essays Toward a Philosophy of History,* trans. H. Weyl [New York: W. W. Norton & Co., 1941], pp. 205–7); *El hombre y la gente* in *Obras Completas,* VII, chaps. 1–4 (Translation: *Man and People,* trans. W. R. Trask [New York: W. W. Norton & Co., 1957], pp. 11–93); Edmund Husserl, *Logical Investigations,* i, §§ 26–27, trans. J. N. Findlay (New York: Humanities Press, 1970), I, pp. 313–20.

10.   Translator's Note: This formula means "What is being?"

11.   Translator's Note: "There-is," "there-are," and their interrogative correlates are here hyphenated on purpose, so as to indicate their sui generis employment. These are translations for *hay,* an impersonal form of the Spanish verb *haber* that is normally used to signify existence or availability, whether physical or ideal. Ortega takes up this everyday sense of the word and carries it to the limit, in order to refer to the absolutely first and totally uninterpreted datum accessible in experience. The hyphenation has the twofold advantage of canceling the connection with *being* (totally missing in *hay* but only too apparent in its usual English translation) and eliminating the possible reference to the traditional understanding of being as *essence,* which at this level of discourse finds no rightful place. Cf. J. Ortega y Gasset, *Unas lecciones de metafísica* in *Obras Completas,* XII, chap. 11. Translation: *Some Lessons in Metaphysics,* trans. M. Adams (New York: W. W. Norton & Co., 1969), pp. 124ff.

12.   Translator's Note: Cf. A. Rodríguez Huéscar, *Perspectiva y verdad,* ii, chap. 4, pp. 147–78.

13.   Cf. J. Ortega y Gasset, "Prólogo a la *Historia de la Filosofía* de Bréhier," *Obras Completas,* VI, pp. 390ff. Translation: "Prologue to a History of Philosophy" in *Concord and Liberty,* trans. H. Weyl (New York: W. W. Norton & Co., 1946), pp. 98ff.

14.   J. Ortega y Gasset, *El tema de nuestro tiempo* in *Obras Completas,* III, p. 201. Translation: *The Modern Theme,* trans. J. Cleugh (New York: Harper & Row, 1933), p. 92.

15.   J. Ortega y Gasset, "Prólogo a la *Historia de la Filosofía* de Bréhier," p. 389. Translation: p. 97.

16.   I may refer here to Manuel García Morente, Xavier Zubiri, José Gaos, Fernando Vela, Luis Recasens Siches, Julián Marías, Manuel Granell, María Zambrano, Manuel Mindán, José Antonio Maravall, Luis Díez del Corral, Paulino Garagorri, and myself. These are just a few, mostly in the field of philosophy, among those who kept in close contact with Ortega and have provided reports of this kind. I do not mention

many first-rank representatives of the arts and sciences who also established a close relationship with Ortega and have contributed valuable
accounts thereof, since any attempt on my part to choose among them
would be arbitrary.

17. (Madrid: Revista de Occidente, 1960). [In *Ortega*, 2d ed.
(Madrid: Alianza Editorial, 1983), I. Translation: *José Ortega y Gasset.
Circumstance and Vocation*, trans. F. M. López-Morillas (Norman: Uni-
versity of Oklahoma Press, 1970)].

18. Translator's Note: Cf. supra, pp. xxi and 158, n. 2.

PART I: A TEXTUAL EXPOSITION OF ORTEGA'S
CRITIQUE OF IDEALISM

1. Translator's Note: *Obras Completas* I, pp. 443ff.
2. Translator's Note: *El Espectador*, iv, *Obras Completas*, II,
pp. 387ff.
3. Translator's Note: *Obras Completas*, VI, pp. 247ff.
4. Translator's Note: *Obras Completas*, I, pp. 309ff.
5. Translator's Note: *El Espectador*, i, *Obras Completas*, II,
pp. 61ff.
6. Translator's Note: *Obras Completas*, IV, pp. 25ff.
7. Translator's Note: *Obras Completas*, VII, pp. 273ff.
8. Translator's Note: *Obras Completas*, V, pp. 461ff.
9. Translator's Note: *Obras Completas*, XII, pp. 11ff.
10. Translator's Note: *Obras Completas*, XII, pp. 143ff.
11. Translator's Note: *Obras Completas*, XII, pp. 487ff.
12. Translator's Note: Obras Completas, III, pp. 141ff.
13. Translator's Note: *Obras Completas*, III, pp. 270ff.
14. Translator's Note: *Obras Completas*, VI, pp. 11ff.
15. Translator's Note: *Obras Completas*, VIII, pp. 411ff.
16. Translator's Note: *Obras Completas*, VII, pp. 69ff.
17. Translator's Note: *Obras Completas*, VIII, pp. 11ff.
18. Translator's Note: *Obras Completas*, V, pp. 517ff.
19. Translator's Note: *Obras Completas*, VIII, pp. 59ff.
20. Translator's Note: *Obras Completas*, I, pp. 244ff.

1. A CONCEPTUAL INTRODUCTION TO ORTEGA'S CRITIQUE
OF IDEALISM

1. Cf. José Ferrater Mora, *Ortega y Gasset. Etapas de una filosofía*
(Barcelona: Seix-Barral, 1958). Translation: *Ortega y Gasset. An Outline
of His Philosophy* (New Haven: Yale University Press, 1957).

162 NOTES

2. Translator's Note: By reason of the author's unforeseen death, I have been unable to ascertain the study he had in mind.

3. Translator's Note: *Obras Completas,* I, pp. 473–93.

4. Ortega's thematic descriptions of human life reappear, in various contexts, throughout his entire work, down to its last phase. It would be a good idea to prepare a chronological and comparative study of such descriptions, in which one would seek to determine how they are related to the respective contexts in which they were formulated, but always keeping in view the evolution of Ortega's thought.

5. J. Ortega y Gasset, "Prólogo para alemanes," *Obras Completas,* VIII, p. 34. Translation: "Preface for Germans" in *Phenomenology and Art,* trans. Ph. W. Silver (New York: W. W. Norton, 1975), p. 43.

6. Ibid., p. 32. Translation: p. 41.

7. Ibid., p. 41. Translation: p. 53.

8. Ibid.

9. Ibid., pp. 41–42. Translation: ibid.

10. Ibid., p. 42. Translation: p. 54.

11. Ibid.

12. Ibid., p. 43. Translation: p. 55.

13. Ibid., p. 45. Translation: p. 57.

14. Ibid. Translation: p. 58.

15. Ibid., p. 47. Translation: p. 60.

16. Cf. ibid., pp. 47–54. Translation: pp. 61–70.

17. [It appeared in the] *Jahrbuch für Philosophie und phänomenologische Forschung.*

18. Translator's Note: *Obras Completas,* XII, pp. 487ff. Translation: "Sensation, Construction, and Intuition," *Phenomenology and Art,* pp. 79ff.

19. Cf. *Revista de libros,* June, July, and September, 1913. [Vide *Obras Completas,* I, pp. 244ff. Translation: "On the Concept of Sensation," *Phenomenology and Art,* pp. 127ff.] The original title of this work by one of Husserl's disciples is *Untersuchungen über den Empfindungsbegriff* [*Archiv für die gesamte Psychologie,* XXVI (1913), nos. 1–2.]

20. Julián Marías, *Ortega, I: Circunstancia y vocación,* p. 418. Translation: pp. 391–92.

21. "Ensayo de estética a manera de prólogo," *Obras Completas,* VI, p. 250. Translation: "An Essay in Esthetics by Way of a Preface," *Phenomenology and Art,* p. 131.

22. Ibid., p. 252. Translation: p. 134.

23. Ibid., p. 253. Translation: p. 135.

24. Ibid., p. 252. Translation: p. 134. The emphasis is mine.

25. Ibid., pp. 252–53. Translation: ibid.

26. Ibid., p. 252. Translation: p. 133.
27. Ibid., p. 253. Translation: p. 135.
28. Ibid., p. 254. Translation: p. 136.
29. Ibid.
30. In his *Meditaciones,* Ortega returns to this topic [and asserts]: "There is an aesthetical verum."
31. "Ensayo de estética a manera de prólogo," pp. 256 [and 255.] Translation: p. 138.
32. Translator's Note: [*Obras Completas,* II, p. 63. Translation: "Consciousness, the Object and Its Three Dimensions," *Phenomenology and Art,* p. 119.
33. "Las dos grandes metáforas," *Obras Completas,* II, p. 387.
34. Ibid.
35. Ibid., pp. 388ff.
36. Cf. ibid., pp. 391ff.
37. Cf. J. Marías, *Ortega, I: Circumstancia y vocación,* especially pp. 285–309. Translation: pp. 265–91.
38. Cf. "Las dos grandes metáforas," pp. 395–96.
39. Ibid., p. 396.
40. Ibid.
41. Ibid.
42. Ibid., p. 397.
43. Ibid.
44. Ibid., p. 398.
45. Ibid., p. 399. [Cf. René Descartes, *Méditations* ii in *Oeuvres de Descartes,* ed. Ch. Adam and P. Tannery; rev. ed. (Paris: J. Vrin, 1964), IX-1, p. 21.]
46. "Las dos grandes metáforas," p. 400.

2. ORTEGA'S STRAIGHTFORWARD CRITIQUE OF IDEALISM PROPERLY SO CALLED

1. Cf. *Obras Completas,* IV, pp. 25ff.
2. Ibid., p. 34.
3. Ibid., p. 39.
4. J. Ortega y Gasset, *¿Qué es filosofía?* in *Obras Completas,* VII, p. 359. Translation: *What is Philosophy?,* p. 135.
5. Translator's Note: By reason of the author's unforeseen death, I have been unable to ascertain which study he specifically had in mind.
6. Translator's Note: Cf. infra, Part II, chap. 4, §§ 4–5, pp. 88ff.
7. Cf. *¿Qué es filosofía?,* p. 362. Translation: p. 139.

8. Cf. ibid., pp. 363–64. Translation: pp. 140–141. [Cf. René Descartes, *Meditationes de prima philosophia* in *Oeuvres de Descartes*, ed. Ch. Adams and P. Tannery, rev. ed., VII, i, pp. 19–20, and vi, p. 89.]

9. *¿Qué es filosofía?*, p. 367. [Emphasis added.] Translation: pp. 146–47.

10. Ibid., p. 370. Translation: p. 151.

11. Ibid.

12. Ibid., p. 371. Translation: ibid.

13. Cf. ibid., pp. 373–74. Translation: pp. 155–56.

14. Cf. ibid., pp. 382ff. Translation: pp. 168ff.

15. Ibid., p. 392. Translation: p. 183.

16. [It is worth noting] that the formulae I have just used are probably the most significant means available to express the notion of the "theme of our times."

17. *¿Qué es filosofía?*, pp. 285–86. Translation: p. 28.

18. Ibid.

19. Ibid., p. 394. Translation: p. 185.

20. Later I shall consider the sense in which one can apply the notion of "performative being" to thinking. [Cf., e.g., infra, pp. 37ff and 90ff.]

21. *¿Qué es filosofía?*, p. 395. Translation: p. 187.

22. Cf. ibid., pp. 395–99. Translation: pp. 188–94.

23. Cf. ibid., pp. 400–406. Translation: pp. 195–204.

24. *¿Qué es filosofía?*, p. 395. Translation: p. 187.

25. Ibid., p. 396. Translation: p. 189.

26. Cf. ibid., p. 399. Translation: p. 193.

27. Ibid. Translation: p. 194.

28. This expression was used especially during the nineteenth century, although its sense ultimately derives from Descartes, even if he in fact never employed the term.

29. *¿Qué es filosofía?*, p. 400. Translation: p. 195.

30. Ibid. Translation: p. 196. In what follows, the essentials of Ortega's critique of idealism will be presented. I mean the most distinctive and original contributions he made towards the critical evaluation of idealism. It was by means of such findings that he rendered available the new manner of reality he was after, namely, the novel modality of being which is characteristic of human life.

31. Ibid., p. 402. Translation: p. 198.

32. Translator's Note: Cf. Martin Heidegger, *Being and Time,* §§ 12, 23, 24–38, and 69.

33. *¿Qué es filosofía?*, p. 403. Translation: p. 199.

34. Ibid. Translation: p. 200.

35. Translator's Note: Cf. J. Ortega y Gasset, *Meditaciones del Quijote*, p. 43 ("Commentary," pp. 266–68).

36.   *¿Qué es filosofía?*, p. 403. Translation: p. 200.
37.   Ibid., pp. 403–4. Translation: p. 201.
38.   Ibid., p. 404. Translation: pp. 201–2.
39.   Ibid., p. 405. Translation: p. 202.
40.   Ibid. Translation: pp. 203–4.
41.   Ibid., pp. 405–6. Translation: p. 204.
42.   Cf. J. Ortega y Gasset, *Unas lecciones de metafísica* in *Obras Completas*, XII, pp. 11ff.
43.   Cf. ibid., p. 103. Translation: p. 125.
44.   Cf. ibid., p. 104. Translation: p. 127.
45.   Cf. ibid., p. 105. Translation: p. 128.
46.   Ibid., p. 106. Translation: p. 130.
47.   Ibid., p. 107. Translation: ibid.
48.   Cf. ibid. Translation: p. 131.
49.   Cf. ibid., p. 112. Translation: p. 138.
50.   Ibid., p. 116. Translation: p. 142.
51.   Cf. ibid., pp. 117–18. Translation: p. 144.
52.   Ibid., p. 118. Translation: pp. 144–45.
53.   Ibid. Translation: pp. 145–46. The emphasis is mine.
54.   Ibid., pp. 118–19. Translation: p. 146. The emphasis is mine.
55.   Ibid., p. 119. Translation: ibid.
56.   Ibid.
57.   Ibid. Translation: p. 147. The emphasis is mine.
58.   Translator's Note: Cf. infra, chap. 3, pp. 51ff.
59.   Unfortunately, I cannot at present dwell any longer on the examination of this issue, to which I shall have to return in other contexts. In fact, I will deal with it in terms of the passage by Ortega that will occupy us next.
60.   Elsewhere I have endeavored to show how the principle at the basis of idealism includes what may serve as a point of departure to overcome it. [Cf. supra, n. 5.]
61.   *Unas lecciones de metafísica*, p. 125. Translation: p. 154.
62.   Ibid.
63.   Ibid., pp. 127–28. Translation: p. 158.
64.   Cf. J. Ortega y Gasset, *Sobre la razón histórica* in *Obras Completas*, XII, pp. 143ff. Translation: *Historical Reason*, trans. Ph. W. Silver.
65.   Ibid., p. 176. Translation: p. 47.
66.   Ibid., p. 177. Translation: ibid.
67.   Ibid. Translation: p. 48.
68.   Ibid. Translation: ibid. [The author has emphasized "but" and "hypothesis" in Ortega's text.]
69.   Ibid., p. 178. Translation: ibid.
70.   Ibid., pp. 183–84. Translation: p. 55.

71.   Ibid., p. 178. Translation: p. 49.
72.   Ibid., p. 179. Translation: p. 50.
73.   Ibid., p. 185. Translation: p. 57.
74.   Ibid., pp. 180–81. Translation: pp. 51–52.
75.   Translator's Note: Cf. "El curso de don José Ortega y Gasset" in Institucíon Cultural Española, *Anales* (Buenos Aires, 1947), I (1919–20), chap. 5, pp. 149ff.
76.   *Sobre la razón histórica,* p. 186. Translation: p. 57.
77.   Ibid., pp. 186–87. Translation: p. 58.
78.   Ibid., p. 187. Translation: p. 59.
79.   Ibid. Translation: pp. 59–60.
80.   Translator's Note: Cf. supra, pp. 20ff.
81.   As a matter of fact, for some time now I have been at work trying to interpret Ortega's notion of performative being by formally substituting the concept of "in-stancy" for that of "sub-stance". Consistent with this, I would describe the world or "things" as that which is converging on me in an active fashion, in-stantly or by way of in-stancies, i.e., by their urging their special point on me. Were it not so extravagant a manner of expression, I would recommend saying that things constitute not so much my "circum-stance," as they do my "circum-in-stance," insofar as they are not just standing-there [*estar*] in my environ-ment, but are in fact engaged in acting on me in the way of in-stancies pressing their point on me. I will return to this issue later, when I find an opportunity to speak of these matters more extensively. [Cf. infra, Part II, chap. 4, § 5B, pp. 104ff.]
82.   *Sobre la razón histórica,* p. 191. Translation: pp. 62–63.
83.   Ibid., p. 193. Translation: p. 67.

3. ORTEGA'S CRITIQUE OF PHENOMENOLOGICAL PHILOSOPHY AS THE MOST RECENT HISTORICAL FORM OF IDEALISM

1.   Translator's Note: Cf. supra, pp. 9–10.
2.   Translator's Note: Cf. supra, p. 11.
3.   Translator's Note: Vide Edmund Husserl, *Ideen zu einer reinen Phänomenologie und phänomenologischen Philosophie. Erstes Buch: Allgemeine Einführung in die reine Phänomenologie,* ed. K. Schumann, 3d ed. (The Hague: Martinus Nijhoff, 1976) in *Husserliana,* III, 1–2. I will be using the English version by F. Kersten throughout this chapter: cf. *Ideas Pertaining to a Pure Phenomenology and to a Phenomenological Philosophy. First Book: General Introduction to a Pure Phenomenology*

(The Hague: Martinus Nijhoff, 1982). Henceforth I shall be referring to this translation as Ideas, I.

4.   [Depending on the edition] it is between ten and twelve pages long.

5.   Translator's Note: Cf. supra, pp. 11f.

6.   J. Ortega y Gasset, "Sobre el concepto de sensación," p. 255. Translation: p. 109.

7.   Ibid., pp. 255–56. Translation: pp. 109–110.

8.   Cf. ibid., p. 251, n. Translation: p. 110, n. 7. [Ortega was confronted with a family of words connected by the basic bond of *leben*. Some of those words are: *das Leben* (life), *leben* (to be living or alive; to dwell), *erleben* (to experience, live, or know from experience), and *das Erlebnis* (a personal experience). On that basis, he had to construct an expression that would be analogous to *Erlebnis*, i.e., to a noun derived from *erleben*. Taking advantage of the fact that the Spanish verb *vivir* corresponds both to *erleben* and *leben*, he fashioned a verbal noun in keeping with a preexisting Spanish pattern, namely, that used in going, say, from *existir* to *existencia*. Hence, he obtained *vivencia* (for *Erlebnis*) from *vivir*.]

9.   J. Ortega y Gasset, "Prólogo para alemanes," p. 47. Translation: p. 61.

10.   Ibid., p. 50. Translation: p. 65.

11.   Ibid., pp. 47–48. Translation: p. 61.

12.   I have in mind the four chapters of Part ii of *Ideas*, I, where the essentials of such doctrines are contained.

13.   E. Husserl, *Ideas*, I, § 30, p. 57.

14.   Ibid., § 31, p. 57.

15.   Ibid.

16.   Ibid., p. 58.

17.   Ibid.

18.   Ibid.

19.   Ibid.

20.   Ibid.

21.   Ibid.

22.   Ibid.

23.   Ibid.

24.   Translator's Note: Cf. infra, pp. 67ff.

25.   E. Husserl, *Ideas*, I, § 31, p. 60.

26.   Ibid., pp. 58–59. [Beginning with this passage and continuing through the one corresponding to n. 30 below,] I have added [or removed] emphasis [as indicated], in order to make it more apparent where Husserl's thinking is undecided or indefinite.

27.   Ibid., p. 59.

28. Ibid.
29. Ibid.
30. Ibid., pp. 59–60.
31. For the expressions just employed, cf. José Gaos, *Introducción a la fenomenología* (Xalapa, Mexico: Universidad Veracruzana, 1960), *passim*.
32. Translator's Note: Cf. E. Husserl, *Ideas*, I, § 53.
33. Translator's Note: Ibid., § 57, p. 133.
34. Translator's Note: Cf. ibid., §§ 37 and 56.
35. Translator's Note: Cf. ibid., § 58.
36. Ibid., § 60, p. 137.
37. Translator's Note: Cf. E. Husserl, *Logical Investigations*, v, § 20, trans. J. N. Findlay, II, p. 586ff.; *Ideas*, I, § 85.
38. Xavier Zubiri, *Cinco lecciones de filosofía* (Madrid: Sociedad de Estudios y Publicaciones, 1963), p. 225.
39. Translator's Note: Cf. infra, pp. 65ff.
40. J. Ortega y Gasset, "Sobre el concepto de sensación," pp. 252-53. Translation: p. 106.
41. J. Ortega y Gasset, *La idea de principio en Leibniz y la evolución de la teoría deductiva*, p. 273, n. 2. Translation: p. 280, n. 3.
42. Ibid., p. 275, n. Translation: p. 281. [Cf. "El curso de don José Ortega y Gasset," pp. 149ff.]
43. J. Ortega y Gasset, "Prólogo para alemanes," p. 48. Translation: pp. 62–63. [Cf. supra, pp. 23–24.]
44. Translator's Note: Cf. J. Ortega y Gasset, "Ideas y creencias," *Obras Completas,* V, pp. 377ff.
45. J. Ortega y Gasset, "Prólogo para alemanes," pp. 48–49. Translation: p. 63.
46. Translator's Note: Here we come across an untranslatable duality of meaning associated with the verb *haber,* on which Ortega plays in order to make an essential point concerning the indivisibility of two correlative aspects of human life, namely, the primordial manner of givenness proper to things (*haber* in the sense of *hay,* i.e., "there-is" or "is-available") and the fundamental significance things have for me (*habérmelas*)—they are that which I have to face by coping or dealing with them, not here or there, or even for the most part, but always, in order simply to live and thus survive, in a biographical (or meaning-based) and, possibly, in a biological sense as well.
47. Translator's Note: Cf. "Prólogo para alemanes," p. 47 (Translation: p. 60); *¿Qué es filosofía?*, p. 414. (Translation: p. 216.)
48. J. Ortega y Gasset, "Prólogo para alemanes," p. 49. Translation: pp. 63–64.
49. Ibid. Translation: p. 64.

50. Ibid. [Cf. E. Husserl, *Ideas*, I, § 46, p. 102.]

51. J. Ortega y Gasset, "Prólogo para alemanes," pp. 49–50. Translation: p. 64.

52. Ibid., p. 50. Translation: p. 65.

53. J. Ortega y Gasset, *Sobre la razón histórica,* p. 181. Translation: p. 52.

54. Translator's Note: "Sobre el concepto de sensación."

55. Translator's Note: Cf. supra, p. 59.

56. I would formulate it in this way, if you only pardon the sheer repetitiousness or redundancy of the expression, for there is in fact no "act" devoid of "actuality."

57. Translator's Note: Cf. supra, p. 64.

58. J. Ortega y Gasset, "Prólogo para alemanes," p. 51. Translation: p. 66.

59. Cf. J. Ortega y Gasset, *La idea de principio en Leibniz y la evolución de la tearia deductiva,* pp. 274–75, n. Translation: p. 280.

60. Ibid., p. 275, n. Translation: p. 281.

61. J. Ortega y Gasset, "Prólogo para alemanes," pp. 52–53. Translation: p. 68.

62. Ibid., p. 53. Translation: p. 69.

63. Ibid., pp. 53–54. Translation: p. 70.

64. Translator's Note: Cf. J. Ortega y Gasset, "Anejo a 'Apuntes sobre el pensamiento. Su teurgia y su demiurgia'," pp. 544ff. (Translation: pp. 80ff.); E. Husserl, *Formal and Transcendental Logic,* trans. D. Cairns (The Hague: Martinus Nijhoff, 1969), p. 5.

65. J. Ortega y Gasset, "Anejo a 'Apuntes sobre el pensamiento. Su teurgia y su demiurgia,'" p. 545. Translation: p. 81. [Cf. supra, n. 8.]

66. [Ibid., pp. 546f., n.; Translation: p. 82]. In fact, what appeared in this journal were the first two parts of what later became volume VI of *Husserliana,* which bears the same title as the above-mentioned lecture, namely, *Die Krisis der europäischen Wissenschaften und die transzendentale Phänomenologie* (1954) [ed. W. Biemel, 2d ed. (The Hague: Martinus Nijhoff, 1962), in *Husserliana,* VI. Translation: *The Crisis of European Sciences and Transcendental Phenomenology,* trans. D. Carr (Evanston: Northwestern University Press, 1970)].

67. J. Ortega y Gasset, "Anejo a 'Apuntes sobre el pensamiento. Su teurgia y su demiurgia,'" p. 547. Translation: p. 82, n.

68. Ibid. [Cf. "Historia como sistema," pp. 11ff. Translation: pp. 163ff.

69. Vide E. Husserl, *Formal and Transcendental Logic.* [Cf. supra, n. 64.]

70. Vide E. Husserl, *Die Krisis der Europäischen Wissenschaften.* [Cf. supra, n. 66].

71. Jean-François Lyotard, *La phénoménologie*, 4th ed. (Paris: Presses Universitaires de France, 1961), p. 36. Naturally, this author was there referring to Husserl's philosophy, which at that point he was examining in a special section devoted to the notion of the "lifeworld."

PART II: ORTEGA'S OVERCOMING OF IDEALISM. TOWARD THE SYSTEM OF LIFE CATEGORIES

1. Translator's Note: Cf. Aristotle, *Categories,* chaps. 3 and 5; *Metaphysics,* 1003 a 28f., 1024 b 10f.; I. Kant, *Critique of Pure Reason,* A 241 / B 300.
2. J. Ortega y Gasset, *¿Qué es filosofía?,* p. 325. Translation: p. 86.
3. Ibid., p. 394. Translation: pp. 185–86.
4. Ibid., p. 408. Translation: p. 206.
5. Ibid., p. 410. Translation: p. 210.
6. Ibid., p. 411. Translation: p. 211.
7. Ibid. (Translation: pp. 211–12.) Here I have made a somewhat extensive use of citations, because there are still some who assert that Ortega was engaged in developing an ontological system and failed.
8. Ibid., pp. 427–28. Translation: pp. 235–36. [Cf. Aristotle, *Metaphysics,* iv, 1003 a.]
9. Translator's Note: Cf. E. Husserl, *Logical Investigations,* i, chap. 3, § 26, pp. 314ff.
10. Translator's Note: Cf. infra, pp. 95ff.
11. J. Ortega y Gasset, *¿Qué es filosofía?,* p. 430. Translation: p. 240.
12. Translator's Note: Cf. supra, p. 78 and n. 8. Emphasis has been added here by Prof. Rodríguez Huéscar.
13. Translator's Note: Cf. supra, n. 10.

4. THE CATEGORIES OF LIFE

1. Translator's Note: Cf. infra, n. 6.
2. Translator's Note: Cf. supra, pp. 62ff.
3. Translator's Note: Cf. supra, pp. 63 and 168, n. 47.
4. Translator's Note: Cf. infra, pp. 104ff.
5. Let me emphasize the fact that expressions like these are only approximately equivalent to Heidegger's notion of "thrownness" or "dereliction" (*Geworfenheit*). [Cf. M. Heidegger, *Being and Time,* p. 174 and § 38.] This is also true of Ortega's concept of "encounter" when one

compares it with Heidegger's idea of "state of mind" or *Befindlichkeit* (and even with his conception of *Grundbefindlichkeit*). [Cf. M. Heidegger, ibid., §§ 29–31, 40, and 68b.] The concepts belonging in Heidegger's philosophy (or, for that matter, in other "existential" doctrines) never coincide with Ortega's own, among other reasons because, ultimately, the fundamental notions constituting their respective points of departure (namely, the concepts of existence and life respectively) are not qualitatively the same and appertain to different metaphysical levels, for, to begin with, the various forms of "existential" philosophy have not been able to go beyond "ontology." Let this general point serve as a cautionary remark to be borne in mind in the following analyses, for undoubtedly we will later come across other conceptual "similarities." [I have been unable to locate the source of the sentence of Ortega's that was quoted by the author in the text.]

6. Translator's Note: Used abstractly, these terms may mislead us and serve as occasions for mistranslation. "*Encontrarme*" is normally employed in phrases like "*encontrarme con*" or "*encontrarme en*," "*percatarme*" in "*percatarme de*," and "*darme cuenta*" in "*darme cuenta de*." The prepositions *con* (with), *en* (in), and *de* (of) refer immediately to the "object" of the "cognitive" action. Hence, the usual translations are "I encounter or come across something" or "I find myself in this or that situation," "I realize something," and "I become aware of something," respectively. However correct these translations may be, they would nonetheless obscure the essential reference to myself the reflexive pronoun *me* designates. Taken in the strong philosophical sense, which is seriously meant here by the author if I have not misunderstood him, the self-reference of the "cognitive" action does not however signify that I would be intently engaged in knowing myself, as it would be the case if the grammatical structure did express a factor overriding everything else. On the contrary, what it means is simply that, in coming across something, or in realizing or becoming aware of something, I would be undergoing an experience containing an implicit component of self-"knowledge" or, more exactly, that in such an experience there would be a spontaneous and reciprocal givenness of self-"knowledge" and "knowledge" of "things", though, to be sure, my "cognitive" action would be focused on the latter only. Cf. supra, § 2: "Encounter," p. 87. "In effect, to live is to *encounter* or come upon *myself living*. But to say this means that I always and inevitably 'encounter' or come upon 'myself' *in connection with* one or another thing."

7. J. Ortega y Gasset, *¿Qué es filosofía?*, p. 414. Translation: p. 216.

8. Ibid.

9. Ibid., p. 415. Translation: p. 217.

10. Ibid., p. 424. Translation: p. 231.
11. Ibid., p. 425. Translation: p. 232.
12. Ibid. p. 428. Translation: p. 236.
13. Ibid., p. 415. Translation: p. 217.
14. Translator's Note: J. Ortega y Gasset, "Meditación prelimi-nar," *Meditaciones del Quijote,* ed. with a commentary by J. Marías, §§ 1–4, pp. 69ff. ("Commentary," pp. 285ff.)
15. Translator's Note: J. Ortega y Gasset, *El hombre y la gente,* chap. 3ff. Translation: pp. 57ff.
16. Translator's Note: Cf. infra, pp. 106–107 and 133f.
17. Translator's Note: Cf. infra, p. 123.
18. Translator's Note: For Aristotle's definition of motion, cf. his *Physics* iii, 1, 201 a 10 and 27–29.
19. Translator's Note: Cf. J. Ortega y Gasset, "Prólogo a *Historia de la Filosofía,* de Emile Bréhier," pp. 409ff. Translation: pp. 118ff.
20. Translator's Note: Cf. infra, § 6, pp. 119ff.
21. Translator's Note: Cf. infra, pp. 104ff.
22. Below I shall be dealing with the ultimate definite sense of "appearing." [Cf. infra, pp. 93ff.]
23. Translator's Note: Cf. supra, n. 6.
24. Translator's Note: Cf. infra, pp. 94 and 95ff.
25. Translator's Note: By means of the interplay between the meanings of "transparent" or "transparency," the author is able to make a subtle but important point. The usual meaning of "transparent" is "capable of being seen through," but its literal or etymological sense is that of "appearing through." One may therefore say that life's transpar-ency allows "things" to be "seen" or to "make an appearance" in its midst (life is thus "transparent" in conformity with the usual meaning of the term), because it consists, to begin with, in "appearing through" things as the medium and agency of their appearing (in view of the literal connotation of the word).
26. Translator's Note: Cf. supra, p. 88 and n. 9.
27. Translator's Note: Cf. *Acts of the Apostles,* 17, v. 28 in *The Holy Bible,* King James version, 1611 (New York: American Bible Soci-ety, 1985), Part II, p. 142.
28. Translator's Note: Cf. infra, pp. 104ff.
29. Translator's Note: Cf. supra, pp. 80f.
30. Translator's Note: Cf. Nicholas of Cusa, *De docta ignorantia,* ii, 3 in *Philosophisch-theologische Schriften,* Studien- und Jubi-läumsausgabe (Latin-German), ed. L. Gabriel, trans. W. Dupré (Vienna: Herder, 1982), I, p. 330.
31. It goes without saying that I have in mind realities insofar as they give-themselves or are "rooted" in my life, the acknowledgment of

‡hich fact leaves the matter of the actual existence of other realities unde-cided. [For the appropriate sources, cf. supra, nn. 14 and 15.]

32. Translator's Note: Cf. infra, pp. 104ff.

33. Let us remember, for example, what Hegel had to say in this connection. [Cf. G. W. F. Hegel, *Wissenschaft der Logik* (Leipzig: Felix Meiner Verlag, 1948), I, i, 1, A.]

34. Translator's Note: Dante Alighieri, *The Divine Comedy,* "In-ferno-1," i, v. 5, trans. and commentary by Charles S. Singleton (Prince-ton, N.J.: Princeton University Press/Bollingen Series, 1970), p. 2. Cf., e.g., J. Ortega y Gasset, "Misión de la universidad", *Obras Completas,* IV, p. 321.

35. Translator's Note: Cf. supra, p. 89 and nn. 14 and 15.

36. Translator's Note: Cf. supra, n. 14; vide A. Rodríguez Huéscar, *Perspectiva y verdad,* Part II.

37. Translator's Note: Cf. J. Ortega y Gasset, "Historia como sistema," viii, pp. 40–41. Translation: pp. 215–16: "We invent for our-selves a program of life, a static form of being, that serves to give a satisfactory answer to the difficulties posed for us by our circum-stance. We essay this form of life, attempt to realize this imaginary character we have resolved to be. . . . But meanwhile the experience has made appar-ent the shortcomings and limitations of the said program of life. . . . With the back view its inadequacy is straightway revealed. We think out anoth-er program of life. But this second program is drawn up in the light, not only of our circum-stance, but also of the first program. We aim at avoiding in the new project the drawbacks of the first. In the second, therefore, the first is still active; it is preserved in order to be avoided. Inexorably we shrink from being what we were. On the second project of being, the second thorough experiment, there follows a third in the light of the second and the first, and so on. We 'go on being' and 'unbeing'— i.e,. living. We go on accumulating being—the past; we go on making for ourselves a being through this dialectical series of experiments. This is a dielectic not of logical but precisely of historical reason—the *Realdialek-tik* dreamt of somewhere in his papers by Dilthey. . . ."

38. Translator's Note: Here, as elsewhere, the author is availing himself of a distinctive linguistic phenomenon for strictly philosophical purposes. Generally speaking, the verbs *ser* and *estar* are translated into English by means of "to be," but this practice obscures a most important differentiation that is peculiar to Spanish at various speech levels. Sim-plifying matters a great deal, I would say that *estar* signifies a transitory attribution or state of affairs, or is employed to refer to a spatial or temporal determination of something, while *ser* is, by contrast, used to designate some feature proper to a thing or some manner of abiding predication about it. In what follows, I shall endeavor, whenever possible,

to keep the reader alive to this differentiation—of which the author tries
to make the most—by translating *ser* and *estar* as "to be" and "to stand"
(and their derivative forms), respectively. It goes without saying that I am
not limiting the sense of "stand" to "being located in space" or to "being
placed in an upright position." Rather, I shall use the word here to mean
the act of occupying a position and holding it for the time being, if
"position" is not limited to its physical connotation. I am thus generally
underscoring the connection between determination and temporality,
which may still be operative in related words like "stable," "state," "station," and the like. This nexus is all-important to the author, especially as
an outcome of doing and projecting.

39.   Cf. José Ferrater Mora, *El ser y el sentido,* chap. 4, § 3 [(Madrid: Revista de Occidente, 1967), p. 111].

40.   Translator's Note: Cf. Kurt Koffka, *Principles of Gestalt Psychology* (New York: Harcourt, 1935), pp. 84ff.; "Perception: An Introduction to the Gestalt Theory," *The Psychological Bulletin,* XIX (1922),
pp. 537ff.; "Probleme der experimentellen Psychologie," *Die Naturwissenschaften,* V (1917), pp. 2ff. and 25ff.; Wolfgang Koehler, "Über
unbemerkte Empfindungen und Urteilstäuschungen," *Zeitschrift für Psychologie,* LXVI (1913); Jean-Paul Sartre, *L'être et le néant* (Paris: Gallimard, 1943), pp. 26ff., 235ff., and 372ff.; Maurice Merleau-Ponty, *Phénoménologie de la perception* (Paris: Gallimard, 1945), pp. 10, 23ff.,
265ff., 302, 306, 361ff., 373ff., and 464; Aron Gurwitsch, *The Field of
Consciousness* (Pittsburgh: Duquesne University Press, 1964), Part II,
§§ 1–2 and pp. 91 and 123ff.

41.   Translator's Note: Cf. A. Gurwitsch, ibid., Part II.

42.   Translator's Note: Cf. A. Rodríguez Huéscar, *Perspectiva y
verdad,* Part II, i, 1.

43.   The term "present," as used in this context, is taken very
narrowly in a sense that could be defined in terms of three determinations, to which I could give expression as follows: that which is "present"
is a. immediately perceptible or "available to the senses"; b. within this
area, it is particularly the zone on which our attention is focused, a fact
which endows it with "objective" unity (this is usually what specifies
perception in every case as, for example, in the "perception of the table");
and c. it has a "temporal" component, namely, "perceptual time" or, as
some psychologists prefer to say, the "time of being present in the mind."
These three determinations are "moments" of "presence" (taking "moment" in Husserl's sense of the word) and, as such, they are in fact
inseparable from one another. [Cf. E. Husserl, *Logical Investigations,*
Vol. I, ii, § 36, pp. 408–10; Vol. II, iii, § 1, p. 436; § 4, p. 440; § 10,
p. 453; § 17, pp. 467–68; § 19, p. 471.] In other words, they are "struc-

tural moments" of it. But, as we already know and will later proceed to clarify, "presence," as an absolute fact of human life, is a dimension the complexity of which cannot be adequately conveyed by this narrow and most simplified notion. [Cf. infra, § 5 B, pp. 104ff.]

44.   Translator's Note: Here the author goes back to the primordial level of our living encounters with "objects," a level that is given expression in the etymological meaning of *objectum,* namely, "that which is thrown in the way" and may "become an obstacle." This is why he establishes a unity of reciprocity between "pro-jective actions" and "circum-stantial *ob-jections,*" a unity disclosive of the uniqueness and oneness of the act of living. Cf. J. Marías, *Ortega. I: Circunstancia y vocación,* iii, chap. iv, § 71, pp. 408ff.

45.   Translator's Note: Cf. supra, pp. 62ff. and 65ff.

46.   Translator's Note: Cf. J. Ortega y Gasset, "Ideas y creencias," pp. 377ff.

47.   Translator's Note: Cf. Alfred Fouillée, *L'évolutionisme des idées-forces,* iii and xii (Paris: 1890); *La morale des idées-forces,* I, chap. 1 (Paris: 1908): *Psychologie des idées-forces* (Paris: 1893), 2 v.

48.   Translator's Note: Cf. supra, pp. 12f; vide pp. 51ff.

49.   Translator's Note: Cf. supra, § 4, pp. 88ff.

50.   Translator's Note: In what follows, the author avails himself of words like *instancia* (instancy), *instante* (instant), *lo instante* (that which is in-stantaneous), and *instar* (to urge, i.e., to "instance" or to exercise an "instancing") in order to make a number of essential points concerning the meaning and experience of life as primordial presence. All of these expressions constitute a "family," that is to say, they are unified with reference to a common etymological origin connected with the Latin verb *stare.* (Cf. supra, n. 38.) The author, deliberately and constantly, keeps this original sense in mind.

51.   Translator's Note: Cf. infra, § 10, pp. 139ff.

52.   Let us bear in mind the meaning of *circum-*, namely, "around" ["about" or "surrounding"], and that of *-stantia,* from *stare,* i.e., to "stand."

53.   Translator's Note: The word is used here in its etymological sense, i.e., as signifying "an offering of a sacrifice, thanksgiving, etc."

54.   By "negative offering" I mean such events as the "self-withdrawal" of something or the "hindering action" it may bring into effect.

55.   Translator's Note: Cf. J. Ortega y Gasset, *El hombre y la gente,* chaps. 3–4. *Prâgma* and its plural *prágmata* are Greek words meaning "something to be done," and even "something fit and right to be done."

56.   Translator's Note: Vide J. Ortega y Gasset, *En torno a Galileo* in *Obras Completas,* V, p. 23; cf. p. 72. Translation: *Man and Crisis,* trans. M. Adams (New York: W. W. Norton & Co., 1958), pp. 23 and 89.

57.   Translator's Note: Cf. J. Ortega y Gasset, "Historia como sistema," p. 41. Translation: p. 216.

58.   Translator's Note: Again, this term is here used etymologically, for "present" derives from *prae-* (before) and *esse* (to be). Accordingly, it is that which—paradoxically—is prior to being.

59.   Translator's Note: Cf. J. Ortega y Gasset, "Historia como sistema," viii.

60.   Translator's Note: Cf. Gabriel Marcel, *Homo viator. Prolégomènes à une métaphysique de l'espérance* (Paris: Aubier-Montaigne, 1944).

61.   Translator's Note: *John* 19:30 in *The Holy Bible,* King James version, Part II, p. 118.

62.   Translator's Note: Cf. Max Scheler, "Repentance and Rebirth," *On the Eternal in Man,* trans. B. Noble (New York: Harper and Brothers, 1960), pp. 33ff.

63.   Translator's Note: Cf. infra, § 6, pp. 119ff.

64.   Translator's Note: Cf. M. Heidegger, *Being and Time,* § 52.

65.   Translator's Note: Or the actual and abiding possession of being.

66.   Translator's Note: Cf. supra, p. 107.

67.   Translator's Note: Cf. J.-P. Sartre, *L'existentialisme est un humanisme* (Paris: Les Éditions Nagel, 1970), p. 17; vide M. Heidegger, *Being and time,* § 9.

68.   Translator's Note: The Greek *parón* is the neuter form of the present participle of *pareinai,* which means "to be present."

69.   Translator's Note: Vide e.g. J. Ortega y Gasset, "Historia como sistema," p. 13 (cf. pp. 32ff); *El hombre y la gente,* p. 104).

70.   Translator's Note: Cf. infra, pp. 113–14.

71.   As used in this locution, the prefix "in" has a negative connotation, as in "in-sensate," "in-decent," "in-temporal," and so on. [The etymological signification of the word "instant" does not however coincide with the author's meaning of the term, though, to be sure, he is perfectly entitled to deviate from the usual, since the expression is here employed in a technical sense. The etymological signification of "instant" is "that which stands in or upon" and thereby "presses" on something. The prefix "in," as a component of "instant," thus has a spatial and "causative" import. This notwithstanding, the etymology of the word is not inconsistent with the sense assigned to it by the author, which may very well be a meaning deriving from or grounded in it.]

72.   Translator's Note: Cf. Aristotle's notion of *tò tí ên eînai* in his *Metaphysics,* I, chap. 10, 993 a 18; II, chap. 2, 994 b 18, etc., Greek/English ed., trans. H. Tredennick (Cambridge, Massachusetts: Harvard University Press/The Loeb Classical Library, 1961), I, pp. 80, 92, etc. Vide Joseph Owens, *The Doctrine of Being in the Aristotelian "Metaphysics,"* 2d ed. rev. (Toronto: Pontifical Institute of Medieval Studies, 1963), pp. 180ff.

73.   Translator's Note: Cf. M. Heidegger, *Being and Time,* §§ 29–30, 40, and 68 b.

74.   Translator's Note: Cf. supra, § 2, p. 87.

75.   Translator's Note: Cf. A. Rodríguez Huéscar, "El temple como acceso a la realidad," *Homenaje a Julián Marías,* ed. F. Chueca Goitía et al. (Madrid: Espasa-Calpe, 1984), pp. 609–28.

76.   The manifold senses of the word "pretension" are here at play.

77.   Translator's Note: Cf. (possibly) infra, pp. 114ff., 130f., 132ff., and 135ff.

78.   Translator's Note: Cf., e.g., J. Ortega y Gasset, "Sobre la leyenda de Goya," § 3, *Goya* in *Obras Completas* (Madrid: Revista de Occidente/Alianza Editorial, 1983), VII, pp. 548ff.

79.   Translator's Note: Cf. infra, § 10, pp. 139ff.

80.   Translator's Note: Cf. supra, p. 113.

81.   Let me reiterate now a point I have made before, for it is no doubt worth repeating time and again. The demands placed upon me by the analysis obligate me—in this context as well as elsewhere in this presentation or, for that matter, in any other—to examine certain things as if they existed "separately," although in fact they not only are unified with each other, but are also given as identified with one another. This caveat would presently apply to logical "resolution" and ethical "resolve," as it did before in the case of "instancy" and "presence" (among others). [A book by Prof. Rodríguez Huéscar on the question of the relation between *éthos* and *lógos* is expected to be published in 1995.]

82.   Translator's Note: Cf. J. Ortega y Gasset, "Ideas y creencias," pp. 383ff.; *El hombre y la gente,* chap. 12; "Un capítulo sobre la cuestión de cómo muere una creencia," *Obras Completas,* IX, pp. 707ff.

83.   Translator's Note: Cf. supra, pp. 104f.

84.   Translator's Note: Cf. supra, p. 106.

85.   Translator's Note: Cf. infra, pp. 122ff.

86.   Translator's Note: Cf. supra, p. 106.

87.   Translator's Note: Cf. G. W. Leibniz, "Système nouveau de la nature et de la communication des substances, aussi bien que de l'union qu'il y a entre l'âme et le corps," 3 in *Die philosophischen Schriften von G. W. Leibniz,* ed. C. I. Gerhardt (Berlin: 1849–63; Hildesheim: Georg Olms, 1960–61), IV, pp. 478–79.

88. Cf. Baruch Spinoza, "Epistola 50," *Spinoza Opera,* ed. C. Gebhardt (Heidelberg: 1925), IV, p. 240, ll. 13–14.

89. Translator's Note: Cf. supra, p. 101.

90. Translator's Note: Cf. supra, p. 106.

91. Translator's Note: Cf. Nicolai Hartmann, *Zur Grundlegung der Ontologie,* 3d ed. (Berlin: Walter de Gruyter & Co., 1948), I, Part II, Section iii.

92. Translator's Note: Cf., e.g., G. W. Leibniz, "On the Reform of Metaphysics and of the Notion of Substance," *Die philosophischen Schriften von G. W. Leibniz,* IV, p. 469; *The Principles of Nature and of Grace,* i, ibid., VI, p. 598; "Système nouveau de la nature et de la communication des substances, aussi bien que de l'union qu'il y a entre l'âme et le corps," ibid., IV, pp. 478–79; *New Essays Concerning Human Understanding,* trans. A. G. Langley, 2d ed. (Chicago: The Open Court Publishing Co., 1916), Appendix 7, p. 702.

93. Translator's Note: Cf. supra, pp. 90–91.

94. Translator's Note: Cf. supra, n. 18.

95. Translator's Note: Cf. G. W. Leibniz, *New Essays Concerning Human Understanding,* p. 702.

96. Translator's Note: Cf. Henri Bergson, *L'évolution créatrice* in *Oeuvres* (Paris: Presses Universitaires de France, 1963), pp. 487ff.; "Introduction à la métaphysique" in ibid., pp. 1392ff.

97. Translator's Note: Cf. supra, pp. 75ff.

98. Translator's Note: Cf. supra, §§ 1–3, pp. 83ff.

99. We will later have an occasion to learn to what degree this is also true when one understands "contingent" in the novel sense the word acquires in the context of the theory of human life. [Cf. infra, § 10A, pp. 140ff. For the contention that human beings have no nature, vide J. Ortega y Gasset, "Historia como sistema," p. 41.]

100. Translator's Note: Cf. supra, p. 90.

101. Translator's Note: Cf. J. Ortega y Gasset, *En torno a Galileo,* p. 23. Translation: *Man and Crisis,* p. 23.

102. In this context, we can see that "possibility" has a connotation different from the one employed when we speak of the "possibilities" available as part and parcel of our "keyboard" or "stock." In point of fact, we ought to distinguish between "transitive possibilities" (or "availabilities") from "permanent possibilities." The latter are, in part, identical with what I have been calling "categories" of human life.

103. Translator's Note: Cf. supra, p. 116.

104. As a matter of fact, this was a discovery made and announced by Ortega long before Sartre gave it currency and renown in Europe. [Cf. J. Ortega y Gasset, "(Prólogo) A una edición de sus Obras," (1932), *Obras Completas* (Madrid: Revista de Occidente/Alianza Editorial, 1983), VI, pp. 349ff.; "Historia como sistema," p. 34; Translation:

p. 203; J.-P. Sartre, *L'être et le néant,* p. 515; *L'existentialisme est un humanisme,* p. 37.]

105.   "Fated" is taken here in Ortega's sense, namely, as meaning "belonging to 'destiny.'"

106.   Translator's Note: Cf. J. Ortega y Gasset, *Meditaciones del Quijote,* pp. 43–44 ("Commentary," pp. 226ff.).

107.   Translator's Note: Cf. J. Ortega y Gasset, *El hombre y la gente,* chap. 3.

108.   Translator's Note: Cf. J. Ortega y Gasset, *Meditaciones del Quijote,* pp. 35, 39, 42–44, 69–83, 106, and 107ff. ("Commentary," pp. 242-49, 252, 256–65, 288–310, 329–30, and 330ff.)

109.   Translator's Note: Cf. E. Husserl, *Ideas,* I, § 27.

110.   I am doing this for the purposes of economy; again, I am taking the word in the broadest sense possible.

111.   Translator's Note: J. Ortega y Gasset, *Meditaciones del Quijote,* p. 42 ("Commentary," pp. 260–63). The emphases have been added by Prof. Rodríguez Huéscar.

112.   I cannot say that this book exhausts the subject matter, but only that it is a most detailed study thereof. Cf. A. Rodríguez Huéscar, *Perspectiva y verdad.*

113.   Again the word is being taken in a broad sense.

114.   Translator's Note: Cf. J. Marías, *Introducción a la filosofía* in *Obras Completas* (Madrid: Revista de Occidente, 1962), II, chap. 1, § 9.

115.   Translator's Note: Cf. J. Marías, *Antropología metafísica,* 2d ed. (Madrid: Alianza Editorial, 1983), chap. 11, pp. 79ff.

116.   Translator's Note: The Latin word means local position.

117.   Translator's Note: Cf. J. Marías, *Antropología metafísica,* chap. 10, p. 75: "The empirical structure is not, then, a *requirement* or set of requirements to be met by *any* human life whatever and [is not therefore] a structure that would be *a priori* with respect to each and every one of the possible lives. Rather, it belongs, as a matter of fact, to all human lives in which I *empirically* happen to find it. I do not however find it just as I would a mere matter of fact, but as something that is also characterized by *stability.* This notwithstanding, an assertion of this sort does not signify that the structure in question is permanent. Accordingly, the empirical structure of life is, in some sense, *a priori,* but not with respect to each and every one of the *possible* lives; hence, it is so only in relation to the many *real* lives I come across in experience. . . . The empirical structure [of life] is thus given as a field of *possible human variation in history.*" Among the components of such a structure, Marías mentions bodiliness, sensibility, temporality, sexuality, and language.

118.   These terms derive from *hic* (meaning "here") and *nunc* (signifying "now"), respectively. I beg the indulgence of the reader for the pedantry involved in employing these neologisms, a procedure so alien to

a linguistic perspective inspired by Ortega, and yet, aside from the fact that I am not Ortega but only a very modest interpreter of his thought, my justification for my decision is that I can find no other abstract nouns to designate these two features more adequately. Moreover, I have in my favor the precedent of a distinguished lexical tradition relevant to my choices, namely, that which extends from Duns Scot's notion of *haecceitas* to Marcel's contemporary concept of *ecceitas*. [Duns Scotus' term derives from *haec* (signifying "this"), and it therefore means "thisness." It is the word by means of which he referred to the principle of individuation. Cf. J. Duns Scotus, *Opus oxoniense*, II, Disputation 3, q. 6, n. 15 in *Opera omnia*, ed. Vivès (Paris: 1891–95), XXII–XXIII. Marcel's expression may derive from *ecce*, which means "behold!" or "lo!"]

119. Translator's Note: Cf. ¿J. Ortega y Gasset, *El hombre y la gente*, p. 125. Translation: p. 74. Ortega's exact words have been slightly modified by Prof. Rodríguez Huéscar. Ortega actually said that ". . . [o]n every moment [of my life, my body keeps] me nailed down to a place and exiles me from the rest [of the world]."

120. Translator's Note: For the notion of occasional expression, cf. E. Husserl, *Logical Investigations*, i, chap. 3, § 26, Vol. I, pp. 313ff.

121. Translator's Note: Cf. infra, pp. 130ff.

122. This is Ortega's own expression for such a boundary line. [Cf. J. Ortega y Gasset, *El hombre y la gente*, pp. 154f. Translation: pp. 112f.]

123. On further consideration, however, we should wonder why we are to be confined to the testimony of sight, for isn't it true that we have an auditive and tactile "horizon" as well?

124. I have formed the Spanish word *percepturible* on the basis of Leibniz's coinage, *percepturitio* [which refers to the perceiver's active capacity to grasp. Cf., e.g., G. W. Leibniz, "A New Method of Learning and Teaching Jurisprudence," *Philosophical Papers and Letters*, trans. and ed. L. E. Loemker (Dordrecht: Reidel, 1969), n. 16, pp. 91–92. The locution appearing in this translation is perceptivity, which is employed in the sense of the subject's power of perceiving, just as activity could be taken to mean the subject's power of acting. In other words, *percepturitio* is "une tendance à nouvelles perceptions" or "a tendency to new perceptions." G. W. Leibniz, *Opera philosophica, quae exstant, latina, gallica, germanica, omnia*, ed. J. E. Erdmann (Berlin: 1840; re-issued—Aalen, 1959), p. 732 and *Briefwechsel zwischen Leibniz und Christian Wolff*, ed. C. I. Gerhardt (Halle, 1860), p. 56, *apud* Ernst Cassirer, *Leibniz' System in seinen wissenschaftlichen Grundlagen* (Marburg, 1902; re-issued—Hildesheim: G. Olms, 1962), pp. 375 and 376; see J. Ortega y Gasset, "Ideas sobre Pío Baroja," *El Espectador*, I (1916), *Obras Completas*, II, 77].

125. Translator's Note: Cf. infra, pp. 132–33. Concerning the first and second factors, vide E. Husserl, *Ideas*, I, § 27.

126. Translator's Note: Cf. supra, pp. 89ff. and 104ff.

127. Translator's Note: For a fuller treatment of the matter, cf. A. Rodríguez Huéscar, "Examen del 'ahora'," *Revista de Filosofía* (Universidad Complutense de Madrid), 3d Epoch, III (1990), No. 4, pp. 69ff.

128. Translator's Note: Cf. supra, p. 200.

129. Translator's Note: Cf. J. Marías, *Antropología metafísica:* "Human life has a structure that I would discover by means of an *analysis* of *my* life. The results of this analysis would constitute a theoretical formulation that is, by virtue of its origin, called the *analytics* [of human life]. Let me insist on the fact that such results are not of themselves something real; the only reality *is* my life, every one's life. Rather, the 'analytics' amounts to being just a theoretical formulation or interpretation about reality which is nonetheless derived from reality. Its contents are the *requirements* or conditions which my life must satisfy if it is to be possible at all; accordingly, it contains the requirements to be met by every one's life. The set of such conditions forms a necessary and *thereby* universal structure . . ." (p. 71). And further: "The necessary structure disclosed by the analytics could therefore be characterized as the *analytical structure* of human life. . . . The analytical structures [of life] would render possible the apprehending of the singular reality of *every one*'s life; they would allow us, say, to compose a *story* about it. Narrating a singular life is possible by means of universal structures, which are to be filled by way of the circum-stantial concretion pertinent to each case. . . . Neither is the [resulting] formula a genuine cognition yet nor is the latter possible without the former. Likewise, the analytics is not itself *real* knowledge, being equivalent solely to the cognition of an irreal structure, and yet concrete reality can only be apprehended by means of such a theoretical formulation" (p. 72). Cf. supra, n. 117.

130. Translator's Note: Cf., e.g., I. Kant, *Critique of Pure Reason,* B 211–12, 233ff., and 257ff.

131. Translator's Note: Cf. supra, pp. 113ff.

132. Translator's Note: Cf. supra, pp. 80f.

133. Translator's Note: Cf. M. Heidegger, *Being and Time,* §§ 65 and 68 a and pp. 377 and 416.

134. Translator's Note: Cf. J. Ortega y Gasset, *En torno a Galileo,* viii, p. 93. Translation: p. 120.

135. Translator's Note: Cf. J. Marías, *Antropología metafísica,* p. 181.

136. An awareness of this fact has always been an integral part of philosophical knowledge. For example, Hedwig Conrad-Martius, well known among Husserl's disciples, has spoken of the "antinomies of the now" in reference to those already identified by Aristotle in Book IV of his *Physics* [chap. 10–14, 218ff. Cf. H. Conrad-Martius, *Die Zeit*

(Munich: Kösel Verlag, 1954), Part I, ii; vide A. Rodríguez Huéscar's translation of this book into Spanish: *El tiempo* (Madrid: Revista de Occidente, 1958)].

137.   Translator's Note: Cf. infra, pp. 139ff.

138.   Translator's Note: Cf. supra, pp. 123ff.

139.   Translator's Note: Cf. supra, pp. 88ff.

140.   Translator's Note: Cf. G. W. Leibniz, *The Principles of Nature and of Grace, Based on Reason,* § 4 in G. W. Leibniz, *Philosophical Papers and Letters,* p. 637; I. Kant, *Critique of Pure Reason,* A 107–08; J. Ortega y Gasset, *Investigaciones psicológicas* in *Obras Completas,* XII, pp. 471ff.; Translation: "Toward a Philosophical Dictionary . . . 3: Apperception," *Psychological Investigations,* trans. J. García-Gómez (New York: W. W. Norton & Co., 1987), pp. 223ff.

141.   Translator's Note: Cf. supra, pp. 100ff.

142.   Translator's Note: Cf. supra, pp. 111 and 113.

143.   Translator's Note: Here the author adds "etc." to underscore the fact that this is just a sketch within an outline of the analysis of the "now."

144.   Translator's Note: Cf. supra, pp. 131ff.

145.   That is to say, the rhythm of one's temper.

146.   Translator's Note: For a further elaboration of the concept of the "now," vide the author's "Examen del 'ahora'" (cf. supra, n. 127).

147.   Translator's Note: Cf. supra, pp. 104ff.

148.   "Vocation" derives from *vocare* [meaning "to call"].

149.   Translator's Note: The term "incorruptible" is the translation I have chosen for *insobornable.* Judging by the context, the reader will be able to verify, however, that the word in question is not used here in a physical sense (as when one speaks of an "incorruptible body") but more in a "moral" vein (as when one says that "a public servant ought to be incorruptible"). This notwithstanding, Ortega's use of the expression goes beyond its "moral" signification, for it has to do with one's genuine constitution or metaphysical foundation, which is to be discovered *as* one invents it. This kernel no doubt has ethical meaning and consequences, which are by no means incidental, and yet its ultimate connotations are metaphysical. Cf. e.g., J. Ortega y Gasset, "Ideas sobre Pío Baroja," *Obras Completas,* II, pp. 75 and 84; "Goethe, el libertador," ibid., IV, p. 425.

150.   Translator's Note: Cf., e.g., Aristotle, *Categories,* trans. J. L. Ackrill, chap. 5, 3 b 33 - 4 a 8 in *The Complete Works of Aristotle,* rev. Oxford ed., ed. J. Barnes (Princeton: Princeton University Press, 1984), I, p. 7: "Substance, it seems, does not admit of a more and a less. I do not mean that one substance is not more of a substance than another (we have said that it is), but that any given substance is not called more, or less, [than] that which it is. For example, if this substance is a man, it will not

be more a man or less than a man either than itself or than another man. For one man is not more a man than another, as one pale thing is more pale than another or one beautiful thing more beautiful than another."

151. Translator's Note: Cf. supra, pp. 139ff.

152. Translator's Note: Cf. J. Ortega y Gasset, *La rebelión de las masas*, chaps. 6ff., *Obras Completas*, IV, pp. 175ff.

153. That is to say, the "fulfilling" aspect, if one is to speak exactly, since the three factors involved are all performative [*ejecutivos*] in character, in Ortega's sense of the term. [Cf. supra, pp. 12f.]

154. Translator's Note: Vide J. Ortega y Gasset, "Vives" (1940), i, *Obras Completas*, V, pp. 495–96; "Historia como sistema," p. 40 (Translation: p. 214); *En torno a Galileo*, p. 23 (Translation: p. 23); *Una interpretación de la historia universal* in *Obras Completas*, IX, p. 89 (Translation: *An Interpretation of Universal History*, trans. M. Adams [New York: W. W. Norton & Co., 1973], p. 108); cf. Alfred Schutz, *The Phenomenology of the Social World*, trans. G. Walsh et al. (Evanston: Northwestern University Press, 1967), chap. 2, §§ 17–18.

155. Translator's Note: Cf. supra, pp. 106f. and 113f.

156. There are, no doubt, various possible approximations to my ideal project. I will address this question below in section E [pp. 147ff.].

157. Translator's Note: D. M. Ausonius, "Quod vitae sectabor iter . . . ," *Edyllia* in *Corpus omnium veterum poetarum latinorum*, ed. P. Brossaeo, 2d ed. (Geneva: S. Crispinnus, 1511), II, p. 658; cf. R. Descartes, ["Le troisième songe de Descartes"], *Olympica* in *Oeuvres de Descartes*, X (1966), pp. 182ff.

158. Making this assertion does not however settle the question as to whether the major project I have chosen is indeed truly my own, if now one assigns to the possessive expression a more radical sense. I will address this matter below. [Cf. section D.]

159. Translator's Note: Cf., e.g., J. Ortega y Gasset, "Introducción a Velázquez," ii, *Obras Completas*, VIII, pp. 467–68.

160. Translator's Note: I have been unable to identify the source of this quote.

161. The problem of the significance of the social in human life, a problem of great proportions that concerned Ortega so much, is a corollary of this question. [Cf. J. Ortega y Gasset, *España invertebrada* (1921), ii, §§ 1, 5, and 7, pp. 91ff., 103ff., and 123ff.; *El tema de nuestro tiempo*, chap. 1; *La rebelión de las masas*, chap. 1.]

162. Translator's Note: Cf. supra, pp. 108, 119ff., and 127.

163. Translator's Note: Cf. supra, p. 143.

164. Translator's Note: Cf. supra, pp. 124–25.

165. Translator's Note: Cf. supra, p. 138 and n. 149.

166. Translator's Note: Cf. ibid.

167. J. Ortega y Gasset, "Pidiendo un Goethe desde dentro," *Obras Completas,* IV, p. 400. [Translation: "In Search of Goethe from Within," trans. W. R. Trask, *The Dehumanization of Art and Other Writings on Art and Culture* (Garden City, N.Y.: Doubleday & Co./Anchor Books, 1956), p. 130]. This piece is of fundamental importance for concepts like "vocation," "destiny," "incorruptible depths," and the like. It is difficult to resist the temptation of dwelling on it in depth, for one may find therein the most felicitous formulations Ortega has proposed concerning this subject.

168.   Translator's Note: Cf. supra, p. 138.

169.   Translator's Note: Cf. supra, pp. 123ff.

170.   Translator's Note: Vide, e.g., J. Ortega y Gasset, *España invertebrada,* ii, § 4, p. 102; cf. *El hombre y la gente,* p. 89 (Translation: p. 25): ". . . our personal individuality is a personage that is never completely realized, a sort of stimulating utopia or secret legend which every human being harbors in the innermost recesses of his heart. No wonder Pindar summarized his heroic ethic in the well-known imperative, *genoío os eidi,* 'become who you are'." Cf. Pindar, "Pythian Ode II," 72 in *The Odes of Pindar Including the Principal Fragments,* trans. J. Sandys (London: William Heinemann/The Loeb Classical Library, 1915), p. 178: "*génoi oîos essi mathón . . .* "; *The Odes of Pindar,* trans. R. Lattimore (Chicago: The University of Chicago Press/Phoenix Books, 1959), p. 50: "Learn what you are and be such."

171.   Translator's Note: Cf. supra, pp. 137ff.

CONCLUSIONS

1.   Translator's Note: Cf. A. Rodríguez Huéscar, *Perspectiva y verdad,* especially Part ii.

2.   It is worth noting that I am saying only that this idea "took shape" on the basis of Ortega's critique of idealism, not that it arose from the critical analysis itself, for the critique developed by Ortega was already guided, at least, by the unequivocal intuitive grasp of the idea in question, or was being elaborated as the latter "matured."

3.   Translator's Note: Cf. E. Husserl, *The Crisis of European Sciences and Transcendental Phenomenology,* Appendix i: "Philosophy and the Crisis of European Humanity," pp. 269ff.

Bibliography

A. PRIMARY

Ortega y Gasset, José. *Obras Completas,* Edición del Centenario (Madrid: Revista de Occidente/Alianza Editorial, 1983), 12 volumes:
"Glosas" (1902), I, pp. 13–18.
"Renan" (1909), I, pp. 443–67.
"Adán en el Paraíso" (1910), I, pp. 473–93.
"Sensación, construcción e intuición" (1913), XII, pp. 487–99. Translation: "Sensation, Construction, and Intuition," *Phenomenology and Art,* trans. Philip W. Silver (New York: W. W. Norton & Co., 1975), pp. 79–94.
"Sobre el concepto de sensación" (1913), I, pp. 244–60. Translation: "On the Concept of Sensation," *Phenomenology and Art,* pp. 95–115.
Meditaciones del Quijote (1914), I, pp. 309–400. Translation: *Meditations on Quixote,* trans. E. Rugg et al. (New York: W. W. Norton & Co., 1961), 192 pp.
"Ensayo de estética a manera de prólogo" (1914), VI, pp. 247–64. Translation: "An Essay in Esthetics by Way of a Preface," *Phenomenology and Art,* pp. 127–50.
Investigaciones psicológicas (1915–16), XII, pp. 331–500. Translation: *Psychological Investigations,* trans. J. García-Gómez (New York: W. W. Norton & Co., 1987), 254 pp.
"Conciencia, objeto y las tres distancias de éste" (1916), II, pp. 61–66. Translation: "Consciousness, the Object, and Its Three Distances," *Phenomenology and Art,* pp. 116–24.
"Ideas sobre Pío Baroja" (1916), *El espectador* (i, 1916), II, pp. 69–102.
"Nada moderno y muy siglo XX" (1916), *El espectador* (i, 1916), I, pp. 22–24.
España invertebrada (1921), III, pp. 35–128.
El tema de nuestro tiempo (1923), III, pp. 141–242. Translation: *The Modern Theme,* trans. J. Cleugh (New York: Harper & Row, 1933), 152 pp.
"Ni vitalismo ni racionalismo" (1924), III, pp. 270–80.

"Las dos grandes metáforas" (1924), *El espectador* (iv, 1925), II, pp. 387–400.

La deshumanización del arte e ideas sobre la novela (1925), III, pp. 351–428. Translation: *The Dehumanization of Art and Other Writings on Art and Culture* (Garden City, N.Y.: Doubleday & Co./Anchor Books, 1956), 187 pp.

"Kant. Reflexiones de centenario" (1929), IV, pp. 23–47.

¿Qué es filosofía? (1929), VII, pp. 273–438. Translation: *What Is Philosophy?*, trans. M. Adams (New York: W. W. Norton & Co., 1960), 252 pp.

"La percepción del prójimo" (1929), VI, pp. 153–63.

"Sobre la expresión fenómeno cósmico" (1930), II, pp. 577–94.

La rebelión de las masas (1930), IV, pp. 111–310. Translation: *The Revolt of the Masses,* trans. anonymous (New York: W. W. Norton & Co., 1932), 190 pp.

"Misión de la universidad" (1930), IV, pp. 311–53.

"En el centenario de una universidad" (1930), V, pp. 461–74.

"[Prólogo] A una edición de sus obras" (1932), VI, pp. 342–54.

"Pidiendo un Goethe desde dentro" (1932), IV, pp. 395–420. Translation: "In Search of Goethe from Within," trans. W. R. Trask, *The Dehumanization of Art and Other Writings on Art and Culture,* pp. 121–60.

"Goethe, el libertador" (1932), IV, pp. 421–27.

Unas lecciones de metafísica (1932–33), XII, pp. 143–330. Translation: *Some Lessons in Metaphysics,* trans. M. Adams (New York: W. W. Norton & Co., 1969), 158 pp.

"Guillermo Dithey y la Idea de la Vida" (1933–34), VI, pp. 165–214. Translation: "A Chapter from the History of Ideas—Wilhelm Dilthey and the Idea of Life," pp. 129–82 in *Concord and Liberty,* trans. H. Weyl (New York: W. W. Norton & Co., 1946), 182 pp.

"Prólogo para alemanes" (1934), VIII, pp. 11–58. Translation: "Preface for Germans," *Phenomenology and Art,* pp. 17–76.

"Historia como sistema" (1935), VI, pp. 11–50. Translation: "History as a System," *History as a System and Other Essays Toward a Philosophy of History,* trans. H. Weyl (New York: W. W. Norton & Co., 1941), pp. 163–233.

En torno a Galileo (1939), V, pp. 13–164. Translation: *Man and Crisis,* trans. M. Adams (New York: W. W. Norton & Co., 1958), 217 pp.

"Meditación de la criolla" (1939), VIII, pp. 411–45.

"Ideas y creencias" (1940), V, pp. 377–409.

Sobre la razón histórica (1940), XII, pp. 143–330. Translation: *Historical Reason,* trans. Philip W. Silver (New York: W. W. Norton & Co., 1984), 223 pp.

"Vives" (1940), V, pp. 493–507.

"Apuntes sobre el pensamiento. Su teurgia y su demiurgia" (1941), V, pp. 517–47. Translation: "Notes on Thinking—Its Creation of the World and Its Creation of God," *Concord and Liberty,* pp. 49–82.

"Prólogo a *Historia de la Filosofía* de Émile Bréhier" (1942), VI, pp. 377–418. Translation: "Prologue to a History of Philosophy," *Concord and Liberty,* pp. 83–128.

"Introducción a Velázquez" (1943), VIII, pp. 457–87.

Una interpretación de la historia universal (1948–49), IX, pp. 9–242. Translation: *An Interpretation of Universal History,* trans. M. Adams (New York: W. W. Norton & Co., 1973), 302 pp.

El hombre y la gente (chap. 1, 1939; 1949–50), VII, pp. 69–272. Translation: *Man and People,* trans. W. R. Trask (New York: W. W. Norton & Co., 1957), 272 pp.

"De Europa meditatio quaedam" (1949), IX, pp. 247–313.

Goya (1950?), VII, pp. 503–73.

"Un capítulo sobre la cuestión de cómo muere una creencia" (1954), IX, pp. 707–25.

La idea de principio en Leibniz y la evolución de la teoría deductiva (1947), VIII, pp. 59–356. Translation: *The Idea of Principle in Leibnitz and the Evolution of Deductive Theory,* trans. M. Adams (New York: W. W. Norton & Co., 1971), 381 pp.

"Algunos temas del 'Weltverkehr'" (1954), IX, pp. 339–43.

_____. *Meditaciones del Quijote,* with a "Commentary" by Julián Marías (Madrid: Universidad de Puerto Rico/Revista de Occidente, 1957), 446 pp.

_____. "El curso de don José Ortega y Gasset" (1916), as summarized in Institución Cultural Española, *Anales* (Buenos Aires, 1947), I (1912–20), chap. 5, pp. 149–208.

_____. *¿Qué es conocimiento?,* 1929–30; 1930–31 (Madrid: Revista de Occidente en Alianza Editorial, 1984), 184 pp.

B. SECONDARY

The Holy Bible, King James Version, 1611 (New York: American Bible Society, 1985).

Aristotle, *The Metaphysics,* Greek/English ed., trans. H. Tredennick (Cambridge, Massachusetts: Harvard University Press/The Loeb Classical Library, 1961), 2 volumes.

_____. *Categories, Physics,* and *Metaphysics* in *The Complete Works of Aristotle,* rev. Oxford trans., ed. J. Barnes (Princeton: Princeton University Press, 1984), 2 volumes.

Ausonius, D. M. "Quod vitae sectabor iter . . . ," *Edyllia* in *Corpus omnium veterum poetarum latinorum,* ed. P. Brossaeo, 2d ed. (Geneva: S. Crispinnus, 1511), II, p. 658.

Bergson, Henri. "Introduction à la métaphysique," *La pensée et le mouvant* in *Oeuvres* (Paris: Presses Universitaires de France, 1963), pp. 1392–1432.

_____. *L'évolution créatrice* in *Oeuvres,* pp. 487–809.

Cassirer, Ernst. *Leibniz' System in seinen wissenschaftlichen Grundlagen* (Marburg: 1902; re-issued—Hildesheim: G. Olms, 1962).

Conrad-Martius, Hedwig. *Die Zeit* (Munich: Kösel Verlag, 1954). Translation: *El tiempo,* trans. A. Rodríguez Huéscar (Madrid: Revista de Occidente, 1958).

Cusa, Nicholas of. *De docta ignorantia* in *Philosophisch-theologische Schriften,* Studien- und Jubiläumsausgabe (Latin-German), ed. L. Gabriel, trans. W. Dupré (Vienna: Herder, 1982), I.

Dante Alighieri. *The Divine Comedy,* trans. and commentary by Charles S. Singleton (Princeton: Princeton University Press/Bollingen Series, 1970), "Inferno-1."

Descartes, René. *Meditationes de prima philosophia* in *Oeuvres de Descartes,* ed. Ch. Adam and P. Tannery, rev. ed. (Paris: J. Vrin, 1964), VII.

_____. *Méditations* in *Oeuvres de Descartes,* IX-1 (1964).

_____. *Olympica* in *Oeuvres de Descartes,* X (1966).

Duns Scotus, John. *Opus oxoniense,* ii in *Opera omnia,* ed. Vivès (Paris: 1891–95), XXII–XXIII.

Ferrater Mora, José. *Ortega y Gasset. Etapas de una filosofía* (Barcelona: Seix-Barral, 1958). Translation: *Ortega y Gasset. An Outline of His Philosophy* (New Haven: Yale University Press, 1957).

_____. *El ser y el sentido* (Madrid: Revista de Occidente, 1967).

Fouillée, Alfred. *L'évolutionisme des idées-forces* (Paris: 1890).

_____. *La morale des idées-forces* (Paris: 1908).

_____. *Psychologie des idées-forces* (Paris: 1893), 2 volumes.

Gaos, José. *Introducción a la fenomenología* (Xalapa, Mexico: Universidad Veracruzana, 1960).

Gurwitsch, Aron. *The Field of Consciousness* (Pittsburgh: Duquesne University Press, 1964).

Hartmann, Nicolai. *Zur Grundlegung der Ontologie,* 3d ed. (Berlin: Walter de Gruyter & Co., 1948), I.

Hegel, G. W. F. *Wissenschaft der Logik* (Leipzig: Felix Meiner Verlag, 1948).

Heidegger, Martin. *Sein und Zeit*, 10th ed. (Tübingen: Max Niemeyer, 1963). Translation: *Being and Time*, trans. J. Macquarrie et al. (New York: Harper & Row, 1962).

Hoffmann, Heinrich. *Untersuchungen über den Empfindungsbegriff* in *Archiv für die gesamte Psychologie*, XXVI (1913), Nos. 1–2.

Husserl, Edmund. *Formale und transzendentale Logik*, ed. P. Janssen (The Hague: Martinus Nijhoff, 1974) in *Husserliana*, XVII. Translation: *Formal and Transcendental Logic*, trans. D. Cairns (The Hague: Martinus Nijhoff, 1969).

―――. *Ideen zu einer reinen Phänomenologie und phänomenologischen Philosophie. Erstes Buch: Allgemeine Einführung in die reine Phänomenologie*, ed. K. Schumann, 3d ed. (The Hague: Martinus Nijhoff, 1976) in *Husserliana*, III, 1–2. Translation: *Ideas Pertaining to a Pure Phenomenology and to a Phenomenological Philosophy. First Book: General Introduction to a Pure Phenomenology*, trans. F. Kersten (The Hague: Martinus Nijhoff, 1982).

―――. *Die Krisis der Europäischen Wissenschaften und die transzendentale Phänomenologie*, ed. W. Biemel, 2d ed. (The Hague: Martinus Nijhoff, 1962) in *Husserliana*, VI. Translation: *The Crisis of European Sciences and Transcendental Phenomenology*, trans. D. Carr (Evanston: Northwestern University Press, 1970).

―――. *Logische Untersuchungen* (The Hague: Martinus Nijhoff) in *Husserliana*, XVII (i, 1975, ed. E. Holenstein) and XIX, 1–2 (ii, 1984, ed. U. Panzer). Translation: *Logical Investigations*, trans. J. N. Findlay (New York: Humanities Press, 1970), 2 volumes.

Kant, Immanuel. *Critique of Pure Reason*, trans. N. K. Smith (New York: St. Martin's Press, 1961).

Koehler, Wolfgang. "Über unbemerkte Empfindungen und Urteilstäuschungen," *Zeitschrift für Psychologie*, LXVI (1913).

Koffka, Kurt. "Perception: An Introduction to the Gestalt Theory," *The Psychological Bulletin*, XIX (1922), pp. 537ff.

―――. *Principles of Gestalt Psychology* (New York: Harcourt, 1935).

―――. "Probleme der experimentellen Psychologie," *Die Naturwissenschaften*, V (1917), pp. 2ff. and 25ff.

Kohák, Erazim. "Jan Patočka: A Philosophical Biography," pp. 1–135 in *Jan Patočka. Philosophy and Selected Writings*, trans. E. Kohák (Chicago: The University of Chicago Press, 1989).

Leibniz, G. W. *Briefwechsel zwischen Leibniz und Christian Wolff*, ed. C. I. Gerhardt (Halle, 1860).

―――. *New Essays Concerning Human Understanding*, trans. A. G. Langley, 2d ed. (Chicago: The Open Court Publishing Co., 1916).

―――. *Opera philosophica, quae exstant, latina, gallica, germanica, omnia*, ed. J. E. Erdmann (Berlin: 1840; re-issued: Aalen, 1959).

———. "On the Reform of Metaphysics and of the Notion of Substance," *Die philosophischen Schriften von G. W. Leibniz*, ed. C. I. Gerhardt (Hildesheim: Georg Olms, 1978), IV.

———. *Philosophical Papers and Letters*, trans. and ed. L. E. Loemker (Dordrecht: Reidel, 1969).

———. *The Principles of Nature and Grace* in *Die philosophischen Schriften von G. W. Leibniz*, IV.

———. "Système nouveau de la nature et de la communication des substances, aussi bien que de l'union qu'il y a entre l'âme et le corps," *Die philosophischen Schriften von G. W. Leibniz*, IV.

Lyotard, Jean-François. *La phénoménologie*, 4th ed. (Paris: Presses Universitaires de France, 1961).

Marcel, Gabriel. *Homo viator. Prolégomènes à une métaphysique de l'espérance* (Paris: Aubier-Montaigne, 1960).

Marías, Julián. *Antropología metafísica*, 2d ed. (Madrid: Alianza Editorial, 1983).

———. *Introducción a la filosofía* in *Obras Completas* (Madrid: Revista de Occidente, 1962), II.

———. *El oficio del pensamiento* in *Obras Completas*, VI (1961).

———. *Ortega, I: Circunstancia y vocación* (Madrid: Revista de Occidente, 1960). This is now Volume I of *Ortega*, 2d ed. (Madrid: Alianza Editorial, 1983). Translation: *José Ortega y Gasset. Circumstance and Vocation*, trans. F. M. López-Morillas (Norman: University of Oklahoma Press, 1970).

———. *Ortega. [II]. Las trayectorias* (Madrid: Alianza Editorial, 1983).

Merleau-Ponty, Maurice. *Phénoménologie de la perception* (Paris: Gallimard, 1945).

Owens, Joseph. *The Doctrine of Being in the Aristotelian Metaphysics*, 2d ed. (Toronto: Pontifical Institute of Medieval Studies, 1963).

Patočka, Jan. *Platon et l'Europe*, trans. E. Abrams (La Grasse: Éditions Verdier, 1983).

Pindar. "Pythian Ode II," *The Odes of Pindar Including the Principal Fragments*, Greek-English ed., trans. J. Sandys (London: William Heinemann / The Loeb Classical Library, 1915); *The Odes of Pindar*, trans. R. Lattimore (Chicago: The University of Chicago Press / Phoenix Books, 1959).

Plato. *Republic*, trans. and ed. F. M. Cornford (New York: Oxford University Press, 1945).

Rodríguez Huéscar, Antonio. "Examen del 'ahora'," *Revista de filosofía* (Universidad Complutense de Madrid), Third Epoch, III (1990), No. 4, pp. 69–81.

———. *Perspectiva y verdad*, 2d ed. (Madrid: Alianza Editorial, 1985).

_____. "El temple como acceso a la realidad" in *Homenaje a Julián Marías,* ed. Fernando Chueca Goitía et al. (Madrid: Espasa-Calpe, 1984), pp. 609–28.

Salas, Jaime de. "Muere el filósofo Rodríguez Huéscar," *ABC* (Madrid), May 2, 1990, p. 50.

Sartre, Jean-Paul. *L'être et le néant* (Paris: Gallimard, 1943).

_____. *L'existentialisme est un humanisme* (Paris: Les Éditions Nagel, 1970).

Scheler, Max. *Formalism in Ethics and Non-Formal Ethics of Values,* trans. M. S. Frings et al. (Evanston: Northwestern University Press, 1973).

_____. *The Nature of Sympathy,* trans. P. Heath (London: Routledge & Kegan Paul, 1954).

_____. "Repentance and Rebirth," pp. 33–65 in *On the Eternal in Man,* trans. B. Noble (New York: Harper and Brothers, 1960).

Schutz, Alfred. *The Phenomenology of the Social World,* trans. G. Walsh et al. (Evanston: Northwestern University Press, 1967).

Spinoza, Baruch. "Epistola 50," *Spinoza opera,* ed. C. Gebhardt (Heidelberg: 1925), IV.

Zubiri, Xavier. *Cinco lecciones de filosofía* (Madrid: Sociedad de Estudios y Publicaciones, 1963).

INDEX